Michael Sullivan
& ASSOCIATES LLP

SULLIVAN ON COMP

Chapter 6: Statutes of Limitations

Michael Sullivan, Esq.
Sure S. Log, Esq.
Prof. David J. Chetcuti

"Sullivan on Comp" is available at a special discount when ordered in bulk quantities. For information contact Michael Sullivan & Associates LLP at 310.337.4480 or SullivanOnComp@sullivanattorneys.com.

This book is designed to provide accurate and authoritative information in regard to the subject matter covered. It is sold with the understanding that the publisher is not rendering legal, accounting, or other professional service. If legal advice or other expert assistance is required, the services of a competent professional person should be sought.

This book went to press in January 2013. Its contents are current through that date; however, any subsequent legislative or case law developments are not reflected in the text for obvious reasons. Subscribers to "Sullivan on Comp" can access the latest version of this continuously updated work online at WorkCompCentral. See http://www.workcompcentral.com/sullivan.

Author: Michael Sullivan
Author: Sure S. Log
Author: David J. Chetcuti
Technical Reviewer: Michael Sliemers
Copy Editor: Ellen Alperstein
Copy Editor: Linda Finestone
Content Index: Mary J. Harper, Access Points Indexing
Content Index: Enid L. Zafran, Indexing Partners LLC
Production: Elizabeth Vo
Production: Michael Bell
Production: Bob Dossa
Programming: Conrad Sollitt, Omnicognic, LLC
Technical Assistance: Tim Ream
Technical Assistance: Stan Wong
Cover Design: Erin Pace-Molina, Exit 74 Designs

Library of Congress Control Number: 2010919402
ISBN 13: 978-0-615-43219-9
ISBN 10: 0-615-43210-9

10 9 8 7 6 5 4 3

Contents

Chapter 6: Statutes of Limitations

INTRODUCTION

Why another treatise on California workers' compensation law?

In a word, *clarity*.

The reader will find a thorough explanation of the law written in straightforward style. It will serve attorneys, claims adjusters, business managers and anyone else in the industry who needs or wants current, complete, accessible information. The text and its footnotes are a powerful resource for in-depth legal analysis.

"Sullivan on Comp" is presented in partnership with WorkCompCentral, whose website is host of the entire work. The treatise will be continually updated online and available via subscription.

The subscription includes a full year of access via WorkCompCentral.com as well as a complete 11-volume set of hard copies consisting of 16 chapters. Once a year, a single-volume yearbook will be sent to active subscribers summarizing important changes to the law during the previous year. In addition, updates of individual volumes will be sent automatically as required by their topics. Subscribers also receive e-mail alerts whenever significant new content is added to the website.

To order, visit http://www.workcompcentral.com/sullivan.

ACKNOWLEDGMENTS

This book was not by any means my work alone. A team of people have worked to make this possible. First, I want to thank my co-authors. Sure Log, a licensed California attorney who recently moved to New Zealand with his family after a distinguished career as a workers' compensation defense attorney, has been of counsel with MS&A for years. As the scope of this project became clear, I knew I could not write this book without help. Sure became a full time co-author, and it is no exaggeration to say that this work could not have been done without him.

I also thank Dave Chetcuti, a WCCP- and BPPE-accredited professor of California Workers' Compensation Insurance Law who has taught the subject at several colleges and universities throughout the state. I have known Dave for years through our work conducting seminars and consulting with several clients. I asked him to join the team because he is someone who thinks deeply about the law, and has unparalleled knowledge of the workers' compensation field.

The staff at Michael Sullivan & Associates has participated in the project from the beginning; of special note is Executive Director Michael Bell, who helped create the idea for the book series, and has been deeply involved in all stages of the work. He helped negotiate the rights to the book, and to establish the relationship with WorkCompCentral. He proofread chapters, directed the copy editing and offered constructive criticism. Responsible for the formatting and presentation, as well as the printing and marketing, Mike created this product out of whole cloth. A good friend, a gifted manager and a great businessman, he is the architect of this grand design. This project would not have happened if not for his intelligence and dedication.

I am grateful to the associate attorneys at MS&A, all of whom, over the years, have discussed critical points of law that helped make this book immediately relevant. So too is this the case with my friends in the industry on both sides of the advocate fence, including judges, particularly those at the Marina del Rey WCAB. The contributions of Yvonne Bar-Yotam of MS&A were notable, especially in marketing and distribution, as were those of our clerical staff. John Sullivan, my brother and our IT director for many years, worked hard on the computer platform to make this book possible. He passed away during the writing, and this book is dedicated to his memory.

Our copy editors, Ellen Alperstein and Linda Finestone, worked hard under unreasonably tight deadlines to render raw copy professional and easier to read. I also thank Erin Pace-Molina, who is responsible for the book's design. Mike Sliemers, who joined us in the late stages, read virtually the entire book, checking citations, proofreading and offering feedback in light of his extensive experience as a claims manager in the industry. He deserves thanks for a real contribution. I also thank computer programmer Conrad Sollitt for writing the needed code that automated the book's format and Bob Dossa, who helped tremendously by refining the final elements of the book production.

I have immensely enjoyed working with David DePaolo, Ronald Haaland, Rob McCarthy, Kristen Chavez and the entire team at WorkCompCentral.

Finally, I offer affection and thanks to my daughter Demetria and wife Staser for all their patience with me and my big ideas. I love you both.

DEDICATION

This book is dedicated to my brother John Sullivan, who passed away in June 2009, during the writing of this book. He is shown here with my daughter Demetria, who loved him as much as we all did.

From the time he was a baby there were two sides to John. He was the brooding thinker. He was the happy-go-lucky boy. As he grew up, the fifth in a family of six children, he demonstrated a formidable mind, one inclined toward logic and philosophy. In college, he redefined the standard for a starving student. He met that challenge by helping others with their computer problems in exchange for food and cigarettes. After four years of nonstop work, he graduated from Loyola Marymount University with a degree in Computer Science, and came to work for me.

I thought I was doing him a favor when I hired him as the IT guy for my new law firm. The opposite turned out to be the case. John was an integral part of building the firm at every stage. As it grew, so did John's role. I have a million wonderful memories of working with him: the two of us stringing wires all weekend in the second office. Playing video games with our buddies. Hanging out at Melody's bar across the street at lunchtime. John and I were close, as we were with the other members of our family who have worked at the firm and the friends we hired and made along the way. I still see John in the large room surrounded by dissembled stacks of computer parts and junk; his disdain for all things organized drove the staff crazy. He would sit slumped in his chair, studying a problem, chewing on the front of his T-shirt, as focused as a laser beam.

Without question, his was a brilliant mind. Maybe even a genius mind. John's efforts at the firm were child's play to him, but he cared a lot about us. He would brainstorm ways to make the firm better, to make my life easier. Shortly before he died, as John's fiancée Kate headed toward graduation from a doctoral program, he was planning to leave the firm. As much as I would have hated to lose him, I always thought that John had so much more to offer than making a modest law firm run. John always wanted to talk about advancement in technology, the progress of humanity, philosophy, ethics ... his interests were many and profound, his mind deeply curious and caring. I have no doubt that had he lived, his contributions would have been real and many.

John's ethic compelled him to charity. Everyone in the building knew him. He was the guy who helped with their computer problems, and did not ask for pay. He was the friendly guy everybody liked, out in the front of the building, chatting with the other smokers, the nicotine rebels. He gathered around him friends that were as loyal as I have ever seen. He allowed my stepson Nick to live on his couch, he forgave rent to errant roommates, he ate fast food and was always sensitive to the feelings of others. He was perceptive, artistic, thoughtful and eccentric.

John's sudden passing was a blow. Many of us still feel his presence and the gaping void he left. At his funeral our brother Bart and his wife Mariana offered the classic Irish blessing, as I do again:

> May the road rise to meet you,
> May the wind be always at your back,
> May the sun shine warm upon your face,
> May the rains fall soft upon your fields,
> And, until we meet again,
> May God hold you in the hollow of His hand.

A NOTE ABOUT STATUTORY AND LEGISLATIVE ABBREVIATIONS

Abbreviations are used throughout the text to reference California legislation, and California and federal legal code statutes. Codes that are less frequently referenced are spelled out. These are the most common abbreviations:

AB - Assembly Bill
BPC - Business and Professions Code
CCR - California Code of Regulations
CCP - Code of Civil Procedure
CFR - Code of Federal Regulations
GC - Government Code
IC - Insurance Code
LC - Labor Code
SB - Senate Bill
UIC - Unemployment Insurance Code
U.S.C. - United States Code
VC - Vehicle Code

A NOTE ABOUT HYPERLINKS

This text includes URLs for a wide variety of web resources, including PDF forms.

Because the web is a dynamic, evolutionary creature, its content shifts. Although the hyperlinks in "Sullivan on Comp" were current at press time, it is possible and even likely that some of them won't work when you enter them into your browser. Generally, the home page addresses are clear, and you might be able to access the information via them. Despite the inoperability of some addresses, we feel that the value of directly referencing most of these resources exceeds the inconvenience you might experience occasionally encountering a broken link.

Chapter 6:

Statutes of Limitations

6.1 STATUTES OF LIMITATIONS — IN GENERAL

A statute of limitations is a restriction of time in which relief may be sought. Simply put, if an application for adjudication of claim or other appropriate document is not filed with the appeals board within certain time periods, the claim for benefits is barred by law.

The purpose of statutes of limitations in workers' compensation is the same as it is in any other area of law — time limits encourage prompt pursuit of legal remedies. There is a need for "diligent prosecution of known claims, thereby providing necessary finality and predictability in legal affairs, and ensuring that claims will be resolved while the evidence bearing on the issues is reasonably available and fresh."[1] In other words, a statute of limitations "[p]revents surprises through the revival of claims that have been allowed to slumber until evidence has been lost, memories have faded, and witnesses have disappeared."[2] Loss of evidence creates problems for all parties involved and the judges who must render decisions. When evidence is old or cannot be produced, it creates a burden on the court to ascertain historical facts. This is an unfair burden on the judicial system, and it would also be unfair for an employee to use time as a weapon by pursuing a remedy long after the employer has the ability to produce otherwise relevant evidence.

The Labor Code provides specific rights and remedies to injured employees. It also provides legally defined time periods in which these rights may be pursued.

[1] *Kaiser Foundation Hospitals/Permanente Medical Group v. WCAB (Webb)* (1977) 42 CCC 302, 306.
[2] *Elkins v. Derby* (1974) 39 CCC 624.

Some statutory time limits apply exclusively to an initial request for commencement of proceedings, and other statutes of limitations apply to a request for the commencement of additional proceedings after a prior WCAB order, decision or award. This chapter examines employees' rights and the employers' defenses on the topic.

Accordingly, several statutes of limitations apply to claims for workers' compensation benefits and to claims for penalties resulting from an industrial injury claim. These are the relevant statutes in the Labor Code:

1. **LC 4903.5**: period for filing a lien;
2. **LC 5405**: commencement of proceedings for medical, temporary disability or permanent disability benefits;
3. **LC 5410**: instituting proceedings (usually by filing a petition to reopen, but sometimes by filing an application for adjudication of claim) on grounds that the injury has resulted in new and further disability or a need for rehabilitation benefits;
4. **LC 5406**: commencement of proceedings for death benefits;
5. **LC 5406.5**: commencement of proceedings for death benefits in case of death from asbestosis;
6. **LC 5406.6**: commencement of proceedings for death benefits in case of death from HIV-related disease;
7. **LC 5408**: commencement of proceedings for an incompetent person or minor;
8. **LC 5803 and LC 5804**: request to reopen a previously closed WCAB case for good cause;
9. **LC 132a**: claim for penalty against the employer and/or its insurance company for discrimination after an injury;[3]
10. **LC 5407**: commencement of proceedings to seek a penalty for serious and willful misconduct of an employer;
11. **LC 5407.5**: commencement of proceedings to seek a penalty against an employee for serious and willful misconduct;
12. **LC 5500.5**: commencement of proceedings to seek contribution from the other co-defendants; and
13. **LC 5814(g)**: commencement of proceedings to seek a penalty under LC 5814.

[3] Note that LC 132a does not have parenthesis around the "a." This is a quirk of the Labor Code.

This chapter discusses these statutes of limitations and the judicially created exceptions that toll them. (When a statute of limitations is "tolled," the clock stops — the period for which an action is required is extended.)

It has been stated that statutes of limitations "are vital to the welfare of society and are favored by the law ... to be viewed as statutes of repose, and as such constitute meritorious defenses."[4] But the appeals board later referred to the statute of limitations as a disfavored affirmative defense[5] because it buys repose at the price of disposing of a cause of action "on procedural grounds" rather than "on the merits" and, in a given case, may buy it at the price of procedurally barring a cause of action that is, in fact, meritorious.[6] But the California Supreme Court subsequently noted that "an affirmative defense based on the statute of limitations should not be characterized by courts as either 'favored' or 'disfavored'" because the two public policies — the one for repose and the other for disposition on the merits — are equally strong.[7]

---

[4] *City and County of San Francisco v. WCAB (Shaughnessy, Maultsby)* (1969) 34 CCC 97, 104.
[5] *Smith v. Johns-Manville Products Corp.* (1981) 46 CCC 557, 560 (appeals board *en banc*); *Nino v. County of Los Angeles* (1982) 47 CCC 370, 372-73 (appeals board *en banc*); *Stephens v. WCAB* (2009) 74 CCC 885 (writ denied).
[6] *Norgart v. The Upjohn Co.* (1999) 21 Cal. 4th 383, 396.
[7] *Norgart v. The Upjohn Co.* (1999) 21 Cal. 4th 383, 396.

6.2 REQUIRED NOTICES FOR THE EMPLOYER AND EMPLOYEE

Employees must have some notice or knowledge of a possible right to receive workers' compensation benefits in order to pursue such benefits. The employer has several independent statutory duties to notify employees of their rights regarding entitlement to workers' compensation benefits. Such notices are explained in this chapter. A failure to provide notice may increase the difficulty of defending the claim on the basis of the statute of limitations.

Notices regarding the employee's potential right to benefits, and instructions on how to claim such benefits if injured, are required to be posted in the workplace in advance of any injury or claim. Once an injury has occurred, notices regarding the employee's rights are required at specific intervals after the employer has received notification of a claimed injury. Notices regarding the employee's entitlement to separate categories of benefits are required during the provision and on termination of payment of such benefits. These notices are collectively designed to enable an injured employee to pursue a claim for workers' compensation benefits before the expiration of any statute of limitations. So each notice provides information regarding alternatives for pursuing resolution of any disputes that may arise, including the employee's right to the services of an officer from the Information and Assistance (I&A) Unit (free of charge), an attorney and the appeals board.

The employer must have some notice of an alleged industrial injury before it becomes liable for workers' compensation benefits. So the Labor Code also imposed certain requirements on employees to give notice of any industrial injury to the employer. The notice requirements for employers and employees, as well as their effect on the statute of limitations, are examined in the forthcoming sections.

6.3 PRE-INJURY NOTICES

POSTING NOTICES

Per LC 3550, the employer is required to post notice regarding an employee's workers' compensation rights. The notice must be posted "in a conspicuous location frequented by employees and where such notice may be easily read by employees during the course of the workday." A broom closet is not a conspicuous location, nor is the supervisor's private office. A lunch room bulletin board or a wall next to a time clock would be appropriate locations. A notice posted at a work site in San Diego would not be "conspicuous" to employees who are employed at a work site in Sacramento. If the employer has multiple work sites, the notice required by LC 3550 must be posted at each.

Note that, if the employer has a medical provider network (MPN), another and broader notice is required to be posted before the MPN is implemented. This is discussed in depth in Section 7.54 MPN — Notice Requirements. Failure to post the notice properly may jeopardize the employer's right to have the applicant treat within the network. This issue is discussed in Section 7.56 Escaping the Network.

CONTENTS OF THE NOTICE

The notice must be easily understandable, and it must be posted in both English and Spanish where there are Spanish-speaking employees. Per LC 3550(d) and CCR 9881, the notice must also include:

1. the name of the employer's current compensation insurance carrier or the fact that the employer is self-insured, and the responsible party for claims adjustment;
2. how to get emergency medical treatment, if needed;
3. emergency telephone numbers for hospital, ambulance, police and firefighting services;
4. the kinds of events, injuries and illnesses covered by workers' compensation;
5. information that the employer may not be responsible for compensation if injury is incurred due to an employee's voluntary participation in an off-duty recreational, social or athletic activity that is not a part of the employee's work-related duties;
6. the injured employee's right to receive medical care;
7. the rights of the employee to select and change the treating physician pursuant to the provisions of LC 4600, including the right to predesignate a physician;
8. the rights of the employee to receive temporary disability indemnity, permanent disability indemnity, supplemental job displacement benefits and death benefits, as appropriate;
9. to whom injuries should be reported;
10. the existence of time limits for the employer to be notified of an occupational injury;
11. the protections against discrimination provided pursuant to LC 132a;
12. the website address and contact information for employees to obtain further information about the workers' compensation claims process and an injured employee's rights and obligations, including the location and telephone number of the nearest information and assistance officer; and
13. a description of medical provider networks, including a predesignation exception, when the employee is to use an MPN physician, the date of coverage and how to request information about the MPN. Also the identifying information for an MPN is to be included, with the address, phone number and website if available.

The required posting is usually printed and provided by the employer's insurance carrier free of charge. In fact, insurers must provide these notices to each of their policyholders, with advice concerning the requirements of LC 3550 and the penalties for a failure to post the notice (LC 3550(f)).

Insurance companies or self-insured employers may post a notice available from the state, or they may reprint the state-published notice with their own logos or other identifying information. A copy of an approved notice from the state is found in CCR 9881.1. Alternatively, employers may devise a form that complies with the notice requirements of LC 3550 that has been submitted to the administrative director of the Division of Workers' Compensation for approval before its use (CCR 9881(c)).

TIME OF HIRE NOTICE

Per LC 3551, the employer is required to give every new employee written notice of the information contained in LC 3550 at the time of hire or by the end of the first pay period. The notice must be easily understandable and available in both English and Spanish. In addition to the information contained in LC 3550, the LC 3551 notice, per CCR 9880, is required to explain:

1. generally how to obtain appropriate medical care for a job injury;
2. the role and function of the primary treating physician; and
3. the form that the employee may use as an optional method for notifying the employer of his or her "personal physician," as defined by LC 4600, or "personal chiropractor," as defined by LC 4601.

Information provided in an employee information pamphlet at the time of hire may no longer be accurate when the employee sustains an injury. For instance, an insured employer may become self-insured after an employee was hired. The employer's posting notice must be changed as necessary to ensure that it is accurate at all times. Although not required, when information in the notice changes to reflect updated circumstances, it's to the employer's benefit to distribute updates to all employees.

Effective in 2012, per LC 2810.5, an employer also is required to provide an employee with information regarding wages and how the employer is obliged to conduct business as well as the name, address and telephone number of the workers' compensation insurance carrier. Specifically, LC 2810.5(a)(1) requires an employer to provide written notice containing this information:

1. the rate or rates of pay and basis thereof, whether paid by the hour, shift, day, week, salary, piece, commission or otherwise, including any rates for overtime, as applicable;

2. allowances, if any, claimed as part of the minimum wage, including meal or lodging allowances;
3. the regular payday designated by the employer;
4. the name of the employer, including any "doing business as" names it uses;
5. the physical address of the employer's main office or principal place of business, and a mailing address, if different;
6. the telephone number of the employer;
7. the name, address, and telephone number of the employer's workers' compensation insurance carrier; and
8. any other information the Labor Commissioner deems material and necessary.

The Labor Commissioner is required to prepare a template that complies with the requirements outlined above.

INAPPLICABLE TO RESIDENTIAL EMPLOYEES

Employers are not required to post or provide the notices defined in LC 3550 or LC 3551 for residential employees as defined by LC 3351(d) (LC 3550(c) and LC 3551(a)). These employees are defined in Section 4.25 Residential Employees.

PENALTIES FOR FAILURE TO POST NOTICE

An employer who fails to keep the notice required by LC 3550 conspicuously posted is guilty of a misdemeanor, and the failure is prima-facie evidence of being uninsured (LC 3550(b)). Any employer who fails to post any notice required by LC 3550 shall be assessed a civil penalty of as much as $7,000 for each violation (LC 6431). Furthermore, the failure to provide the notice as required by LC 3550 shall automatically permit the employee to be treated by his or her treating physician with respect to an injury occurring during that failure (LC 3550(e)). The effect when there is a medical provider network in place is discussed in Section 7.56 MPN — Escaping the Network.

EFFECT ON THE STATUTE OF LIMITATIONS

Neither LC 3550 nor LC 3551 discusses whether the failure to post notice of an employee's right to compensation benefits has an effect on the statute of limitations. The employer's failure to post the required notices could have an adverse effect on a statute of limitations defense to a claim. This is because an employee should not be barred from receiving workers' compensation benefits if the employer never informed the employee of his or her compensation rights and how to pursue them. As discussed later in this chapter, a series of cases hold that if an employer has knowledge of an industrial injury, the statute of limitations is tolled if the employer fails to provide the employee with a claim form pursuant to LC 5401.[1]

In an unpublished opinion, the Court of Appeal also held that if an employer fails to post the notice of employee' workers' compensation rights required by LC 3550, and the employee is otherwise unaware of them, the statute of limitations is tolled until the employee gains actual knowledge that he or she may be entitled to benefits.[2] In that case, an employee claimed a cumulative trauma (CT) injury to her psyche ending in July 1999. The doctors told her in 1998 and 1999 that the stress was work related and she went off work due to stress. So the date of injury pursuant to LC 5412 was in 1999. The employee did not file her claim until 2003, asserting that she was unaware of her rights and did not know that her problems were covered. The employer disputed the claim on the grounds that the employee failed to file her claim within one year from the date of injury as defined by LC 5412. The employer did not admit that it failed to post notice of workers' compensation rights, nor did it produce evidence that it did post such a notice, nor evidence that it provided the applicant with an individual notice of her rights.[3]

The Court of Appeal annulled the appeals board's decision and found that the claim was not barred by the statute of limitations. The court noted that the case demonstrated the need for posted notices to protect employees' rights under the workers' compensation law because the employee testified that she did not file a claim because she did not know her injury might be covered and was unaware of her rights. The court acknowledged that tolling the statute of limitations for failing to post notices under LC 3550 could frustrate the policy supporting the statute of limitations because memories fade, witnesses may no longer be available and evidence may be lost. The court added, however, that other principles overrode the statute of limitations considerations and added that in cases in which no individual can testify to seeing a posted notice, the employer may be able to establish posting by other evidence including habit and custom. Finally, the court found that there was no authority to support the employer's

[1] See *Reynolds v. WCAB* (1974) 39 CCC 768; *Kaiser Foundation Hospitals, Permanente Medical Group v. WCAB (Martin)* (1985) 50 CCC 411.

[2] *Pugh v. WCAB* (2008) 73 CCC 1561, 1562-64 (Court of Appeal opinion unpublished in official reports).

[3] *Pugh v. WCAB* (2008) 73 CCC 1561, 1562-64 (Court of Appeal opinion unpublished in official reports).

argument that the civil and criminal penalties enumerated in LC 3550 were the only consequences for an employer's failure to post the required notice.[4]

So although LC 3550 provides for a misdemeanor conviction and a civil penalty of $7,000 for each violation, an additional consequence of the failure to post a required notice under LC 3550 may be the tolling of the statute of limitations for filing an employee's workers' compensation claim until the employee gains actual knowledge of his or her right to benefits.

[4] *Pugh v. WCAB* (2008) 73 CCC 1561, 1564-67 (Court of Appeal opinion unpublished in official reports).

6.4 DUTY OF THE EMPLOYEE TO REPORT INJURY

The employee may not know the difference between industrial and nonindustrial injuries. But if the employer has complied with all pre-injury notice requirements, the employee will have been advised in advance to report all injuries that may be industrially related to the employer. The employee may also have received optional notifications that the employer voluntarily provided, such as information disseminated at safety meetings.

If the employee believes an injury or condition may be work related, he or she is obligated to put the employer on notice of it – the employee has a basic obligation to notify the employer of an injury. The employer is entitled to notice and an opportunity to timely investigate the injury.

TIMING OF EMPLOYEE'S REPORT OF INJURY

LC 5400 provides that no claim for compensation shall be maintained unless the employer is served in writing with notice that an injury claimed to have caused disability or death has occurred. This notice must be served within 30 days after the injury occurs, and this requirement includes dependents of a deceased employee. LC 5400 does not require that the written notice be issued in any particular form, and in practice, it is rarely done.

LC 5402 sets forth an exception to the written notice requirement established in LC 5400. Under LC 5402, an employer's knowledge of the injury from any source, or knowledge that a claim is being asserted, substitutes for the written notice required by LC 5400.[1] (What constitutes knowledge of injury is discussed in depth in Section 6.5 Post-Injury Notices.) So the employee bears the initial burden of notifying the employer of an injury, unless such notice is unnecessary because the employer already knows of the injury or claimed injury from other sources.[2] An employee's failure to give written notice has no consequence if an employer otherwise gains knowledge of the injury. But if the employer does not gain such knowledge, it may move to dismiss the claim under LC 5403.[3]

DISMISSAL OF CLAIM FOR EMPLOYEE'S FAILURE TO TIMELY REPORT

If the employee fails to provide the employer notice under LC 5400 and the employer does not have knowledge of the injury from any source under LC 5402, the employer can move to dismiss an untimely claim under LC 5403. That statute states that a failure to give notice under LC 5400, or any defect or inaccuracy in a notice, is not a bar to recovery unless the employer was misled or prejudiced by the failure to provide notice. Put differently, a claim may be barred for a failure to give notice under LC 5400 only if the employer was misled or prejudiced by the lack of notice. The employer bears the burden of proving prejudice.[4]

Dismissals under LC 5403 are rare because of the broad notice provisions of LC 5402 and the employer's heavy burden of proving prejudice for lack of notice.[5] It does not appear that any cases have outlined circumstances under which prejudice may be demonstrated under LC 5403.[6]

But a couple of cases have described circumstances in which the assertion of prejudice was not proved. In one, an applicant reported an injury to his left wrist due to a specific injury. The medical reporting demonstrated that the injury occurred as a result of a cumulative trauma injury rather than a specific injury. The appeals board denied benefits because the applicant only alleged a specific

[1] *Honeywell v. WCAB (Wagner)* (2005) 70 CCC 97, 101.
[2] *Honeywell v. WCAB (Wagner)* (2005) 70 CCC 97, 102.
[3] *Kaiser Foundation Hospitals, Permanente Medical Group v. WCAB (Martin)* (1985) 50 CCC 411, 417.
[4] LC 5705(e); *Pacific Employers Insurance Co. v. IAC (Huffman)* (1949) 14 CCC 82.
[5] *Kaiser Foundation Hospitals, Permanente Medical Group v. WCAB (Martin)* (1985) 50 CCC 411, 417, fn. 7. See *Charter Oak Unified School District v. WCAB (Mangone)* (1996) 61 CCC 103 (writ denied); *Summers v. WCAB* (2004) 69 CCC 645 (writ denied).
[6] The defense worked in at least one writ-denied case, *Valensolo v. WCAB (McGuinness)* (1977) 42 CCC 569 (writ denied). But that case did not describe any specific prejudice or the standard that could be used to determine it. In an unpublished opinion, the court held that LC 5403 did not apply when a claim was barred by the post-termination defense under LC 3600(a)(10)(A), because an employee's failure to give notice of injury within 30 days under LC 5400 is separate from issue of whether injury claim was filed subsequent to employee's notice of termination or layoff. *Chavez v. WCAB* (2007) 72 CCC 307 (Court of Appeal opinion unpublished in official reports).

injury and there was no evidence to support that claim. The Court of Appeal held that the appeals board abused its discretion in not considering the CT claim. The court noted that although a claim could not be maintained unless an employer is given notice in writing under LC 5400 and LC 5401, the employer knew that the applicant was suffering a cumulative trauma injury based on the medical evidence. So because the employer had timely knowledge of the nature of the employee's injury, it was not prejudiced only because the injury was improperly claimed as a specific injury rather than a cumulative trauma injury.[7]

In another case, an employee slipped and fell at work on May 16, 2001, injuring his wrists. He did not report the injury or miss any time from work. In October 2002, the applicant complained of increased wrist pain and underwent surgery in December 2002. A doctor opined that the applicant's injury was due to the May 2001 fall at work. Before going off work for surgery, the applicant did not report his injury to the employer. The appeals board ultimately decided the claim was compensable because the employer was not misled or prejudiced by the applicant's failure to report the injury. The appeals board stated that the applicant received no medical treatment until late 2002. It noted that the applicant's deposition was taken fewer than five months after the surgery, and the employer had a full and fair opportunity to question the applicant about the circumstances of the accident and his medical condition. It added that because there were no witnesses to the accident, the employer was not prejudiced by an inability to obtain statements from others. Furthermore, all of the medical records regarding the applicant's condition were available to the employer. The appeals board also concluded that the claim was not barred by the statute of limitations under LC 5405 (discussed in detail in Section 6.13 One-Year Statute of Limitations) because the case involved a latent specific injury and the applicant filed his claim within one year of learning that the condition was industrial.[8]

It is very difficult to have a claim dismissed under LC 5403. In practice, the defense is frequently raised and seldom successful. But the 30-day limitation period is not completely worthless or totally disregarded by judges — it can bar or reduce the employee's compensation in the very few cases in which the employer is able to prove prejudice. For the purposes of LC 5403, "prejudice" means prejudice to a proper defense of the claim. The type of prejudice likely contemplated by LC 5403 would be the inability to effectively investigate the claim due to the unreasonable delay in reporting the injury. If the statutory criteria for the application of LC 5403 can be established, there is no reason for

---

[7] *Beckstead v. WCAB* (1997) 62 CCC 1646.

[8] *Save Mart Supermarkets v. WCAB (Hixson II)* (2007) 72 CCC 509 (writ denied).

the employer to disregard this potentially valuable defense. If the defense is established, it will completely bar the applicant's claim.

6.5 POST-INJURY NOTICES

After receiving knowledge of an injury, either in writing (LC 5400) or from any source (LC 5402), the employer is required to provide information to the employee about his or her rights to workers' compensation benefits. In the case of death, an employer is required to provide the information to the employee's dependents.

If there is no knowledge of injury, there is no obligation to provide this information, with one exception: An employer is required to give any employee who is a victim of a crime that occurred on work premises written notice that the employee is eligible for workers' compensation for injuries, including psychiatric injuries, that may have resulted from the crime (LC 3553).

CLAIM FORM AND NOTICE OF POTENTIAL ELIGIBILITY

The initial post-injury notice that the employer is required to provide to the employee (or dependents in the event of death) is a claim form and a notice of potential eligibility for benefits. A claim form is a simple, one-page document that identifies the parties as well as the nature and part of body affected by the claimed injury. The notice of potential eligibility for benefits will advise the employee of the various rights and benefits available for workers' compensation injuries, and must be understandable and available in English and Spanish (LC 5401). The contents include, but are not limited to:

1. how to commence proceedings for the collection of compensation;
2. a description of the different types of workers' compensation benefits;
3. what happens to the claim form after it is filed;

4. from whom the employee can obtain medical care for the injury;
5. the role and function of the primary treating physician;
6. the rights of an employee to select and change the treating physician pursuant to LC 3550(e) and LC 4600;
7. how to get medical care while the claim is pending;
8. the protections against discrimination pursuant to LC 132a;
9. these written statements:
    a. You have a right to disagree with decisions affecting your claim.
    b. To obtain importation information about the workers' compensation claims process and your right and obligations, go to [applicable Internet Web site(s)], or contact an information and assistance (I&A) officer for the state Division of Workers' Compensation. You can also hear recorded information and a list of local I&A offices by call [applicable information and assistance telephone number(s)].
    c. You can consult an attorney. Most attorneys offer one free consultation. If you decide to hire an attorney, his or her fee will be taken out of some of your benefits. For names of workers' compensation attorneys, call the State Bar of California at (telephone number of the State Bar of California's legal specialization program, or its equivalent).

The claim form must also advise that "[a]ny person who makes or causes to be made any knowingly false statement or material misrepresentation for the purpose of obtaining or denying workers' compensation benefits or payments is guilty of a felony (LC 5401.7). The form and content of the claim form and notice have been prescribed by the administrative director after consultation with the Commission on Health and Safety and Workers' compensation. Copies of the claim form and notice may be found in CCR 10139.

The employer portion of the form may also include other information pertinent to the claim, including a logo or other employer identifying information, but such information shall in no way impose additional duties or prohibitions on the employee or delay the processing of the claim (CCR 10138).

The mechanics of the claim form are described in CCR 10138 - CCR 10140. It is a one-page white form with carbon copies attached; the employer generally retains the original. The second page is pink and goes to the employee. The third page is yellow and goes to the claims administrator. The final copy is green and labeled a receipt. It is to be retained by the employee. The employee fills out the top of the form and the employer fills out the bottom. Note that the information regarding benefits and procedures is printed on the back of the temporary receipt. That information can be needed to show proper notice to the employee, so it is important that he or she be given that last green copy.

KNOWLEDGE OF INDUSTRIAL INJURY

Per LC 5401(a), an employer must provide a claim form and notice of potential eligibility within one working day of receiving notice or knowledge of an injury under LC 5400 or LC 5402 that results in lost time beyond the employee's work shift or that results in medical treatment beyond first aid. The pertinent question is: What constitutes "knowledge of injury"? If the employer hears gossip from co-workers that there was an injury, is that enough? Or does the employer have to witness it? In other words, under what circumstances is knowledge of injury imputed to the employer?

First, the knowledge must be obtained by a managing agent, superintendent, foreman or other person in authority (LC 5402(a)). A co-worker is not a person of authority for the purposes of LC 5402.[1] Furthermore, in an unpublished opinion, the Court of Appeal held that a union representative could not be regarded as an agent or other person of authority.[2]

Next, the employer clearly has knowledge on receipt of written notice of an injury pursuant to LC 5400. But per LC 5402, the employer also has awareness on receipt of "knowledge of an injury, obtained from any source ... or knowledge of the assertion of a claim of injury sufficient to afford opportunity to the employer to make an investigation into the facts." So knowledge of an industrial injury may come from any source and is not limited to written notice from the employee. This is the rule that is a source of much confusion.

Previously, courts held that knowledge for the purposes of LC 5402 was not limited to actual knowledge, but included constructive knowledge of the injury.[3]

---

[1] See *Hall v. WCAB* (1996) 61 CCC 1072 (writ denied).
[2] *United Parcel Service v. WCAB (White)* (1999) 64 CCC 1369 (Court of Appeal opinion not published in official reports).
[3] *Kaiser Foundation Hospitals, Permanente Medical Group v. WCAB (Martin)* (1985) 50 CCC 411; *Sidders v. WCAB* (1988) 53 CCC 445, 450. See *Buena Ventura Gardens v. WCAB (Novak)* (1975) 40 CCC 434 (employer did not have precise medical knowledge of the employee's condition, but knew that the disability was sustained during the period of employment, that it was permanently disabling and that it *might* be related to the employment).

In *Honeywell v. WCAB (Wagner)*,[4] however, the California Supreme Court concluded that an employer's duty under LC 5401 to provide a claim form and notice arises when it has notice in writing of an injury by the employee, or knows of the injury or claim from another source. The court continued that the duty does not arise whenever the employer learns facts that would lead a reasonable person to conclude with some certainty that an industrial injury has occurred or is being asserted. Instead, the court concluded that the duty arises when the employer actually knows of an injury or claim, not when it should have known.[5]

In *Honeywell,* an applicant's wife called the employer in October 1998. She left a message that the applicant had been hospitalized for psychiatric problems, and that the work supervisor had pushed the applicant over the edge with his "head games." Four days later disability forms were submitted to the employer, which made reference to both personal problems and "work problems" as a subject for "continued work in aftercare." The risk managers at the employer testified that in that October that they were "reasonably certain" that the applicant was reporting a work-related injury. The claim form was not provided until the following January 1999, when a medical form was received checking a box, indicating that the injury was work related. The claim was denied the following March, which lent the question, did the reporting in October amount to employer knowledge of injury? The timeliness of the denial turned on the question.

The appeals board in an *en banc* decision concluded that "reasonable certainty" constituted employer knowledge and triggered the obligation to provide a claim form. But the Court of Appeal, and the Supreme Court in *Honeywell,* reversed, holding that "The employer's duty under section 5401 arises ... (when it) has 'knowledge' of the injury or claim form from another source (5402(a)); it does not arise whenever the employer learns of facts that would 'lead a reasonable person to conclude with some certainty that an industrial injury .... has occurred or is being asserted.'" "The duty arises when the employer knows of an injury or claim, not when it should have known. ..."[6]

The *Honeywell* court suggests that only actual knowledge triggers an employer's duty to provide a claim form. So witnessing an injury would be enough, but hearing a rumor from employees would not. Of course, even after *Honeywell,* one can envision many situations in which it is not clear whether the employer has

---

[4] (2005) 70 CCC 97.
[5] *Honeywell v. WCAB (Wagner)* (2005) 70 CCC 97, 107.
[6] *Honeywell v. WCAB (Wagner)* (2005) 70 CCC 97, 107, quoting *Wagner v. Allied Signal Aerospace* (2001) 66 CCC 483, 489.

actual knowledge. Case law does give us some examples. In a decision before *Honeywell,* the California Supreme Court held that an employer had knowledge when a supervisor witnessed an employee's heart attack on premises.[7] The appeals board has also held that an employer had knowledge of an industrial injury when it received a copy of a doctor's first report of occupational injury or illness,[8] and when a civil suit was filed that articulated a work-related injury.[9]

In one case subsequent to *Honeywell,* a farm worker began suffering symptoms after pruning grape vines. She complained to the foreman that her hands were blistered and painful. She also told the vineyard manager that she could not sleep because of pain in her hands. The vineyard manager told the applicant it was her decision whether or not to keep working. In an unpublished opinion, the Court of Appeal stated that the applicant's report of pain and her supervisors' reactions to her comments appeared to establish that the employer was on notice that she was injured and entitled to workers' compensation. The case was remanded for further proceedings to determine whether the employer was on notice that the applicant was suffering from work-related injuries.[10]

In another unpublished opinion, in 2001 an employee noticed pain from her groin radiating to her right leg and eventually told her supervisor that she could not perform her duties. The employee received state disability benefits augmented by the employer's short- and long-term disability policies. In 2004, when her long-term disability insurance coverage ended, the employee filed for workers' compensation benefits. The court held that she was not barred by the statute of limitations because the employer failed to advise the employee of her rights to file a workers' compensation claim. The court noted that the applicant's symptoms should have been so obvious that the employer should have known she sustained a work-related injury because she complained to her supervisor and continually was absent from work. Also, the court added that the employer should have been aware of her condition through its sponsored health plan and short- and long-term disability plans.[11] Both of these unpublished opinions cited *Honeywell,* but neither is binding or even citable.

In contrast, in a panel decision, the appeals board found that the employer did not have notice of an injury, even though it had notice of an incident involving

---

[7] *Reynolds v. WCAB* (1974) 39 CCC 768.
[8] *Bailey v. WCAB* (1997) 63 CCC 52 (writ denied); *City of Anaheim v. WCAB (Hagan)* (1995) 60 CCC 1017 (writ denied).
[9] *Gorelik v. Norris Industries* (1991) 20 CWCR 13 (board panel decision).
[10] *Arciga v. WCAB* (2007) 72 CCC 1 (Court of Appeal opinion unpublished in official reports).
[11] *Federal Express v. WCAB (Uhlik)* (2006) 71 CCC 1703 (Court of Appeal opinion unpublished in official reports).

the applicant. It was undisputed that the applicant reported his fall from a ladder to his immediate supervisor before termination. The immediate supervisor, however, testified that when the applicant reported the incident to him, the applicant said he was fine. The applicant missed no time from work and did not request or seek medical treatment before his termination. Based on these facts, the appeals board concluded that the employer did not have notice of an injury.[12]

MEDICAL TREATMENT BEYOND FIRST AID

An employer is not required to provide a claim form to an employee for a minor injury. (The definition of injury is covered in Chapter 5.) An employer is only required to provide a claim form and notice of potential eligibility to an employer for an injury that results in lost time beyond the employee's work shift or *medical treatment beyond first aid.* LC 5401 defines "first aid" as "any one-time treatment of minor scratches, cuts, burns, splinters, or other minor industrial injury, which do not ordinarily require medical care." One-time treatment, and a follow-up visit for the purpose of observation, is considered first aid even when provided by a physician or registered professional personnel. The employer's duty to provide the employee with a claim form and notice of potential rights to benefits (and concurrently file a report of injury with its insurer) is contingent upon the type of treatment that the employee receives, not the qualifications of the person providing treatment.

LC 5401 states that a "minor industrial injury" "does not include serious exposure to a hazardous substance as defined in subdivision (i) of Section 6302."[13] In one case, the appeals board held that X-rays, an ice pack, a sling and an afternoon off work did not trigger the requirement of LC 5401 that an injured employee be provided with a claim form.[14]

The parties do well to remember that the care given is an issue of fact that requires proof. In one case the appeals board concluded that an applicant's visits to the company nurse were sufficient to trigger the defendant's obligation to provide a claim form. The defendant argued that the applicant received only first

[12] *Palacios v. Upside Management Co., Inc.*, 2011 Cal. Wrk. Comp. P.D. LEXIS 495. *Palacios* dealt with notice of an injury under LC 3600(a)(10) for the purposes of the post-termination defense. Because the knowledge required to give rise to an employer's duty to provide a claim form is the same as that required under LC 3600(a)(10)(A) (both rely on LC 5400 and LC 5402), the standard in *Honeywell* also would apply to cases involving the post-termination defense under LC 3600(a)(10).

[13] LC 6302(i) defines a "serious exposure" as "any exposure of an employee to a hazardous substance when the exposure occurs as a result of an incident, accident, emergency or exposure over time and is in a degree or amount sufficient to create a substantial probability that death or serious physical harm in the future could result from the exposure."

[14] *Cottrell v. WCAB* (1998) 63 CCC 760 (writ denied).

aid — but had failed to prove that point in court. The WCAB panel explained that any records of the applicant's visits to the company nurse should be in the defendant's possession, and if the defendant wished to prove that only first aid was provided, it could have offered those records into evidence. So the defendant failed to show that only first aid was provided at the visit. Because the defendant did not show that notice of the applicant's workers' compensation rights were furnished properly, the panel concluded that the applicant's claim was not barred by the statute of limitations.[15]

FURNISHING THE CLAIM FORM

An employer is not required to provide a claim form and notice of potential eligibility for workers' compensation benefits unless the employee loses time beyond his work shift or requires medical treatment beyond first aid, and the employer is aware that the circumstances of work caused or contributed to the injury.[16] But for the sake of consistency and to protect a potential statute of limitations defense, it could be in the employer's best interest to routinely provide a claim form for every claim of injury.

Once the claim form is furnished, it is often filled out by the employee on the spot. The employer is then under the obligation to fill out its portion, sign it and deliver it to the claims adjuster with copies to the employee as described above (CCR 10140). If the claim form is not returned in person, then these functions are usually performed by mail. There seems to be no direct legal impact if the employer does not fill out its portion of the form or deliver it. It is the provision of the claim form and notice of rights that matters for purposes of the statute of limitations.

If the employer is required to furnish a claim form to an employee, it must be furnished within one working day of receiving notice or knowledge of injury. The form must be furnished personally or by first-class mail. An employer is not required to provide additional claim forms each time a medical report identifies another symptom or injured body part.[17] But an employer is required to provide a claim form any time it obtains knowledge of a new injury.[18]

If an injured applicant is not an employee as in the case of an association, or is both an employer and an employee, as in the case of a partnership, the notice

[15] *Palafox v. Textron Inc.*, 2011 Cal. Wrk. Comp. P.D. LEXIS 389.
[16] *Bailey v. WCAB* (1997) 63 CCC 52 (writ denied).
[17] *Wildermuth v. WCAB* (1995) 60 CCC 666 (writ denied).
[18] *Crown Cork & Seal v. WCAB (Fields)* (2002) 67 CCC 175 (writ denied).

requirements are not applicable. This is because a person with knowledge of a potential claim is not required to give notice to himself or herself.[19] But if the employer is a corporation, the notice requirements of LC 5402 would apply.[20]

If the employer does not provide the claim form, the duty to do so can fall to the insurance carrier. If the claims administrator obtains knowledge that the employer has not provided a claim form or notice of potential eligibility for benefits to the employee, it must provide one to the employee within three working days of knowing that the form was not provided. If the claims administrator cannot determine if the employer has provided the required forms to the employee, the claims administrator shall provide one to the employee within 30 days of the administrator's date of knowledge of the claim (LC 138.4(b)(c) and CCR 10140(b)(c)). As a practical matter, most insurance adjusters provide the claim form and other documentation upon knowledge of a claim.

EFFECT ON THE STATUTE OF LIMITATIONS

It is very important that a claim form and notice of potential eligibility for benefits is provided to the employee if one is required, as this will trigger the statute of limitations to file the claim. If the employer has met its statutory and regulatory obligations to provide legally required notices, the employer becomes entitled to the finality and repose the statue of limitations is intended to provide.[21] If, however, the employer fails to provide a claim form and notice of potential eligibility for benefits, the statute of limitations will be tolled until the employer ultimately provides the required notices or until the employee gets actual notice of his or her workers' compensation rights.[22] This will be discussed in Section 6.17 Estoppel Based on Failure to Provide Notice.

[19] *Sidders v. WCAB* (1988) 53 CCC 445, 453.
[20] *Sidders v. WCAB* (1988) 53 CCC 445, 453.
[21] *Stephens v. WCAB* (2009) 74 CCC 885 (writ denied).
[22] *Kaiser Foundation Hospitals, Permanente Medical Group v. WCAB (Martin)* (1985) 50 CCC 411, 416.

6.6 FILING THE CLAIM FORM AND EFFECT ON RIGHTS

FILING THE CLAIM FORM

The completed claim form can be filed with the employer by the injured employee, or, in the case of death by a dependent of the injured employee, by an agent of the employee or dependent. Note that the employee does not have to fill out and deliver the claim form, nor does he or she have to file a claim form. But to file a workers' compensation claim, one must deliver the form. The claim form is deemed filed when it is personally delivered to the employer or received by the employer by first-class or certified mail (LC 5401(d)). Although the employee is supposed to file a completed claim form with the employer, a claim form filed directly with the employer's insurer or claims administrator will be deemed to have been filed with the employer.

The completed claim form must include the employee name, address, Social Security number, date of injury, a description of where the injury happened and a description of the injury and the part(s) of body affected. Upon receipt of the completed claim form, the employer must date the form, and a dated copy must then be provided by the employer to the employer's insurer and to the employee, dependent or agent who filed the form (LC 5401(d)). The employer should provide the dated copy to the employee and its claims administrator within one working day of receipt (CCR 10140).

The claims administrator must keep a copy of the claim form showing the date the employer received knowledge of the claim of injury, the date the form was provided to the employee and the date a completed form was received from the employee. If the employee does not return a completed claim form to the employer, the claims administrator must document the date the employer provided a claim form to the employee or, if one was not furnished by the employer, the date the claims administrator provided the claim form to the employee (CCR 10101.1). The employer's documentation of the date the form was provided to the employee is an important piece of evidence should the employee later seek benefits after expiration of a statute of limitations.

EFFECT ON RIGHTS

The filing of the claim form by an employee is the filing of a workers' compensation claim. This act carries legal implications in the system. Filing the claim form allows the injured worker to begin receiving certain payments and to request a medical evaluation.[1] A claim form must be filed with the employer before the injured employee's entitlement to late payment supplements under LC 4650(d), commonly referred to as a "self-imposed penalty," or a request for a medical-legal evaluation under LC 4060, LC 4061 and LC 4062. In addition, the filing of a claim form triggers the 90-day period under LC 5402 for the employer to investigate and evaluate the claim. If the employer does not reject liability within that period, the injury is presumed compensable, and the presumption is only rebuttable by later discovered evidence.[2] (The presumption of injury is discussed in detail in Section 5.16 Presumption of Injury — 90-Day Rule.)

Note that the filing of a claim form is not required for the employer to be obligated to provide benefits, including reasonable medical care (CCR 10137), which must be provided upon notice of injury. Unless there is genuine reasonable doubt as to the need for medical care, it must be provided regardless of whether the claim form is filed. It remains unclear how long this duty lasts, but the employer does seem entitled at some point to have a claim actually filed.

There is some statutory guidance, which demonstrates the importance of the claim form. Per LC 5402(c), within one working day after an employee files a claim form under LC 5401, the employer must authorize the provision of all reasonable medical treatment for the alleged injury. LC 5402(c) does not force an employer to provide medical care that is unnecessary or unreasonable. (Medical treatment is discussed in depth in Chapter 7.) But the employer must continue to provide for the reasonable treatment until the date liability for the claim is

[1] *Honeywell v. WCAB (Wagner)* (2005) 70 CCC 97, 102.
[2] *Honeywell v. WCAB (Wagner)* (2005) 70 CCC 97, 102.

accepted or rejected. Until that time, the employer's liability for medical treatment is limited to $10,000. Of course, liability ends at the time of denial, and so the defense is motivated to move quickly to a decision if the case seems to warrant possible denial.

If there is a bona fide dispute as to provision of medical treatment under LC 5402(c), the applicant is entitled to an expedited priority hearing and decision pursuant to LC 5502(b) and CCR 10136.[3] No determination of whether or not an industrial injury has occurred will be made at an expedited hearing conducted under LC 5402(c). The issues are limited to:

1. whether the employee filed a claim form and the date and receipt by the employer;
2. whether the employer has accepted or rejected liability, and the date of acceptance or rejection; and
3. whether or not medical treatment must be provided generally under LC 5402(c), the liability for that medical treatment and the intervals of such liability.[4]

At any expedited hearing defined LC 5402(c), the parties may request the case to be continued for a priority conference (if the employee is represented) or a status conference (if the employee is not represented) in order to address the issue of injury arising out of and in the course of employment (AOE/COE).[5]

EFFECT ON STATUTE OF LIMITATIONS

The filing of a claim form with an employer also tolls the statute of limitations established in LC 5405 and LC 5406, until the claim is denied by the employer or the injury becomes presumptively compensable pursuant to LC 5402 (LC 5401(d)). If the employer denies the claim, the statute of limitations begins to run from the date of the denial.[6] Per LC 5402, unless a claim has been denied within 90 days after a claim form is filed, it is rebuttably presumed to be compensable. Unless the presumption is rebutted, benefits are owed and the employee may file a timely claim within one year from the last provision of benefits.

---

[3] DWC/WCAB Joint Implementation Memorandum on Labor Code 5402(c) (June 16, 2004).
[4] DWC/WCAB Joint Implementation Memorandum on Labor Code 5402(c) (June 16, 2004).
[5] DWC/WCAB Joint Implementation Memorandum on Labor Code 5402(c) (June 16, 2004).
[6] *McDaniel v. WCAB* (1990) 55 CCC 72.

6.7 DENIAL LETTER

The filing of a claim form triggers the 90-day period under LC 5402 for the employer to investigate and evaluate the claim. If the employer does not reject liability within that period, the injury is presumed compensable, and the presumption is only rebuttable by later discovered evidence. The form and substance of the denial letter and the ramifications for an untimely denial are discussed in Section 5.16 Presumption of Injury — 90-Day Rule. The 90-day period and the denial letter are also important in their effect on the statute of limitations.

Per LC 5401(d), the filing of a claim form tolls the statute of limitations established in LC 5405 and LC 5406. That is, the period that the applicant has to file his case with the WCAB is suspended when the claim form is filed. The period does not begin to run again until the claim is denied by the employer or the injury becomes presumptively compensable 90 days later. Of course, the claim may be accepted and then the statute will run from the last payment of benefits, as discussed in the next sections.

Unlike a denial sufficient to avoid the presumption of compensability under LC 5402, a denial for the purpose of ending the tolling of the limitations period must be in writing and conform with the notice regulations enumerated in CCR 9810 et. seq. (CCR 10142).[1] CCR 10142 provides that the date of denial for the purposes of ending the tolling of the limitations period is the date the written denial notice

[1] CCR 9812(i) specifically provides that if a claims administrator denies liability for the payment of all workers' compensation benefits for any claim except a claim for death benefits, including medical-only claims, the claims administrator shall advise the employee of the denial and the reasons for it. The notice shall be sent no later than 14 days after the determination to deny was made, and a copy of the most recent version of the DWC informative pamphlet QME/AME Fact Sheet shall be provided with the notice.

is personally served, or if the denial is mailed, then five days after the denial is placed in the mail if the address is within California, 10 days if the address is outside of California and 20 days if the address is outside of the United States.[2]

Note that an employer is not precluded from denying a claim simply because it has paid the applicant workers' compensation benefits. A claim may be denied if a subsequent investigation reveals that the injury was not compensable, even in some cases in which the 90-day investigation period has expired, particularly if the benefits were procured by fraud. If an employer voluntarily furnishes benefits, but subsequently informs the claimant that it is denying liability for the alleged industrial injury, the claimant has one year from the date notice of denial was given to commence workers' compensation proceedings.[3]

---

[2] See *McDaniel v. WCAB* (1990) 55 CCC 72, 76.

[3] *Kaiser Foundation Hospitals, Permanente Medical Group v. WCAB (Webb)* (1977) 42 CCC 302. See also *Lockheed Missiles & Space Co. v. WCAB (Buckman)* (1991) 56 CCC 84 (Court of Appeal opinion unpublished in official reports) (claim filed more than one year after employer provided benefits and then denied liability was barred by the statute of limitations).

6.8 COMMENCEMENT OF PROCEEDINGS

The claim form must be given to the employer. An employee can do that and still end up violating the statute of limitations. Ultimately, in order to avoid a statute of limitations problem, an employee must commence proceedings with the appeals board within certain time limitations. What does that mean? Proceedings are commenced before the appeals board by filing an application for adjudication.[1]

Appeals board proceedings include hearings (trials), conferences or arbitration. Proceedings are not commenced simply because an applicant has filed a claim form with the employer.[2] The taking of a deposition is not the commencement of proceedings.[3] Likewise, sending an employer a letter indicating that an applicant would be seeking compensation benefits is insufficient to constitute the commencement of proceedings because the intention is not the performance of

---

[1] This has been so throughout the history of California workers' compensation, except for the "window period." This was the period between Jan. 1, 1990 and Dec. 1, 1993; an ill-fated attempt at reform changed the rules on this point for dates of injury within this period. During window-period cases, the claim form and not the application was filed to commence proceedings. The claim form was still used for its other purposes, which created a lot of confusion. When the 1989 Reform Act was, in essence, reversed as of 1994, it was provided that, once again, the application should be filed with the WCAB to commence proceedings, for all dates of injury. So for window-period cases, if a claim form had ever been filed with the appeals board, the application was again the correct document to file.

[2] See *San Joaquin Community Hospital v. WCAB (McMahan)* (2002) 67 CCC 1653 (writ denied) (appeals board discussing how the one-year statute of limitations begins with the filing of an application for adjudication and not a claim form, but holding that the claim was timely when the employer did not provide adequate notices regarding the applicant's workers' compensation rights); *Banks v. WCAB* (1999) 64 CCC 1457 (writ denied) (claim barred when applicant filed a claim form, but not application).

[3] *Barragan v. WCAB* (2011) 76 CCC 356 (writ denied); *Sanchez v. System Services of America,* 2011 Cal. Wrk. Comp. P.D. LEXIS 341.

the act.[4] Instead, LC 5500 states, "[T]he filing of an application for adjudication and not the filing of a claim form shall establish the jurisdiction of the appeals board and shall commence proceedings before the appeals board for the collection of benefits." The application is like the complaint in a civil lawsuit. In a sense, filing the application is filing the lawsuit and the employee does not have forever to do so.

The statute of limitations requirements in workers' compensation are complicated and will be explained in this chapter one element at a time. LC 5405 defines the basic one-year time period for filing an application for workers' compensation benefits, and invoking the board's original jurisdiction.[5] The timely filing of an application renders the statute of limitations inoperative to any subsequent proceedings for benefits referable to the same injury.[6] Once a timely application has been filed, all further proceedings are governed by the five-year limitations period provided in LC 5410 and LC 5804.[7] If the application is filed in the wrong local WCAB office, the filing remains valid for the purposes of the statute of limitations. In that situation, the presiding workers' compensation judge should simply refer the matter to the proper office.[8]

What does it mean to file an application? Filing is defined under CCR 10301(r), which says to file a document is to "deliver a document or cause it to be delivered to the district office with venue ... for the purpose of having it included in the adjudication file." Generally, the appeals board has a machine that date stamps all documents delivered to it each day. It has been held that stamping in the document is sufficient for filing; a case number need not be assigned until later.[9] It is best to ensure proof of delivery by creating and keeping a conformed copy, and best to have the document filed by hand instead of mail. If the appeals board does not receive the document, it can go badly for the applicant, and can be a malpractice trap for applicant attorneys. In one case, the application was sent by mail with a cover letter. The clerks there were behind and the application was not "officially filed" until past the deadline. It was held that the application

---

[4] *Gonzales v. WCAB* (2008) 73 CCC 519 (writ denied).
[5] *Sanchez v. WCAB* (1990) 55 CCC 179.
[6] LC 5404; *Sanchez v. WCAB* (1990) 55 CCC 179. See *Charter Oak Unified School District v. WCAB (Mangone)* (1996) 61 CCC 103 (writ denied) (amendment to claim not barred by the statute of limitations when the original claim was not barred).
[7] *Sanchez v. WCAB* (1990) 55 CCC 179.
[8] *Noble v. City of Oakland Police Department* (1982) 47 CCC 1 (appeals board *en banc*).
[9] *Main Tool & Die, Inc. v. WCAB (Allen)* (1999) 64 CCC 1488 (writ denied).

was barred by the statute of limitations.[10]

[10] *Gardner v. WCAB* (1986) 51 CCC 145 (writ denied). But see *Torres v. WCAB* (1993) 58 CCC 417 (Court of Appeal opinion unpublished in official reports) in which an LC 132a petition could not be found in the WCAB file. It was proved that it was timely served on defendants, and the WCJ stated his opinion that the appeals board likely misfiled it. Although there was no proof that it was timely filed with the WCAB, it was held as a matter of law that it was. See also *Pizza Hut/Yum Brands v. WCAB (Babayants)* (2007) 72 CCC 1025 (writ denied) (application sent by mail with proof of service was deemed filed when the application was not processed or a case number assigned due solely to clerical error).

SECTIONS 6.9 THROUGH 6.12 ARE RESERVED FOR FUTURE USE

6.13 ONE-YEAR STATUTE OF LIMITATIONS

The statute of limitations in California consists of several provisions with varying limits of time depending on the particular situation (LC 5404 - LC 5412). LC 5405 establishes the basic time limit for commencing proceedings (filing the application for adjudication with the WCAB) and invoking the appeals board's original jurisdiction. It provides that the limit for normal benefits (medical and disability) is one year from the longest of these periods: (1) the date of injury; (2) the date of last indemnity payment for temporary or permanent disability; or (3) the date of last furnishing of any hospital and medical benefits.[1]

If an employer or its workers' compensation insurance carrier, knowing of a potential claim, furnishes treatment or advances sums for purposes bearing a clear relationship to an industrial injury, the one-year statute of limitations under LC 5405(a) will be tolled.[2] For example, if a claim form was filed and immediately denied, the applicant would have one year to file the application with the WCAB. If the claim was accepted and medical benefits were paid, the applicant would have one year from the last provision of treatment to file the application.

There is also a five-year statute of limitations in workers' compensation, which will be discussed in depth in subsequent sections. The five-year statute can have an effect on the one-year statute. When the one-year statute of limitations of LC

[1] *Youngblood v. WCAB* (1989) 54 CCC 489; *McDaniel v. WCAB* (1990) 55 CCC 72, 75 both citing 2 Hanna, Cal. Law of Employee Injuries and Workmen's Compensation (2nd rev. ed. 1989) Section 18.03[1], pps. 18-12-18-13.

[2] *Kaiser Foundation Hospitals/Permanente Medical Group v. WCAB (Webb)* (1977) 42 CCC 302, 304.

5405(a) is tolled by the voluntary furnishing of benefits, the five-year rule of LC 5410 is triggered.[3] LC 5410 extends the period within which an original proceeding may be instituted from one year to five years after the date of injury on the grounds of new and further disability, if the employer furnishes workers' compensation benefits either voluntarily, or pursuant to an award.[4] The reasoning here is that the "new and further disability" to which LC 5410 refers is a disability in addition to that for which the employer previously provided benefits as required by statute.[5]

Sometimes an application is never filed. A claim is made and benefits are paid, sometimes for years. In that instance, the five-year statute becomes irrelevant to the analysis. LC 5405(b)(c) may operate to extend the time for filing original claims beyond the five-year limitations of LC 5410 when benefits continue to be paid voluntarily, without award.[6] That is, if the employer voluntarily provides medical treatment and compensation benefits to the employee more than five years after the date of injury, the employee may commence proceedings by filing an application within one year from the date of the last benefit payment. Furthermore, as long as the employer's conduct reasonably suggests that the filing of an application is unnecessary, the tolling of the statutory time period is entirely proper and in accord with LC 5410 and LC 5405(b)(c).[7] This concept is called estoppel and it is also discussed in the next sections.

Once a potential claimant has been fully informed that the employer and its carrier disclaim compensation liability for an industrial injury — once the claim is denied — the five-year statute of limitations of LC 5410 ceases and the one-year statute of limitations to commence proceedings begins. The statute of limitations begins to run no later than the date on which the notice denying liability was given.[8] So if an employer voluntarily furnishes benefits, but subsequently informs the claimant that it is denying liability for the alleged

[3] *Youngblood v. WCAB* (1989) 54 CCC 489; *McDaniel v. WCAB* (1990) 55 CCC 72, 75; *Sanchez v. WCAB* (1990) 55 CCC 179.

[4] *Youngblood v. WCAB* (1989) 54 CCC 489; *Standard Rectifier Corp. v. WCAB (Whiddon)* (1966) 31 CCC 340, 341; *Sanchez v. WCAB* (1990) 55 CCC 179. Compare *Chandler Furniture Co. v. WCAB (Meeks)* (1990) 55 CCC 248 (writ denied) (claim filed four years after the date of injury was timely when employer provided TD benefits within one year of filing the application) with *Kelley v. WCAB* (2002) 68 CCC 84 (writ denied) (claim filed Dec. 3, 1999 for injury of May 21, 1993 was barred by the statute of limitations of LC 5410, even though employer paid some TD and medical benefits, because it was filed more than five years after the date of injury).

[5] *Standard Rectifier Corp. v. WCAB (Whiddon)* (1966) 31 CCC 340, 342.

[6] *Sanchez v. WCAB* (1990) 55 CCC 179; *Youngblood v. WCAB* (1989) 54 CCC 489; *State of California, SIF v. IAC (Busch)* (1962) 27 CCC 14; *SIF v. IAC (Ferguson)* (1960) 25 CCC 26; *City of Long Beach v. WCAB (Bramlett)* (1985) 60 CCC 1021 (writ denied).

[7] *Kaiser Foundation Hospitals/Permanente Medical Group v. WCAB (Webb)* (1977) 42 CCC 302, 307.

[8] *Kaiser Foundation Hospitals/Permanente Medical Group v. WCAB (Webb)* (1977) 42 CCC 302, 307; *McDaniel v. WCAB* (1990) 55 CCC 72, 76.

industrial injury, the claimant has one year from the date notice was given to commence workers' compensation proceedings.[9]

For example, in *Kaiser Foundation Hospitals/Permanente Medical Group v. WCAB (Webb),*[10] an employee developed a hernia during the course of employment and treated with a medical facility that became a lien claimant. The employer referred the employee for an examination whose conclusion was that the hernia was not job-related. As a result, the employer notified both the employee and the lien claimant that it was rejecting liability for the claim. The employee underwent a hernia repair, and a claim for reimbursement of medical expenses was filed more than one year after notification of rejection of liability, but less than one year after the lien claimant's last rendition of medical services. The California Supreme Court held that the claim was barred by the statute of limitations, reasoning that the potential claimants had been fully advised that the employer was denying liability for the claim. The court held "that the statute of limitations, embodied in LC 5405, begins to run against a potential claimant no later than the date on which the claimant is notified of a disclaimer by an employer or its insurance carrier."[11] After the denial, "a claimant can no longer be fairly said to harbor any false hopes engendered by the employer, but must thereafter be deemed fully aware that resort must be had to the formal statutory remedies in order to vindicate any claimed benefits."[12]

[9] *Kaiser Foundation Hospitals/Permanente Medical Group v. WCAB (Webb)* (1977) 42 CCC 302. See also *Lockheed Missiles & Space Co. v. WCAB (Buckman)* (1991) 56 CCC 84 (Court of Appeal opinion unpublished in official reports); *Lopez v. Barrett Business Services*, 2011 Cal. Wrk. Comp. P.D. LEXIS 41; *Sanchez v. System Services of America*, 2011 Cal. Wrk. Comp. P.D. LEXIS 341.

[10] (1977) 42 CCC 302.

[11] *Kaiser Foundation Hospitals/Permanente Medical Group v. WCAB (Webb)* (1977) 42 CCC 302, 307.

[12] *Kaiser Foundation Hospitals/Permanente Medical Group v. WCAB (Webb)* (1977) 42 CCC 302, 307.

6.14 ONE YEAR FROM DATE OF INJURY

If the employer has not voluntarily furnished indemnity or medical benefits, the employee has a maximum period of one year from the date of injury to file an application for adjudication of claim with the appeals board.[1] The date of injury for the purposes of the statute of limitations is defined by LC 5411 and LC 5412.

STATUTE OF LIMITATIONS FOR SPECIFIC INJURIES

LC 5411 controls the date of injury for specific injuries for the purposes of the statute of limitations. It says that the date of a specific injury is "that date during the employment on which occurred the alleged incident or exposure, for the consequences of which compensation is claimed." Usually the date of specific injury is not in dispute, as a specific injury results from one incident or exposure (LC 3208.1). The employee could bump a knee on a desk or be overcome by noxious fumes. Regardless of the cause, by incident or exposure, the injury occurs on a specific date. The consequences of the injury can be traced to some specific event that occurred on a certain date. The statute of limitations period commences to run on this date. If there is conflicting evidence as to the date of a specific injury, the appeals board's finding on the matter is binding.[2]

If an application for workers' compensation benefits is filed more than a year from the date of injury, and the employer has made no payments and furnished

[1] See *Huanosto v. WCAB* (1986) 51 CCC 427 (writ denied) (claim barred by LC 5405 when it was not filed within one year of the date of injury and no benefits were furnished).
[2] *U.S. Casualty Co. v. IAC (Moynahan)* (1954) 19 CCC 8.

no benefits to the employee, the claim will generally be barred by the statute of limitations.[3] This is especially so when an employee suffers from symptoms immediately following the injury resulting in disability or the need for medical treatment. But if an employee suffers an industrial injury as result of a specific incident or exposure that has latent effects, the issue is not as clear. That is, if the employee suffers a specific injury but the effects of the injury are not felt until sometime after the injury, there is conflicting case law as to whether the limitations period commences on the date of injury, or at the point when the employee manifests symptoms and understands the relationship between the disability and the employment. Based on current case law, it appears clear that the "latent injury theory" is viable.

In an older case, the Court of Appeal held that if an injury did not fall under LC 5412, the date of injury for the purposes of the statute of limitations would be governed by LC 5411.[4] So if an injury is not cumulative, it must be treated as specific. In that case, a recreational director took 12 girls to the beach and complained of "having been cold and uncomfortable all day." More than three weeks later, the employee entered a hospital, was diagnosed with polio and informed that her polio was due to her employment. More than a year after the incident, the employee filed her application for workers' compensation benefits. The Court of Appeal held that the claim was barred by the statute of limitations of LC 5405(a) because the applicant's polio was not a cumulative occupational disease and therefore, the limitations period begins to run from the time of the exposure.[5]

In another case, the appeals board confirmed that the statute of limitations for a specific injury with latent effects was controlled by LC 5411. An employee sustained a specific injury when a crane broke and fell 50 feet onto his head. The employee was informed by a doctor that he only had a scalp wound and that he would be all right. Nearly a year later, the applicant treated for headaches and dizziness and was informed that the symptoms were related to stomach troubles. More than 5 1/2 years after the accident, the applicant was treated by a neurologist who diagnosed him with cervical root syndrome resulting in headaches, dizziness and neck symptomology, and advised the employee that the condition was a result of the industrial injury. The applicant filed an application for compensation benefits for the injury. The appeals board held that

[3] See *Ratner Clothes Corp. v. WCAB (Saborio)* (1977) 42 CCC 365 (Court of Appeal opinion unpublished in official reports).

[4] *Johnson v. IAC* (1958) 23 CCC 54. At the time *Johnson* was decided, LC 5412 covered only occupational diseases. That statute was not amended to cover cumulative trauma injuries until 1973.

[5] *Johnson v. IAC* (1958) 23 CCC 54.

the claim was barred by the statute of limitations because the claim was not based upon an occupational disease, and therefore the date of injury was the date of the incident. The appeals board added that the amendments to the Labor Code in 1947 foreclosed the doctrine of latent injury in specific injury cases.[6]

This thinking was explicitly upheld in the case of *Horn v. WCAB*.[7] An applicant had a specific injury and filed the application 11 years later. In rejecting his claim that the effects of the injury were latent, it was noted, "The Appeals Board rejected the notion that in latent injuries the statute of limitations does not begin to run until the compensable consequences of the injury are discovered."[8]

Nevertheless, the appeals board has made exceptions to this rule. The appeals board held that a workers' compensation claim for the development of an HIV infection filed seven years after the needle prick that prompted the infection was not barred by the statute of limitations. In that case, the appeals board found that the applicant's HIV infection resulted from a specific industrial injury but relied on evidence that the incubation period for the disease was seven to 10 years. The appeals board reasoned that because the applicant did not know that she had the HIV virus until seven years after the needle prick, the filing of the claim was timely. This was because the delay in filing the claim was due to the incubation period, and not any failure to act on the applicant's part.[9] This case may be plausibly reconciled with the cases above on the grounds that the applicant's HIV infection was an occupational disease. Although the appeals board found a specific injury, the applicant's HIV could be regarded as an occupational disease for which the date of injury would be defined per LC 5412.[10]

But more recent cases are more difficult to reconcile and suggest that a specific injury resulting in latent effects should be governed by the principles of LC 5412. In one case, the appeals board held that an applicant's claim for workers' compensation benefits filed on Jan. 29, 2003, for an injury to his wrists on May 16, 2001, was not barred by the statute of limitations when it was filed within a year of the applicant needing medical treatment and becoming temporarily disabled. The applicant sustained an industrial injury to his wrists when he slipped and fell. Although he felt slight pain at the time of the injury, he did not report the injury to the employer, sought no medical treatment and missed no time from

[6] *Mack v. WCAB* (1971) 36 CCC 661 (writ denied).
[7] (1983) 48 CCC 33 (writ denied).
[8] *Horn v. WCAB* (1983) 48 CCC 33, 34 (writ denied).
[9] *County of Los Angeles/USC Medical Center v. WCAB* (1995) 60 CCC 1105 (writ denied).
[10] See *County of Los Angeles v. WCAB (Gleason)* (2002) 67 CCC 1049 (writ denied) (needle stick resulting in hepatitis C assessed under LC 5412 for the purposes of the statute of limitations). This same mechanism was used in *Palazzi v. Plumas Lumber Co.* (1966) 32 CCC 175 (panel decision) with regard to hearing loss.

work. More than a year after the injury, the applicant complained of increased wrist pain, and underwent X-rays that revealed fractures in both wrists. The doctor opined that the applicant fractured his wrists when he fell at work. The applicant filed a workers' compensation claim.[11]

The appeals board held that the claim was not barred by the statute of limitations because the applicant did not sustain a knowable industrial injury until there was a consequence from the injury allowing a claim for compensation. That is, the appeals board believed that the applicant did not sustain a "specific injury," pursuant to LC 3208.1, until the applicant obtained medical treatment and incurred temporary disability. The appeals board reasoned that in the case of latent specific injuries under LC 5411, an employee's claim is not barred by the statute of limitations unless he or she knew or reasonably should have known that the disability was caused by the employment. The appeals board stated, "We ... do not find in the statutes any intention by the Legislature to deny injured worker's [*sic* et al] with latent specific injuries the same protection of the worker's compensation law provided employees with other specific injuries, cumulative injuries and occupational diseases."[12] So the appeals board held that in cases involving latent specific injuries, the statute of limitations does not begin to run until the employee knew or should have known that disability was industrial in nature.[13]

In another case, an applicant, while participating in wild fire training, stepped on a rattlesnake. He ran down the hill to avoid being bitten, fell and hit the left side of his body on a cement culvert. He felt minor pain in his shin immediately after the event, but did not believe he had sustained a serious injury. A report was made of the incident, which was witnessed by co-workers. As time passed, the applicant felt pain in his foot and left hip, but did not connect the symptoms with his earlier fall. Eleven months after the incident, the applicant went to his family doctor because of the hip and foot pain. An X-ray was taken, which revealed degenerative arthritis in the left hip. The applicant lost no time from work. More than a year after the incident, he was evaluated by an orthopedist who, based on his examination and the history provided, concluded that the arthritis was a

---

[11] *Save Mart Supermarkets v. WCAB (Hixson II)* (2007) 72 CCC 509 (writ denied).

[12] *Save Mart Supermarkets v. WCAB (Hixson II)* (2007) 72 CCC 509 (writ denied).

[13] In an earlier unpublished opinion in this case, *Save Mart Supermarkets v. WCAB (Hixson I)* (2006) 71 CCC 171 (Court of Appeal opinion unpublished in official reports), the appellate court stated, "Under Section 5411, the date of a specific injury is 'that date during the employment on which occurred the alleged incident or exposure,' with no statutory exception comparable to Section 5412 extending the date of injury to the date the employee either knew or should have known the disability was industrial in nature." In a panel decision, the appeals board recognized that the concept of a latent specific injury and the effect of that latency on the statute of limitations were considered in *Hixson*. But the case was remanded for a more in-depth discussion on the concept of a latent specific injury. *Salas v. Zacky Farms*, 2010 Cal. Wrk. Comp. P.D. LEXIS 444.

consequence of the fall. The applicant filed a workers' compensation claim. The defendant argued that the claim was barred by the statute of limitations. The appeals board affirmed a decision that it was not.[14]

The panel explained that the purpose of a statute of limitations is to avoid prejudice to the defendant by ensuring that claims are resolved "while the evidence bearing on the issues is reasonably available and fresh." It found that the defendant did not assert that it was prejudiced because the claim was filed more than a year after the incident, and nothing in the record suggested that the delay between the date of the fall and the applicant's awareness of its connection to his hip condition caused any worsening of the injury. Citing the Supreme Court's decision in *Marsh v. IAC,*[15] the panel explained that in construing LC 5405, it was guided by the principle that for the purposes of the running of a statute of limitations on a workers' compensation claim, "it is almost universally the rule that the injury is not deemed to occur until ascertainable disability results."[16] The panel then relied on the California Supreme Court's decision in *Fruehauf Corp. v. WCAB (Stansbury).*[17] Although recognizing that *Stansbury* addressed the language of former LC 5411 and LC 5412 as applied to cumulative trauma injuries, and that the holding in that case did not directly relate to industrial injuries suffered as a result of a specific incident but that have latent effects, the panel found that in 1973, when LC 3208.1, LC 5411 and LC 5412 were amended to their current form, the Legislature continued to encompass the basic principles described in *Marsh* and *Stansbury* that there is not a knowable industrial injury until there is a consequence from the injury allowing a claim for compensation along with knowledge of the connection to employment. It noted that LC 3208.1 describes a specific injury as "occurring as the result of one incident or exposure *which causes disability or the need for medical treatment*" (emphasis added). So the panel stated, "Under the *Stansbury* analysis, the date of injury pursuant to section 3208.1 did not occur until the 'consequence of which compensation is claim' as described in section 5411 manifests themselves, and applicant reasonably became aware of the industrial causation."[18]

In addressing the applicability of LC 5411 to latent specific injuries, the panel found it appropriate to apply the "fundamental rule" expressed in *Marsh* "that an employee is not barred by the statute of limitations applicable to workmen's

---

[14] *Young v. City of Ventura Fire Department,* 2011 Cal. Wrk. Comp. P.D. LEXIS 408.
[15] (1933) 217 Cal. 338.
[16] *Young v. City of Ventura Fire Department,* 2011 Cal. Wrk. Comp. P.D. LEXIS 408 quoting *Marsh v. IAC* (1933) 217 Cal. 338, 345-346.
[17] (1968) 33 CCC 300.
[18] *Young v. City of Ventura Fire Department,* 2011 Cal. Wrk. Comp. P.D. LEXIS 408.

compensation claims unless he knew, or in the exercise of reasonable diligence should have known, that his disability was caused by his employment." It added, "We also do not find an intention by the Legislature to deny injured worker's with latent specific injuries the same protection of the worker's compensation law provided employees with other specific injuries, cumulative injuries and occupational diseases," and that "it would be inconsistent with the principle of liberal interpretation expressed in *Stansbury* and *Marsh* to construe the limitations statute in that way."[19]

So, in these two recent cases, the appeals board has crafted an exception for latent specific injuries similar to what LC 5412 established. The appeals board has concluded that the limitations period for a latent specific injury is the date on which the applicant suffers disability, and either knows or should have known that the injury was industrial in nature. This language does not appear in LC 5411 itself. So it is likely this issue will be tested further in the courts.

STATUTE OF LIMITATIONS FOR CUMULATIVE TRAUMA INJURIES AND OCCUPATIONAL DISEASES

The statute of limitations for a cumulative trauma injury or occupational disease is the same as that for a specific injury. Employees generally have one year from the date of injury to file an application for adjudication when benefits are not provided. But unlike a specific injury that occurs on a specific date, pinpointing the date for a CT injury or occupational disease is not easy. There is no one episode or event that produces an injury. Per LC 3208.1, a cumulative trauma injury occurs as a result of "repetitive mentally or physically traumatic activities extending over a period of time." The date of injury for occupational diseases and CT injuries for the purposes of the statute of limitations is defined by LC 5412.

Per LC 5412, "[T]he date of injury in cases of occupational disease or cumulative injury is that date upon which the employee first suffered disability ... and either knew, or in the exercise of reasonable diligence should have known, that such disability was caused by his present or prior employment." So the date of an occupational disease or a cumulative trauma injury requires the concurrence of two elements: (1) compensable disability, and (2) knowledge of industrial causation.[20] These elements present questions of fact to be determined by the

[19] *Young v. City of Ventura Fire Department*, 2011 Cal. Wrk. Comp. P.D. LEXIS 408.
[20] *Chavez v. WCAB* (1973) 38 CCC 174; *Bassett-McGregor v. WCAB* (1988) 53 CCC 502, 507.

appeals board, with the burden of proof resting with the employer.[21] For a thorough discussion on pinpointing the date of injury pursuant to LC 5412, see Section 5.5 Cumulative Injury.

Compensable Disability

Generally, disability for the purposes of LC 5412 requires either compensable temporary disability or permanent disability.[22] Temporary disability is a replacement for wage loss because the applicant is too hurt to continue doing his or her work. Permanent disability is money paid to compensate both for actual incapacity to work and for physical impairment of the worker's body, which may or may not be incapacitating.[23] When the employee is receiving temporary disability benefits or has a ratable permanent disability, an employee has clearly suffered disability for the purposes of LC 5412.[24]

The issue is not as clear, however, when the employee receives medical treatment, but is returned to modified work without missing any time from work. The Court of Appeal has held that modified work alone is not a sufficient basis for compensable temporary disability, as actual wage loss is required for temporary disability. But modified work may indicate a permanent impairment of earning capacity, especially if the worker is never able to return to the original job duties.[25] Although medical treatment alone does not automatically indicate disability, it may be evidence of compensable permanent disability.[26]

Knowledge of Industrial Causation

Proving the date of knowledge pursuant to LC 5412 can often be more difficult than proving the date of disability. An employee is not charged with knowledge just because he had some symptoms.[27] Generally, an applicant is not deemed to have knowledge of a cumulative trauma injury unless so advised by a

[21] *Bassett-McGregor v. WCAB* (1988) 53 CCC 502, 507.
[22] *Chavira v. WCAB* (1991) 56 CCC 631, 639; *SCIF v. WCAB (Rodarte)* (2004) 69 CCC 579, 582.
[23] *J.T. Thorp, Inc. v. WCAB (Butler)* (1984) 49 CCC 224, 228; *Western Growers Insurance Co. v. WCAB (Austin)* (1993) 58 CCC 323, 327.
[24] *Chavira v. WCAB* (1991) 56 CCC 631; *SCIF v. WCAB (Rodarte)* (2004) 69 CCC 579, 583.
[25] *SCIF v. WCAB (Rodarte)* (2004) 69 CCC 579, 584; *County of Fresno v. WCAB (McFadden)* (1982) 47 CCC 1349; *Anderson v. County of Fresno* (1983) 48 CCC 871.
[26] *SCIF v. WCAB (Rodarte)* (2004) 69 CCC 579, 584.
[27] *Pacific Indemnity Co. v. IAC (Rotondo)* (1950) 15 CCC 37, 39; *Chambers v. WCAB* (1968) 33 CCC 722, 724; *Lewis v. City and County of San Francisco* (1981) 46 CCC 206; *Jordan Potash, Inc. v. WCAB (Ward)* 48 CCC 472 (1983) (writ denied).

physician.[28] Furthermore, the Court of Appeal has stated, "[A]n applicant will not be charged with knowledge that his disability is job related without medical advice to that effect unless the nature of the disability and the applicant's training, intelligence and qualifications are such that applicant should have recognized the relationship between the known adverse factors involved in his employment and his disability."[29] So medical records or reporting of some sort is often necessary before the court will be willing to find that the applicant had knowledge of continuous trauma injury.[30]

But a medical opinion stating that a disability is work related is not required in all cases.[31] Furthermore, in some cases, no special training or expertise is necessary for an employee to determine that there is a connection between the disability and the employment. If the injury claimed does not involve some exotic disease, if the situation is more prosaic, such as when an employee experiences pain performing a physically stressful activity, and the employee correlates the disability to the employment, the employee may be charged with knowledge for the purposes of LC 5412 even without medical advice.[32]

---

[28] *City of Fresno v. WCAB (Johnson)* (1985) 50 CCC 53, 56. Compare *First Bank & Trust v. WCAB (Ziegler)* (2006) 71 CCC 533 (writ denied) (CT claim not barred by the statute of limitations when applicant first learned that her employment was causing the disability within one year of being advised by her treating physician); *ExpoServices/San Francisco Expo Services v. WCAB (Cratty)* (2004) 69 CCC 260 (writ denied) (CT claim not barred by the statute of limitations when it was filed within a year of the first medical report discussing the cumulative nature of the injury); *Doris v. WCAB* (2001) 66 CCC 1459 (Court of Appeal opinion unpublished in official reports) (nurse's aide did not have the requisite knowledge under LC 5412 until retaining counsel); *Modesto City Schools v. WCAB (Finch)* (2002) 67 CCC 1647 (writ denied) (claim not barred because applicant first learned of CT injury in a physician's report); *Northrop Grumman Corp. v. WCAB (Elachkar)* (2012) 77 CCC 187 (writ denied) (no evidence of knowledge before filing her application of adjudication) with *Price v. WCAB* (2007) 72 CCC 1687 (writ denied) (claim barred by statute of limitations when applicant had knowledge of CT injury from AME but did not timely file application); *Hopper, Inc. v. WCAB (Larkins)* (1997) 62 CCC 67 (writ denied) (statute of limitations arose when applicant was advised by AME that her carpel tunnel was related to the employment).

[29] *City of Fresno v. WCAB (Johnson)* (1985) 50 CCC 53, 57-58. See also *Sperry Corp. and Gab Business Services, Inc. v. WCAB (Malkowski)* (1988) 53 CCC 333 (writ denied); *CBS v. WCAB (White)* (1979) 44 CCC 777 (writ denied); *City of Los Angeles v. WCAB (Calvert)* (1978) 43 CCC 1280.

[30] See *Pacific Indemnity Co. v. IAC (Rotondo)* (1950) 15 CCC 37; *Hanna v. WCAB* (1973) 38 CCC 321; *City of Bakersfield v. WCAB (Ragusa)* (1984) 49 CCC 247 (writ denied); *Koel v. WCAB* (1987) 52 CCC 426 (Court of Appeal opinion unpublished in official reports); *City of Los Angeles (Fire Department) v. WCAB (Johns)* (2010) 75 CCC 755 (writ denied); *Zenith Insurance Co. v. WCAB (Yanos)* (2010) 75 CCC 1303 (writ denied); *Atria Senior Living, dba Hillsdale Manor v. WCAB (Cohen)* 77 CCC 484 (writ denied).

[31] See *Alford v. IAC* (1946) 11 CCC 127 (employee asked to be released from the plant because the work was detrimental to his health and might be fatal; it was deemed he had knowledge of the employment connection).

[32] See *Nielsen v. WCAB* (1985) 50 CCC 104; *Cucamonga Unified School District v. WCAB (Ingram)* (1996) 61 CCC 1384 (Court of Appeal opinion unpublished in official reports); *The County of San Bernardino v. WCAB (Schroeder)* (2007) 72 CCC 1365 (Court of Appeal opinion unpublished in official reports). See *City of Santa Ana v. WCAB (Smith)* (2008) 73 CCC 460 (Court of Appeal opinion unpublished in official reports) (applicant knew or should have known of the connection between his skin cancer and his employment without medical advice, as he had a 30-year history of skin problems and received medical treatment and advice during this time).

Particular Determinations

Whether an employee knew or, in the exercise of reasonable diligence, should have known, that his or her disability was caused by the employment is a question of fact for the appeals board.[33] The appeals board's determination will be upheld if it is supported by substantial evidence including reasonable inferences to be drawn from the evidence.[34]

For example, a police officer's workers' compensation claim filed after a heart attack in 1971 was not barred by the statute of limitations even though he retired in 1962 and had periods of disability before his heart attack. His claim was allowed when it was determined that he did not have knowledge of the industrial connection between the employment and his heart problems until so informed by his physicians after the heart attack.[35]

The appeals board has held that an applicant's claim for a CT injury was not barred by the statute of limitations defined in LC 5405 and LC 5412, as a doctor's advice that his condition *might* be work related was not evidence that the applicant knew his condition was work related. In that case, the appeals board also relied on the applicant's testimony that he missed no time from work as a result of the injury.[36] In another case, a claim was not barred when a doctor led the applicant to believe that his pulmonary disease was not related to his employment.[37] Also, the appeals board has held that an applicant does not have sufficient knowledge if physicians did not tell him that his condition was caused by work, only that his activities at work were making the condition worse.[38]

---

[33] *Chambers v. WCAB* (1968) 33 CCC 722; *Pacific Indemnity Co. v. IAC (Rotondo)* (1950) 15 CCC 37.

[34] *Nielsen v. WCAB* (1985) 50 CCC 104.

[35] *Hanna v. WCAB* (1973) 38 CCC 321. See also *City of Santa Ana v. WCAB (Smith)* (2008) 73 CCC 460 (Court of Appeal opinion unpublished in official reports) (claim for heart injury filed in 2003 was timely even though the applicant retired in 1991 and had symptoms in the early 1990s; his coronary heart disease was not diagnosed until 2003); *McCleary v. WCAB* (1994) 59 CCC 841 (Court of Appeal opinion unpublished in official reports) (employer had knowledge when told by a physician); *County of Orange v. WCAB (Barrow)* (2012) 77 CCC 559 (writ denied) (knowledge in 2009 when AME found the cumulative trauma was industrially related, even though applicant filed a DWC 1 claim form in 2001 after his cancer diagnosis).

[36] *U.S. Airways v. WCAB (Hale)* (2004) 69 CCC 844 (writ denied). See also *Commercial Union Insurance Co. v. WCAB (Medina)* (1984) 49 CCC 143 (writ denied) (claim not barred by statute of limitations when it was filed more than a year after the applicant suspected he had an asbestos-related disease, but within a year after he was first told by a physician his difficulties were work related; the problems had not caused the applicant to lose time from work); *City of Chico v. WCAB (Scholar)* (2012) 77 CCC 440 (writ denied) (applicant did not know of his industrial cancer until filing his claim in 2008 because he was given several diagnoses and told that the mass could be congenital; although cancer was suspected, early medical reports were not definitive).

[37] *Kalomiros v. Agilent Technologies (aka Varian, Inc.)*, 2011 Cal. Wrk. Comp. P.D. LEXIS 576.

[38] *Olson v. Gelson's Market*, 2012 Cal. Wrk. Comp. P.D. LEXIS 530. See also *Hughes Aircraft Co. v. WCAB (Zimmerman)* (1993) 58 CCC 220 (writ denied); *Kaiser Foundation Health Plan v. WCAB (Bradford)* (1986) 51 CCC 355 (writ denied).

In one case, an applicant/police officer filed a claim form for hypertension in 2003 which was denied on the grounds it was nonindustrial. The applicant did not file an application for adjudication following the denial. In 2005, the applicant filed a second claim for a CT injury to his heart and associated injuries. The defendant argued that the subsequent claim was barred by the statute of limitations. The appeals board first noted that the 2005 claim was substantially different from the 2003 claim because the 2003 claim alleged only high blood pressure, and not damage to the heart in the form of left ventricular hypertrophy that was alleged in the 2005 claim. This was important because the LC 3212.5 presumption of industrial causation applied, and the applicant's heart trouble could not be attributed to the 2003 hypertension claim that developed before the manifestation of the heart injury. Also, the evidence established that the applicant first suffered disability and was informed that the disability was caused by the employment in 2006. So the claim was not barred by LC 5405.[39] This case raises the distinction between the concept of injury and the concept of body parts injured, which is discussed in other parts of this book.[40]

In another case, an applicant's claim for a cumulative trauma injury from 1994 to Dec. 6, 1999, filed in 2002 was not barred by the statute of limitations, even though the applicant had a specific injury Dec. 6, 1999, that was resolved by way of compromise and release. In that case, the employer argued that the applicant should have known that the disability was caused by the employment based on an Oct. 2, 2000, report by the applicant's treating physician. But the appeals board determined that because the treating physician reported that the applicant's disability resulted from a specific injury, and did not mention a cumulative trauma injury, there was no evidence that the applicant should have known she sustained a CT injury.[41]

In an unpublished opinion, the Court of Appeal held that a claim was not barred by the statute of limitations when the employee was aware that his industrial injury was work related more than a year before filing his worker's compensation claim, but the employer failed to prove that the employee had sustained a compensable disability. In that case, the applicant experienced stress

---

[39] *Tanksley v. City of Santa Ana* (2012) 40 CWCR 72 [2012 Cal. Wrk. Comp. P.D. LEXIS 105].

[40] For example, the "90-day rule" is governed by dates of injury, rather than body parts injured; see Section 5.16 Presumption of Injury — 90-Day Rule. Also relevant is the discussion on the distinction in Section 5.65 Compensable Consequence Injuries.

[41] *Lennox Hearth Products, Inc. v. WCAB (Escalante)* (2008) 73 CCC 395 (writ denied). See also *Fekete v. WCAB* (2000) 65 CCC 637 (Court of Appeal opinion unpublished in official reports) (prior workers' compensation claim did not establish knowledge of industrial relationship); *Weibl v. St. Louis Cardinals*, 2012 Cal. Wrk. Comp. P.D. LEXIS 107 (prior shoulder stiffness and prior specific injury to applicant's shoulder do not constitute knowledge he sustained a cumulative industrial injury).

symptoms as a result of his employment and took off limited amounts of time for medical visits and stress relief more than one year before filing his claim. The court held that the claim was timely because it determined that the applicant's missed days from work and medical visits for reporting work-related stress did not constitute substantial evidence of compensable disability — it was not shown that those days were related to the industrial problem.[42]

But the Court of Appeal held that an applicant's claim was barred by the statute of limitations when he sustained an injury within a week of starting an assignment to disassemble and reassemble a bottle rack, and took off work in 1981 but did not file a claim until 1983. The court noted that the injury was to the employee's lower back and his employment duties involved frequent bending and lifting heavy objects, thereby suggesting that there was a clear connection between the employment and the injury. Based on the applicant's testimony that he was of the opinion that the injury was industrially caused from the first day, the court concluded that the applicant knew or should have known in the exercise of reasonable diligence that his condition was industrially caused as of the day he took off work in 1981. This was despite the absence of medical evidence at that time. So the claim was barred by the statute of limitations because the compensable disability and knowledge of industrial causation were concurrent and occurred more than one year before the filing of the claim.[43]

In an unpublished opinion, the Court of Appeal held that a workers' compensation claim was barred by the statute of limitations when the applicant testified that doctors told him that his injury was work related more than a year before filing his claim. Again, this was despite the absence of medical reports stating that his condition was work related.[44]

In another unpublished opinion, the Court of Appeal held that a cumulative trauma claim filed 2 1/2 years after the applicant last worked for the employer was barred by the statute of limitations when the applicant testified that he believed that his problems were industrially caused.[45]

---

[42] *County of Mariposa v. WCAB (Johnson)* (2006) 71 CCC 1499 (Court of Appeal opinion unpublished in official reports).

[43] *Nielsen v. WCAB* (1985) 50 CCC 104.

[44] *American Tissue Corp. v. WCAB (Sarabia)* (2005) 70 CCC 771 (Court of Appeal opinion unpublished in official reports).

[45] *The County of San Bernardino v. WCAB (Schroeder)* (2007) 72 CCC 1365 (Court of Appeal opinion unpublished in official reports). See also *Price v. WCAB* (2007) 72 CCC 1687 (writ denied) (claim barred by LC 5405 when AME reported cumulative trauma but applicant did not file application until more than a year later, and knowledge was inferred because applicant was represented by counsel at the time of the AME report); *Morell v. WCAB* (2001) 66 CCC 947 (writ denied) (applicant's claim barred by the statute of limitations when he testified that he knew his employment was causing his pain and did not file a claim until more than

In light of these cases, it appears that proving that the employee knew of the industrial connection between an injury and the employment without medical support will generally require an admission from the employee to that effect.

Applicability to Lien Claimants

In *County of Los Angeles v. WCAB (Rottman),*[46] the Court of Appeal suggested that the statute of limitations could commence earlier for a lien claimant if it knew or should have known that an employee's disability was work related before the employee obtained said knowledge. The court stated that the employer bears the burden of proving that the employee and/or the lien claimant knew or should have known that the disability was work related more than one year before the claim was filed. The court noted that although there was no reason to require the provider of medical services to have greater insight into whether the disability is work related than an employee as long as both are apprised of the same facts, it went on to state, "If a provider can be shown to have greater knowledge in that respect than that of the employee, the provider's claim may be precluded as a lien."[47] The court indicated that if a lien claimant had the requisite knowledge under LC 5412 of the causal connection between the disability and the employment before the employee, then the statute of limitations on the claimant's lien would commence before the employee's knowledge, and therefore, before the date of injury pursuant to LC 5412.

But the California Supreme Court, in *Kaiser Foundation Hospitals, Permanente Medical Group v. WCAB (Martin),*[48] subsequently stated that "there is but one limitations period for any particular workers' compensation claim, and that is the period applicable to the injured employee."[49] The court held that the tolling of the statute of limitations due to the an employer's failure to notify an employee of his or her workers' compensation rights also tolled the statute of limitations as to a lien claimant, regardless of its own prior knowledge of the workers'

one year after he stopped working because of the pain); *Escalante v. WCAB* (2000) 66 CCC 173 (writ denied) (statute of limitations barred a claim when the applicant testified that he knew there was a causal connection between his job and his injury at the time the problem started); *Fairchild Semiconductor Corp. v. WCAB (Cole)* (1983) 48 CCC 625 (Court of Appeal opinion unpublished in official reports) (cumulative injury barred by the statute of limitations when it was filed more than one year after the date of disability and the date the applicant was advised by a physician that the disability was related to the employment).

[46] (1982) 47 CCC 951.

[47] *County of Los Angeles v. WCAB (Rottman)* (1982) 47 CCC 951, 954.

[48] (1985) 50 CCC 411.

[49] *Kaiser Foundation Hospitals, Permanente Medical Group v. WCAB (Martin)* (1985) 50 CCC 411, 419.

compensation laws.[50] The court, in a footnote, commented that the Court of Appeal's statements in *Rottman* regarding the applicability of the statute of limitations to lien claimants were in dicta and presumed that the court meant that a lien claimant could be barred by laches if it unreasonably delayed.[51] Consequently, it appears that the statute of limitations for a lien claimant to initiate workers' compensation proceedings is also governed by the worker's knowledge of industrial causation, rather than its own.

Separate Cumulative Trauma Periods

Suppose the employer establishes a date of injury for a cumulative trauma injury under LC 5412, but the employee continues to work for several years after the date of injury and does not file a workers' compensation claim until the injury becomes worse. An employee might become aware of a CT injury and suffer some disability, such as time lost from work. That employee may then decide to continue to work. Time goes on, there is more injurious exposure and the employee gets worse. Finally, he or she decides to file a claim. In this scenario, the employee would seem to be barred by the statute of limitations. This can present a problem, as it seems that the employee who works on diligently and in good faith is punished by a technical rule. LC 5412 as it defines the date of injury for a cumulative trauma claim is indeed helpful when it comes to questions of dividing liability between defendants and simplifying litigation. But, is it really meant to deprive an applicant of his or her rights?

In one case the Court of Appeal attempted to solve the problem by holding that, in such cases, there may be separate periods of cumulative trauma. In *Hooker v. WCAB,*[52] a state traffic officer who worked from 1954 to 1970 suffered dizziness and headaches. He sought treatment in 1967, was diagnosed with sinus trouble and informed that the problems were connected to his employment. Between 1967 and June 19, 1970, he used 159 hours of sick leave in connection with his problem. He ultimately requested changing his job and finally filed an application for adjudication on Sept. 14, 1970. The applicant was declared permanent and stationary Jan. 2, 1971. The appeals board held that the applicant's claim was barred in its entirety by the statute of limitations because the date of injury as defined by LC 5412 and LC 3208.1 was in 1967. So the date of injury occurred more than one year before the filing of the application on Sept. 14, 1970.

---

[50] *Kaiser Foundation Hospitals, Permanente Medical Group v. WCAB (Martin)* (1985) 50 CCC 411, 419.
[51] *Kaiser Foundation Hospitals, Permanente Medical Group v. WCAB (Martin)* (1985) 50 CCC 411, 419 fn. 10.
[52] (1974) 39 CCC 75.

The Court of Appeal did not agree. It held that the applicant would be barred from receiving any benefits that were incurred more than one year before the application was filed. The court also held that the applicant would not be barred from receiving benefits that would be due within that one-year period and continuing, reasoning that the applicant should not be precluded from recovering for the cumulative disability that did not and could not manifest itself until the applicant had undergone further exposure. The court stated, "It is irrational to rule that the employee who shrugs off the effects of the initial stages of industrial trauma forfeits the right to recover from the cumulative effect of the trauma which ultimately renders him unable to carry on his regular duties."[53]

The court noted that in 1967, the applicant first used his sick leave for a cumulative trauma injury that he either knew or in the exercise of reasonable diligence should have known occurred as a result of repetitive mentally or physically traumatic activities over a period from 1954 through 1967. So claims for benefits for such disability were barred by the statute of limitations. But the court also noted that the disability could not embrace a more severe and more disabling injury from the continued traumatic activities in the period from 1967 to 1970, to which the employee could not possibly have been exposed in 1967. The court added that the disability reached its climax in 1970 when the applicant had to forgo the performance of normal job duties, and that the applicant did not have compensable permanent disability until his condition stabilized Jan. 2, 1971. The court stated, "[S]o long as the combined effect of the repetitive mentally or physically traumatic activities extending over a period of time cause an ever-increasing disability or need for medical treatment there are separate periods of cumulative injury. Recovery for time lost from work or medical treatment incurred more than one year from the filing of the application may be barred because the employee knew or should have known that such disability was caused by his employment. Nevertheless, so long as the repetitive trauma continues to cause further disability, recovery may be had for such disability as had occurred within one year of filing of the application."[54] In that case, the court held that the applicant's claim was not barred insofar as it claimed TD and medical benefits for a period no earlier than one year before filing the application, and PD benefits as they did not accrue until Jan. 2, 1971.[55]

---

[53] *Hooker v. WCAB* (1974) 39 CCC 75, 80. See also *Schaadt v. WCAB* (1973) 38 CCC 511 (employee with varicose veins had problems but bore the pain; the CT date was not determined until he finally left the workplace).
[54] *Hooker v. WCAB* (1974) 39 CCC 75, 80-81.
[55] *Hooker v. WCAB* (1974) 39 CCC 75, 81.

This is a subtle ruling. It must be said that its reasoning, in light of subsequent cases, is suspect, and may not currently be good law. In Section 5.6 Defining Multiple Injury Dates, the subject of multiple cumulative trauma dates is discussed in depth. In particular, the issue of whether, given a certain set of facts, there should be identified one cumulative injury or two is explored. A foundational case in this area was decided well after the *Hooker* case, and has been steadily followed since — *Western Growers Insurance Co. v. WCAB (Austin).*[56] In particular, the *Austin* case contained facts very close to that of *Hooker*; briefly, an applicant had disability and treatment, left work for hospitalization and returned only to suffer further injurious exposure. The Court of Appeal reversed the appeals board in finding only one cumulative injury, and not two. It was held that the date of injury as defined under LC 5412 was present in the first period, and the subsequent injurious exposure periods were irrelevant. The carrier on the risk at the time of the first exposure had to pay for the entire claim.

The *Austin* case did not mention *Hooker,* nor has *Hooker* been mentioned by the series of cases following *Austin.* So one could argue that *Hooker* has been supplanted. In studying the two cases, however, one cannot fail to see an explicit and salient difference: *Austin* dealt with the issue of two cumulative trauma periods and determining liability between employers, whereas *Hooker* dealt with the issue of two cumulative trauma periods for the purposes of barring an employee's claim to compensation per the statute of limitations. It has been noted that because the statute of limitations is a disfavored defense, it may result in one finding for one purpose and different findings for a different purposes.[57]

The courts have been willing to apply LC 5412 strictly in cases where two or more employers or carriers are struggling to avoid liability. That is so even if one party ends up with what some might see as an unfair portion of the liability. But a different standard has been applied when an injured worker faces the harsh consequences of a statute of limitations prohibition. The courts are more flexible with the law in applying it to a statute of limitations.[58]

At this juncture there does not appear to be a clear rule of law for these unique cases. But nothing in the *Austin* decision alters the reasoning of the *Hooker* decision — that an applicant should not be precluded from recovering for the

---

[56] (1993) 58 CCC 323.

[57] *Smith v. Johns-Manville Products Corp.* (1981) 46 CCC 557, 560 (appeals board *en banc*); *Nino v. County of Los Angeles* (1982) 47 CCC 370, 372-73 (appeals board *en banc*).

[58] See *Ferguson v. City of Oxnard* (1970) 35 CCC 452 (appeals board *en banc*) (appeals board interpreting the law as permitting the employee to claim benefits for *any* disability, but applying to the statute of limitations only for a *compensable* disability).

cumulative disability that did not and could not manifest itself until the applicant had undergone further exposure. Applicants will continue to press for legal reasoning as presented in *Hooker*. The defense will take the position that LC 5412 must be applied uniformly and that the *Hooker* case is an exemplar of the old adage. No doubt the issue will be heard further in litigation.

SPECIFIC INJURY OR PART OF A CONTINUOUS TRAUMA?

It is not unusual, especially in long employment relationships, to see a continuous trauma claim made — sometimes coinciding with a plan to retire. In these situations a personnel file may be replete with "medical only" injuries — claims filed over the years for minor complaints of pain that, according to the applicant, are part and parcel of a continuous trauma claim. But the defense, to reduce its liability, will be inclined to see these as separate specific injuries. The defense may then argue that any benefits due from these injuries may not come into play, as they are barred by the statute of limitations. How is an employer to discern the specific injury from those linked in the chain of a continuous trauma?

Under the literal definitions of specific injury (one incident of exposure causing the need for medical treatment or disability) and continuous, or cumulative, trauma (repetitive traumatic activities that over time combine to cause the need for medical treatment or disability), it seems that some events that result in a claim could meet both definitions.[59] The courts recognize that under LC 3208.2 each injury must be examined on its own and liability must be assigned accordingly. But and despite the strict language of the statute, they have tended in these gray areas to find continuous trauma injuries rather than a horde of specific ones. It appears that the courts want to avoid the splintering of claims into so many pieces as to create impractical or unfair situations in litigation.

In the *en banc* decision of *Ferguson v. City of Oxnard,*[60] the appeals board held that "disability" for purposes of defining a specific injury in this situation means "compensable disability" — lost time from work that would result in temporary or permanent disability; it also held that a resulting need for medical care only, without disability, was not enough.[61] In other words, a specific injury for the purposes of the statute of limitations requires either a compensable temporary or

[59] LC 3208.1 states, "An injury may be either: (a) 'specific,' occurring as the result of one incident or exposure which causes disability or need for medical treatment; or (b) 'cumulative,' occurring as repetitive mentally or physically traumatic activities extending over a period of time, the combined effect of which causes any disability or need for medical treatment." See Chapter 5 for a thorough discussion of these terms.

[60] (1970) 35 CCC 452.

[61] *Ferguson v. City of Oxnard* (1970) 35 CCC 452 (appeals board *en banc*). See also *Beaver Insurance v. WCAB (Chandler)* (1992) 57 CCC 730 (writ denied).

permanent disability. The appeals board noted that an employee has an immediate right of action against the employer when the injury caused either disability or the need for medical treatment. But the statute of limitations does not immediately run against the medical-only claim because the date of injury for a cumulative trauma requires a compensable disability.

Note that this interpretation of the law can result in more than one definition for a date of injury. An applicant claiming an injury certainly shows enough to obtain workers' compensation benefits when the incident results in the need for medical care alone. But the appeals board felt justified in creating a higher standard for defining a specific injury for purposes of the statute of limitations defense, requiring that a specific injury result in compensable disability. The appeals board stated, "It is reasonable that the law be more restrictive in defining the accrual date of a cause of action for the purpose of the statute of limitations than it is for determining when an employee may prosecute a claim for benefits. If it were otherwise an employee's claim might be barred before he even knew of its existence. For example, where employment activities have caused a need unknown to the employee for medical treatment, a separate injury has occurred. If after the passage of over a year additional employment activities combine with the earlier activities to contribute to the employee's ultimate disability, giving rise to a second injury, it would be a harsh law indeed that would require a portion of the employee's right to such disability indemnity and medical benefits to be debarred on account of the running of the statute of limitations on the first injury."[62]

Ferguson has been cited with approval in numerous Court of Appeal decisions for the proposition that for statute of limitations purposes, the date of injury for a cumulative trauma is the date the employment activities cause compensable disability. This continues to be the law.[63] So an employee may sustain "medical only" injuries that would be compensable as specific injuries. But unless the injuries resulted in compensable disability, either temporary disability or permanent disability, such injuries may be merged into a cumulative trauma injury when they ultimately result in a compensable disability.

---

[62] *Ferguson v. City of Oxnard* (1970) 35 CCC 452, 458 (appeals board *en banc*).
[63] See *Aetna Casualty and Surety Co. v. IAC (Coltharp)* (1973) 38 CCC 720; *Hooker v. WCAB* (1974) 39 CCC 75; *Norton v. WCAB* (1980) 45 CCC 1098; *SCIF v. WCAB (Rodarte)* (2004) 69 CCC 579.

AMENDED CLAIMS

As a general principle of pleading, an amended application or other pleading supersedes the original. But the amended pleading does not wholly nullify the original pleading. The time of filing the original is still the date of commencement of the action for the purposes of the statute of limitations, except when a wholly different case is pleaded by the amendment.[64] This means that amendments may be filed after the statute of limitations has expired for filing an original application. (For a full discussion of amendments to applications, see Section 15.3 Amendment and Interpretation of the Application.)

In *Bassett-McGregor v. WCAB*,[65] the Court of Appeal held that an applicant was allowed to amend a claim that was originally pleaded as a specific injury to one alleging a cumulative trauma injury, even though more than a year had passed between the date of injury and the date of the amended application. This was because the disability alleged in the amended application arose from the same set of facts, and did not allege a new and different cause of action. The amended application superseded the original application, and related back to the original filing date for the purposes of the statute of limitations.[66]

But the amendment only relates back to the date of the original filing if it is not a wholly different case. So in one case, an applicant sustained multiple specific injuries and a cumulative trauma injury during the course of employment, but filed an application only for the CT claim. The specific injury claims were not filed until nearly four years later. The appeals board held that the specific injury claims were barred by the statute of limitations, explaining that the specific injury claims did not arise from the same set of facts as the cumulative trauma claim because, although the specific injury claims involved injury to the same body parts, the specific injury claims each differed from the ending date of the applicant's CT injury.[67]

An applicant's amended application more than one year after the date of injury to correct the name of the employer, who was erroneously named in the original application, relates back to the timely filed application.[68]

---

[64] *Bassett-McGregor v. WCAB* (1988) 53 CCC 502, 513.
[65] (1988) 53 CCC 502.
[66] *Bassett-McGregor v. WCAB* (1988) 53 CCC 502, 512-14. See also *The Southern California Gas Co. v. WCAB (Roberson)* (1997) 62 CCC 232 (writ denied).
[67] *Cooke v. WCAB* (2003) 68 CCC 1703 (writ denied). But see *Smith v. Johns-Manville Products Corp.* (1981) 46 CCC 557, 562 (appeals board *en banc*) (appeals board stated, "Amendment of an application alleging a cumulative injury to allege a specific injury causing the same disability does not constitute a new cause of action or result in prejudicial lack of notice to the employer.").
[68] *Scandinavian Airlines v. WCAB (Berg)* (1989) 54 CCC 457 (writ denied).

6.15 ONE YEAR FROM LAST PROVISION OF BENEFITS

Once the employer provides medical or disability benefits, the employee's time to commence proceedings for normal benefits with the appeals board is extended. Per LC 5405, the statute of limitations is a one-year period, but the starting date is not the date of injury when benefits are paid. The employee may file a timely claim within one year from either the "expiration of any period" of payment for temporary or permanent disability benefits, or the "date of last furnishing of any" medical benefits. The one-year statute of limitations will begin to run on the date the last workers' compensation benefit is provided and will expire after a year has elapsed without any further benefit being provided. Should a dispute arise, the employer must prove that benefits were not provided for more than one year.

The purpose of provisions extending the statute of limitations beyond the initial year after the date of injury to the longer period of one year after the date of the last payment of indemnity benefits and medical treatment is to protect an "injured employee from being lulled into a sense of security by voluntary payments of benefits until the time to commence formal proceedings with the [appeals board] has expired."[1] That is, LC 5405 prevents a potential claimant from being misled by an employer's voluntary acts that reasonably indicate an acceptance of responsibility for the employee's injury.[2] So those provisions prevent an employer from giving the employee a false sense of security that all

---

[1] *Pacific Employers Insurance Co. v. IAC (Bracchi)* (1944) 9 CCC 284, 286; *Kaiser Foundation Hospitals/Permanente Medical Group v. WCAB (Webb)* (1977) 42 CCC 302, 304.
[2] *Kaiser Foundation Hospitals/Permanente Medical Group v. WCAB (Webb)* (1977) 42 CCC 302, 305.

elements of a claim will be resolved satisfactorily by furnishing medical treatment or disability benefits, and then while treatment is underway or shortly after it terminates, invoking the statute of limitations.[3]

Note that because benefits can and often are provided indefinitely, this rule can provide the employee with an indefinite period of time in which to timely file an initial WCAB claim for workers' compensation benefits. Each time the employee receives medical treatment or the employer issues a payment for disability benefits, the employee gets a new one-year period. In some cases, there will never be more than a year between the provision of medical benefits. In nonlitigated cases, where the employer is voluntarily providing payment of a permanent disability life pension, the employee can commence proceedings before the WCAB any time during his lifetime.

ONE YEAR FROM THE LAST PROVISION OF INDEMNITY BENEFITS

If the employer provides disability benefits, the employee's time to commence proceedings with the appeals board is extended beyond the date of injury. Per LC 5405(b), the statute of limitations is a one-year period from the "expiration of any period" of payment for temporary or permanent disability benefits.

Usually, there's a definite date a final payment is issued for indemnity benefits. The one-year statute of limitations will begin to run on the date the last workers' compensation benefit is provided and will expire when a year goes by without any further benefit being provided.

Indemnity benefits are generally provided on the date the claims administrator issues a payment by placing it in the mail (usually the date that appears on the check, but the appeals board may rely on a postmarked envelope as evidence that payment was made on a subsequent date). If disability checks are mailed late, the statute of limitations period can be extended. Furthermore, if a disability payment covers future benefits, such as when a lump sum payment of temporary disability indemnity is paid, the statute of limitations commences from the end of the period for which compensation had been paid, rather than the date of the payment.[4] Payments of compensation under the laws of another state are also

[3] *SIF v. IAC (Clubb)* (1957) 155 Cal. App. 2d 288, 290.
[4] *U.S. Fidelity and Guaranty Co. v. IAC (Frazier)* (1928) 204 Cal. 88.

treated as payment within the meaning of LC 5405 sufficient to toll the statute of limitations.[5]

Payment of Wages or Salary

Payments to an employee needn't be designated as either temporary disability or permanent disability benefits in order to toll the statute of limitations. The courts have liberally defined what constitutes a benefit for the purposes of LC 5405(b), because the statute of limitations is not a trap to defeat a just claim, but a mere rule to limit the time for a claim to be presented. The rule was adopted for the purpose of encouraging diligence and preventing injustice.[6]

In many cases, wages or salary paid to an employee during a period of disability has been held to constitute compensation for the purposes of tolling the statute of limitations. The California Supreme Court has stated "that whenever compensation is due as a matter of fact ... then payments for the benefit of the injured employee shall be treated as disability indemnity, whatever the motive may have been in paying them, and whether or not there was any acknowledgment of liability to pay compensation or of payment as compensation."[7] So if an employee is totally disabled and the employer continues to pay wages during the period of disability, the courts will view the payments not as wages or gratuities, but as payments of compensation that operate to toll the statute of limitations while they are paid.[8] This is so even if the claimant deliberately decides to defer the filing of the claim.[9]

The purpose of this is to avoid victimizing the claimant. The employer is not allowed to make payments that can be construed as compensation and then surreptitiously apply the statute of limitations. When the applicant is not placed in this position, payment of wages will not be seen as made in lieu of compensation. So the payment of salary by the employer during a period that the employee was off from work does not constitute the payment of compensation if the employer did not know and the employee did not claim that the absence was due to injury.[10] Moreover, the payment of wages during the period of disability for work previously performed does not lead to the conclusion that the payments

---

[5] *Industrial Indemnity Exchange v. IAC (Waggoner)* (1947) 12 CCC 110.
[6] *Morrison v. IAC* (1938) 3 CCC 182, 186.
[7] *Bulger v. IAC* (1933) 218 Cal. 716, 725.
[8] *London Guarantee & Accident Co., LTD. v. IAC (Read)* (1928) 92 Cal. App. 298; 301; *Bulger v. IAC* (1933) 218 Cal. 716, 725; *Morrison v. IAC* (1938) 3 CCC 182, 185; *Rendleman v. IAC* (1966) 31 CCC 172.
[9] *Astrocraft v. WCAB (Kayden)* (1989) 54 CCC 359 (writ denied).
[10] *Morrison v. IAC* (1938) 3 CCC 182, 186 quoting 1 Campbell's Workmen's Compensation, section 947.

were made in lieu of temporary disability.[11] And the mere fact that an employer permits an employee to return to his old position at full pay does not give rise to a claim that a portion of the pay was compensation for the industrial injury, unless it is shown that there was an agreement to that effect or that the payments received were more than the value of the services.[12]

In one case, a firefighter and two police officers of the city of San Francisco sustained industrial injuries and were paid disability and retirement benefits for the injuries in compliance with a city charter. The California Supreme Court addressed the issue of whether the payments constituted compensation within the meaning of the Labor Code so as to toll the statute of limitations. It determined that the payments received at the time of disability that were due under the Labor Code were "compensation" and served to toll the statute of limitations. But the payments that were made after the city had fully satisfied and discharged its liability to the injured employees under the Labor Code were not compensation and did not toll the statute of limitations.[13]

In an unpublished opinion, the Court of Appeal held that the payment of wages while an employee was not working due to an industrial injury did not toll the statute of limitations. In that case, the employee was not confused or misled by the receipt of the wage, and was aware of her workers' compensation benefits, but chose, for personal reasons, not to timely file a claim.[14]

ONE YEAR FROM THE LAST PROVISION OF MEDICAL BENEFITS

Per LC 5405(c), the statute of limitations may also be tolled if the employer or insurance carrier, knowing of a claim or potential claim, furnishes medical treatment or advances sums for a purpose bearing a clear relationship to an industrial injury.[15] LC 4600 provides that the employer must provide all "[m]edical, surgical, chiropractic, acupuncture, and hospital treatment, including nursing, medicines, medical and surgical supplies, crutches, and apparatuses, including orthotic and prosthetic devices and services, that is reasonably required to cure or relieve the injured worker from the effects of his or her

[11] *Glenn v. WCAB* (1972) 37 CCC 385 (Court of Appeal opinion unpublished in official reports).
[12] *Hunt v. IAC* (1919) 43 Cal. App. 373, 375.
[13] *City and County of San Francisco v. WCAB (Quinn, Page)* (1970) 35 CCC 390, 395.
[14] *SCIF v. WCAB (Murphy)* (1984) 49 CCC 295 (Court of Appeal opinion unpublished in official reports). See also *Arthur v. WCAB* (1987) 52 CCC 391 (writ denied).
[15] *Kaiser Foundation Hospitals/Permanente Medical Group v. WCAB (Webb)* (1977) 42 CCC 302, 304; *McDaniel v. WCAB* (1990) 55 CCC 72, 75.

injury." Under LC 5405(c), the employee must commence proceedings within one year from the date of last furnishing of medical care.

What exactly constitutes the "furnishing" of medical care? Does this refer to when the applicant sees the physician, or when the claims adjuster or employer pays the bill? Or does it refer to when the care was authorized? In one case, the Court of Appeal indicated that LC 5405(c) would apply from "the last rendition of medical services to [the applicant]," but did not specifically address the issue.[16]

In one case, the appeals board interpreted the word "furnished" to mean the date treatment was furnished, and not the date payment for treatment was made.[17] In cases in which treatment is furnished because premiums for group health care are paid by the employer (discussed below), the implication is that paying the premium constitutes the furnishing of medical treatment.[18] But this issue will need to be clarified by the courts.[19]

Medical Treatment

What exactly constitutes medical treatment under LC 4600 that may toll the statute of limitations under LC 5405(c)? The furnishing of treatment does not toll the statute of limitations unless it is made as compensation for a workers' compensation claim.[20] Obviously, if an employer refers an employee for professional medical treatment following an industrial injury, it would generally qualify as medical treatment for the purposes of LC 5405(c). In one case, the appeals board held that treatment at a union clinic, which was funded jointly by

---

[16] *Kaiser Foundation Hospitals/Permanente Medical Group v. WCAB (Webb)* (1977) 42 CCC 302, 303. Note that in *Webb*, the court found the claim barred because it was filed more than one year after notice of rejection but less than one year after the last furnishing of benefits to the injured employee.

[17] *Records v. Waste Management*, 2012 Cal. Wrk. Comp. P.D. LEXIS 96. See also *Sun Harvest v. WCAB (Carrizales)* (1988) 53 CCC 95 (writ denied).

[18] *Mihesuah v. WCAB* (1972) 37 CCC 790; *Pizza Hut of San Diego, Inc. v. WCAB (Bailey)* (1978) 43 CCC 70; *Nielsen v. WCAB* (1985) 50 CCC 104.

[19] There is a troublesome series of older cases in which the employer or carrier did not explicitly notify the applicant that no further medical care would be provided. It was held that the employer was estopped from raising the statute of limitations because of this violation, and implied that the last furnishing of benefits ran only from the denial of any further care. *Viking Freight Systems v. WCAB (Coutee)* (1997) 62 CCC 123 (writ denied); *Texture Coatings of America v. WCAB (Alaia)* (1984) 49 CCC 707 (writ denied) (failure to inform applicant that medical benefits were terminating tolled the statute of limitations); *San Diego Unified School District v. WCAB (Peterson)* (1996) 61 CCC 1220 (writ denied); *McAfee v. WCAB* (1997) 62 CCC 1395; *Texture Coatings of America v. WCAB (Alaia)* (1984) 49 CCC 707 (writ denied). But all of these cases were premised on CCR 9859, which required notification when medical treatment was denied. That CCR has been repealed, so it appears that none of these cases today is good law on the point. A failure to notify the applicant of the termination of medical treatment benefits should not affect the ability of the defense effectuate a statute of limitations defense.

[20] *Nielsen v. WCAB* (1985) 50 CCC 104.

the union and the employer, constituted treatment that could toll the statute of limitations.[21]

Generally, the courts have taken a liberal view as to what constitutes medical treatment. For example, it has been held that the furnishing of pain pills by a supervisor with knowledge that they were to alleviate a condition caused by work constituted the furnishing of medical treatment.[22] Furthermore, first aid rendered to an injured employee by an employer's nurse has also been held to be medical treatment.[23] It has also been held that an employer furnished medical care for an employee following an industrial injury when it provided transportation to a doctor's office, even though it did not pay the doctor for the services.[24]

But the appeals board has held that the employer did not furnish medical treatment for the purposes of LC 5405 when an employee self-procured ibuprofen from the first aid kit in the employees' break room without the knowledge of a supervisor. The appeals board concluded that the mere availability of nonprescription pain medicine at the workplace did not constitute the furnishing of medical treatment for an injury when the employer did not know that the employee was taking the medication and/or did not know of the claimed injury.[25] Likewise, when an employee cut himself and cleaned the wound with water and paper towels, it was found that the employer did not provide medical treatment.[26]

In another case, the Court of Appeal held that until the employer denied the claim, an employer's payment of a medical treatment lien constituted the furnishing of medical treatment that tolled the statute of limitations. The court also held that the voluntary provision of medical treatment triggered the five-

[21] *Sun Harvest v. WCAB (Carrizales)* (1988) 53 CCC 95 (writ denied).
[22] *Standard Rectifier Corp. v. WCAB (Whiddon)* (1966) 31 CCC 340.
[23] *Pacific Indemnity Co. v. IAC (Wimmer)* (1948) 13 CCC 112. See also *Blakeley v. WCAB* (1970) 35 CCC 498 (taking aspirin on the advice of an employer's nurse was medical treatment by the employer and tolled the statute of limitations). It must be considered that in 1990, LC 5401 was amended to provide that provision of a claim form was not required unless the injury results in lost time beyond the date of injury or that results in medical treatment beyond first aid. So the prior cases holding that provision of pain pills or first aid may toll the statute of limitations may no longer be controlling.
[24] *Sullivan v. WCAB* (1971) 36 CCC 163.
[25] *Gordon v. WCAB* (2003) 68 CCC 657 (writ denied). See also *Stevens v. IAC* (1963) 28 CCC 39 (writ denied).
[26] *Dorsey v. WCAB* (1973) 38 CCC 427 (writ denied). Compare *American Solvents & Chemical Corp. v. IAC (Susanj)* (1936) 1 CCC 160 (examination by a physician without provided treatment not enough) with *Craigie & Zeller Motors v. WCAB (Pouget)* (1956) 21 CCC 6 (writ denied) (examination by treating physician may be enough to constitute provision of medical treatment).

year statute of limitations of LC 5410.[27] This is discussed in Section 6.24 Five-Year Statute — Original Jurisdiction.

The provision of medical treatment for a workers' compensation claim is an issue of fact, and the burden is on the employer to establish the last date of treatment. So when the employer denies payment of medical expenses, but there is evidence that the employer paid medical expenses related to an industrial injury, the appeals board may find that the statute of limitations is tolled under LC 5405(c).[28] If the employer provides medical treatment but does not provide any evidence as to the last date the medical benefits were provided, the employer cannot prove that the claim is barred by LC 5405(c).[29]

It is of special note that the Legislature in 2004 enacted SB 899, which includes the new LC 5402(c). It requires an employer to provide medical care during the period in which a claim is being investigated. This is discussed in depth in Section 7.24 Immediate Medical Care. Under this provision of the code, the employer is compelled to provide medical care before it has decided whether the claim should be accepted or denied. It probably would be disadvantageous to the defense to have this count as medical treatment for purposes of extending the statute of limitations, but there have been no cases on this issue to date. Nevertheless it is most likely that this medical treatment will be found to affect the statute of limitations analysis. It is of note that LC 5402(d) specifically provides that medical treatment provided under subdivision (c) does not give rise to a presumption of compensability of the claim; but this speaks to liability, and says nothing about the statute of limitations. Of course, if the employer denies the claim, the clock begins to run from the date of denial. Since the time delay/investigatory period is only 90 days, this consideration should not have a huge effect in most denied cases.

Medical Treatment Paid by Employer's Group Insurance

In some cases, medical treatment paid under the employer's group insurance, rather than workers' compensation insurance, may also constitute the furnishing of medical treatment for the purposes of LC 5405(c). This can happen when the employer knows of the injury, provides medical benefits through a nonworkers' compensation policy and does not deny the injury. For example, in *Mihesuah v. WCAB*,[30] an employee was injured while on his way home from work, and the

[27] *McDaniel v. WCAB* (1990) 55 CCC 72.
[28] *Kohagen v. WCAB* (1997) 62 CCC 1492, 1500 (Court of Appeal opinion unpublished in official reports).
[29] *New York Yankees v. WCAB (Montefusco)* (2001) 66 CCC 291 (writ denied).
[30] (1972) 37 CCC 790.

employer treated the injury as a nonindustrial injury. But the employer did not inform the employee that it had decided to treat his accident on a nonindustrial basis. The employer furnished benefits under its own medical plan for almost two years, and paid the employee benefits from its own pension and disability fund. The employee only filed an application for adjudication when he was notified that his benefits would be terminated. The Court of Appeal held that medical payments made under an employer's group medical program tolled the statute of limitations. Although the issue of whether the injury occurred within the scope of employment was not on appeal, the Court of Appeal concluded that if the injury was industrial, the employer's contributions to its group insurance policy constituted benefits under LC 4600. So in that case, the court held that the claim was timely filed.[31]

But medical treatment received by an employee under a medical plan to which the employer contributes does not constitute medical treatment under LC 5405(c) if an employer fully informs the employee that it is rejecting liability for the claim.[32] Furthermore, it has been held that an employer's payment of medical treatment charges under an employer's insurance plan did not toll the statute of limitations when the employer had no knowledge of an industrial injury that gave rise to the treatment. In that case, an employee injured his back and left leg, but did not inform the employer that the injury was related to the employment. Instead, he informed his supervisor that the injury was caused by kickboxing. The employee's medical charges were paid by employer's group insurance carrier. More than a year after the date of injury, the employee filed a claim for workers' compensation benefits. He relied on the *Mihesuah* holding that the payment of medical charges under the employer's group medical insurance constituted the furnishing of compensation within the meaning of LC 5405 for the purposes of tolling the statute of limitations. The Court of Appeal, however, held that the claim was barred by the statute of limitations, noting that in *Mihesuah,* the employer knew of the injury, knew of the surrounding facts and should have realized the industrial character of the injury, but decided to treat the injury as nonindustrial and furnished benefits, including medical expenses under its group medical program. The court concluded that it was for this reason that the employer in *Mihesuah* was estopped to claim that it had not provided the benefits as compensation. But in the case at bar, the court noted that the

[31] *Mihesuah v. WCAB* (1972) 37 CCC 790. See also *Pizza Hut of San Diego, Inc. v. WCAB* (1978) 43 CCC 70, *Hartford Accident & Indemnity Co. v. WCAB (Miran)* (1979) 44 CCC 872 (writ denied), *State of California, Department of Mental Hygiene v. WCAB (Trigueiro)* (1976) 41 CCC 160 and *Maryland Casualty Insurance Co. v. WCAB (Taylor)* (1979) 44 CCC 480 (writ denied) (treatment under a group insurance policy for which the employer paid premiums constituted furnishing of medical treatment).

[32] *Kaiser Foundation Hospitals/Permanente Medical Group v. WCAB (Webb)* (1977) 42 CCC 302; *Muntzel v. WCAB* (1983) 48 CCC 642 (writ denied).

payments under the group medical policy did not indicate that the employer had accepted liability for the injury. This was because there was no evidence that the employer knew the injury was work related nor any evidence that the employer voluntarily furnished medical benefits to the employee as compensation. So there was no evidence that the employee was misled by the payment of medical expenses that caused him to delay in filing his claim.[33]

Medical Treatment for Multiple Injuries

When an employee sustains multiple injuries to the same body part, the statute of limitations for a subsequent injury is not automatically tolled. When the employer furnishes medical treatment for a prior injury for which the employee has received an award of continuing medical care, there is no tolling.[34] But if the medical treatment is designed to relieve the employee from the effects of the subsequent injury, then the statute of limitations may be tolled.[35]

Medical-Legal Examinations

The statute of limitations is not tolled every time an employee is evaluated by a physician for an industrial injury. Not all medical examinations are done for the purposes of treatment; some are done to prove or disprove a claim or an issue in a claim. Such examinations commonly are called medical-legal examinations, and they do not constitute medical treatment if no treatment or medication is provided.[36] Employers have a statutory right to determine their liability before providing any benefits or payments. As long as the examining physician restricts the examination to a determination of merits of the claim without providing treatment, the examination will not toll the statute of limitations.

For example, in one case, an applicant alleged that he sustained an industrial CT injury ending in 2009. The employer denied the claim on the grounds of the statute of limitations but advised the applicant of his right to obtain a panel QME. The applicant did so Nov. 16, 2009, and the panel QME reported that he sustained an industrial low-back injury. The applicant did not file a claim form, but filed an application for adjudication more than a year after the report issued. Because the employer did not pay temporary or permanent disability benefits,

[33] *Nielsen v. WCAB* (1985) 50 CCC 104. See also *Ingram v. WCAB* (1987) 52 CCC 442 (writ denied); *Mayberry v. WCAB* 45 CCC 1178 (writ denied).
[34] *Martin v. WCAB* (2004) 69 CCC 814 (writ denied).
[35] *Plotnick v. WCAB* (1970) 35 CCC 13, 15-16; *Chandler Furniture Co. v. WCAB (Meeks)* (1990) 55 CCC 248 (writ denied).
[36] *Hunt v. IAC* (1919) 43 Cal. App. 373. For a full discussion of medical-legal evaluations see Chapter 14: Discovery and Settlement.

and did not provide medical treatment, no voluntary furnishing of benefits was made. The panel QME evaluation did not constitute medical treatment. The appeals board also found that the applicant was aware that his condition was industrial on receipt of the panel QME report. So because the application was not filed within one year of the date of injury, it was barred by the statute of limitations.[37]

In the present environment, medical-legal examinations are performed pursuant to LC 4060, LC 4061, LC 4062, LC 4062.1 and LC 4062.2. In the past, however, employers were permitted to refer employees for examination with their own doctors to determine issues of causation. Again, such examinations did not constitute medical treatment. In one case, an employee underwent several examinations with an employer's physician but testified that he received no treatment or medication during any of these visits. As a result, the Court of Appeal held that there was no service that could be construed as compensation, and therefore no basis for a tolling of the statute of limitations.[38]

EMPLOYER'S ACTIONS BIND THE INSURANCE CARRIER

If the employer tolls the statute of limitations either by providing medical treatment or disability benefits to the employee, such acts are binding on the insurance carrier. That is, if the employer cannot successfully plead the statute of limitations, the insurance carrier is likewise barred from doing so.[39] Along these lines, it has been held that if one carrier pays benefits, the statute is tolled for another carrier on the risk.[40] If the employer on its own or through a carrier pays benefits to the applicant that can reasonably be related to the claim, benefits are considered paid for purposes of the statute of limitations. The employer and its carriers stand in each other's shoes.

---

[37] *Battle v. Gulfstream Aerospace*, 2012 Cal. Wrk. Comp. P.D. LEXIS 332.

[38] *Hunt v. IAC* (1919) 43 Cal. App. 373, 376. See also *American Solvents & Chemical Corp. v. IAC (Susanj)* (1936) 1 CCC 160. But see *Southern California Gas Co. v. WCAB (Penn)* (1966) 31 CCC 205 (writ denied) (recommendation by company's doctor that employee wear a lumbosacral corset was treatment).

[39] *U.S. Fidelity & Guaranty Co. v. IAC (Avila)* (1925) 195 Cal. 577.

[40] *The Hartford v. WCAB (Schwartz)* (2000) 65 CCC 407 (writ denied).

6.16 ESTOPPEL TO PLEAD THE STATUTE OF LIMITATIONS

Bad behavior on the part of the employer can negate or at least delay the statute of limitations defense. A concept in law called "estoppel" applies to the statute of limitations. Simply put, an employer may be estopped, or prevented, from raising the statute of limitations if its behavior would make raising the defense unfair to the employee. In cases in which estoppel applies, the employer has either intentionally or by failure to perform some duty, misled the applicant. The applicant relies on the representations of the employer to his or her detriment.

Generally, the concept of estoppel applies to the one-year statute of limitations under LC 5405. As discussed in Section 6.30 Estoppel and the Five-Year Statute there is some question as to whether it applies to the five-year statute of limitations. When an employer is found to be estopped, the applicant does not have forever to file the application and initiate the case. Rather, the statute of limitations is tolled until such time as the employer's bad behavior is corrected or the applicant becomes aware of his or her rights. Estoppel is a common response of applicants when the defense raises the statute of limitations, and is often effective.

The next two sections examine the specific grounds for estoppel in this area. If the employer fails to provide notice to the applicant of his or her rights as required by law, estoppel can apply. As defined in LC 5405(b)(c), the Legislature has determined that the statute of limitations will be tolled by the voluntary furnishing of temporary or permanent disability or the furnishing of medical or hospital benefits. But the courts have also determined that the statute of limitations will be tolled when an employer with knowledge of an industrial injury fails to provide an employee with required statutory notices.[1]

Estoppel also will apply when the employer engages in acts that lead the employee to believe that liability for the injury is admitted and will not be contested. As long as the employer's conduct reasonably suggests that the filing of a claim is unnecessary, the tolling of the statutory time period can occur.[2] There are also instances in which the employer by word or action misrepresents to the employee or fraudulently conceals from him material facts upon which liability depends. As long as the falsehood is maintained, the running of the statute of limitations may be tolled.[3]

[1] *Reynolds v. WCAB* (1974) 39 CCC 768.
[2] *McDaniel v. WCAB* (1990) 55 CCC 72, 76.
[3] *Pacific Employers Insurance Co. v. IAC (Bracchi)* (1944) 9 CCC 284, 286.

6.17 ESTOPPEL BASED ON FAILURE TO PROVIDE NOTICE

Under LC 5405, a claim for workers' compensation benefits must generally be filed within one year of either the date of injury or the last date specified benefits were provided. But in *Reynolds v. WCAB,*[1] the California Supreme Court held that an employer may not raise the statute of limitations defense if the employer knew that an employee's injury was industrially related, but failed to provide the employee with the required notices.[2] The court stated that the rules and regulations regarding the employer's notice requirements were implemented "to protect and preserve the rights of an injured employee who may be ignorant of the procedures or indeed, the very existence of the workmen's compensation law. Since the employer is generally in a better position to be aware of the employee's rights, it is proper that he should be charged with the responsibility of notifying the employee ... that there is a possibility he may have a claim for workmen's compensation benefits."[3] In *Reynolds,* the employer was estopped from raising the statute of limitations because it had failed to comply with its statutory notification duties.[4] After *Reynolds,* LC 138.3 was added and LC 5402 was amended to approve of the results reached in that case.[5] The idea that notices must be sent or estoppel applies has been reiterated in many cases.[6]

---

[1] (1974) 39 CCC 768.

[2] *Reynolds v. WCAB* (1974) 39 CCC 768. See also *Rivas v. WCAB (Rodriguez)* (1980) 45 CCC 303 (writ denied).

[3] *Reynolds v. WCAB* (1974) 39 CCC 768, 770.

[4] See also *Buena Ventura Gardens v. WCAB (Novak)* (1975) 40 CCC 434; *Hughes Aircraft Co. v. WCAB (Zimmerman)* (1993) 58 CCC 220 (writ denied).

[5] *Kaiser Foundation Hospitals, Permanente Medical Group v. WCAB (Martin)* (1985) 50 CCC 411, 415.

[6] *Balcom, dba Thee Coffee Shop v. WCAB (Vandevort)* (1985) 50 CCC 2 (writ denied); *Johnson v. WCAB* (1997) 62 CCC 625 (Court of Appeal decision not published in official reports) (sending the applicant a letter

Subsequently, in 1985, the California Supreme Court, in *Kaiser Foundation Hospitals, Permanente Medical Group v. WCAB (Martin)*,[7] added to the rule articulated in *Reynolds* and held that the statute of limitations would be tolled by the breach of an employer's duty to notify only if the employee is prejudiced by the breach. The court stated, "An employee would be prejudiced without the tolling if he has no knowledge that his injury might be covered by workers' compensation before he receives notice from the employer. Requiring prejudice to toll the limitations period promotes the policy behind the notification statutes: to protect those unaware of their rights."[8] Because the court added the element of prejudice to the analysis, if an employee gains actual knowledge of his workers' compensation rights, the statute of limitations will not be tolled, even if an employer breaches its duty to provide a claim form and notice of potential eligibility. The employee is not prejudiced by the employer's breach.

If, in contrast, the employee remains ignorant of his workers' compensation rights, the employee will be prejudiced from the date of breach until the employee gains actual knowledge that he may be entitled to benefits under the workers' compensation system.[9] Once a breaching employer notifies an injured employee of his workers' compensation rights, the tolling ends no later than the date the notice is received. The tolling period may end before the date notice is received only if the employer proves that the employee gained the requisite knowledge of his workers' compensation rights before he received the employer's notices.[10] So the employer has the burden not only to assert the running of the statute of limitations, but also to establish either that written notice was given to the employee or the employee had actual notice of his workers' compensation rights.[11] If the employer cannot prove that it provided an employee with notice of workers' compensation rights and procedures, it may

---

saying that a pamphlet describing his rights was available upon request was not enough to avoid estoppel); *Pomona College v. WCAB (Robusto)* (2009) 74 CCC 1284 (writ denied).

[7] (1985) 50 CCC 411.

[8] *Kaiser Foundation Hospitals, Permanente Medical Group v. WCAB (Martin)* (1985) 50 CCC 411, 416. See *Vanover-Lopez v. Kelly Staff Leasing*, 2011 Cal. Wrk. Comp. P.D. LEXIS 301 (WCAB rescinded WCJ's finding that defendant failed to prove that applicant's claim was barred by statute of limitations even though defendant failed to meet its burden of proving that it provided all requisite notices to applicant; WCJ did not assess whether applicant had been prejudiced by the breach of the notice requirements).

[9] *Kaiser Foundation Hospitals, Permanente Medical Group v. WCAB (Martin)* (1985) 50 CCC 411, 416. See *New York Yankees v. WCAB (Montefusco)* (2001) 66 CCC 291 (writ denied) (baseball player ignorant that he could file a claim in California due to jurisdictional questions; no notice given by the ball club and estoppel applied, despite the fact that the claim was filed nine years after the fact); *Pic-A-Bagel, Inc. v. WCAB (Hercz)* (2009) 74 CCC 307 (writ denied) (claim not barred when applicant filed application two years after his injury when employer did not provide claim form and never advised applicant or his workers' compensation rights based on erroneous determination that applicant was an officer who was excluded from workers' compensation coverage).

[10] *Kaiser Foundation Hospitals, Permanente Medical Group v. WCAB (Martin)* (1985) 50 CCC 411, 416-17.

[11] *Sidders v. WCAB* (1988) 53 CCC 445, 452.

not rely on the affirmative defense of the statute of limitations to defeat an employee's claim.[12]

In *Martin*, an employee slipped and fell at work and was taken to a hospital where medical treatment was provided. The hospital sent a first report of work injury to the insurance carrier nearly two months after the injury. Two and a half months later, the adjuster sent the employee a letter rejecting liability for the injury, and advising him that if he was not satisfied he could contact the state Division of Industrial Accidents or consult an attorney. A copy of the letter was sent to the hospital. The hospital filed an application for adjudication as a medical lien claimant more than a year after the employee's injury, but less than one year after the employer notified the employee of his workers' compensation rights. The appeals board found that the claim was barred by the statute of limitations. The California Supreme Court annulled the decision, finding no evidence that the employee knew of his workers' compensation rights and presumed that he was ignorant of those rights until he received notice of them from the adjuster. Because the employer breached its duty and the employee was ignorant of his workers' compensation rights until he received notice, the statute of limitations was tolled and the application for adjudication was timely filed.[13]

INADEQUATE NOTICE

The practitioner must be very careful when it comes to providing notice to the applicant. Generally, providing the claim form and the notice of rights as spelled out and sanctioned in CCR 10139 (see Section 6.5 Post-Injury Notices) is sufficient to place the applicant on notice. In a vacuum, proper notices are enough to avoid estoppel,[14] and notices sent to the applicant submitted to the court at trial are sufficient to meet the employer's burden of proof.[15] An employer is not required to provide notice to an applicant beyond what is required by the law. An employer cannot reasonably be expected to guess what kind of notice it should provide to an injured worker, particularly when the administrative director has promulgated clear regulations on that issue.[16]

Historically, a series of cases held that estoppel applied when the applicant was not specifically notified that he had only one year to file an application. This was

[12] *Hampton v. WCAB* (2001) 66 CCC 1269 (Court of Appeal opinion unpublished in official reports).
[13] *Kaiser Foundation Hospitals, Permanente Medical Group v. WCAB (Martin)* (1985) 50 CCC 411, 417-18. See also *Hampton v. WCAB* (2001) 66 CCC 1269 (Court of Appeal opinion unpublished in official reports); *Rubin v. Delta Airlines*, 2011 Cal. Wrk. Comp. P.D. LEXIS 188.
[14] *Bridges v. WCAB* (1984) 50 CCC 3 (writ denied).
[15] *Lawson v. WCAB* (1985) 50 CCC 445 (writ denied).
[16] *Stephens v. WCAB* (2009) 74 CCC 885 (writ denied).

so despite the fact that the applicant had been given all other notices required by law.[17] Those cases were based on a regulation, CCR 9882, that has since been repealed; right now there is no CCR requiring such language. Accordingly, if an employer provides the appropriate claim form and notice of potential eligibility, which do not indicate the applicable statute of limitations, the employer is not estopped from asserting the statute of limitations defense just because it does not notify the applicant of the applicable statute of limitations.[18]

But inadequate or misleading notices of workers' compensation rights may act to toll the statute of limitations.[19] If benefit notices sent to an applicant are misleading or even ambiguous in regard to an applicant's rights and lull an applicant into a false sense of security, the employer risks being estopped from raising the statute of limitations.

For example, in *SCIF v. WCAB (Mahan)*,[20] a case that should concern all defendants, the state fund sent an applicant notice that temporary total disability (TTD) was ending because the applicant was returning to work. The letter stated that the State Compensation Insurance Fund (SCIF) would pay for his future medical care, and that "You may be entitled to further workers' compensation benefits." This was held to be enough to mislead the applicant into believing that he did not have to prosecute his claim within the statutory time frame.

Another good example is the case in which the appeals board held that an employer was estopped to raise the statute of limitations defense, even though it sent a pamphlet advising the nonlitigated employee that his claim could be barred if he waited more than a year from the notice of denial to file a claim with the appeals board. The defense failed to advise him that he had a right to choose from the entire list of panel qualified medical evaluators (QMEs) under former LC 4060(d). Also, the denial letter that was sent under CCR 9812(i) allowed that the denial might be reconsidered.[21]

---

[17] *San Joaquin Community Hospital v. WCAB (McMahan)* (2002) 67 CCC 1653 (writ denied); *Galloway v. WCAB* (1998) 63 CCC 532; *Times Mirror Co. v. WCAB (Berke)* (1987) 52 CCC 124 (writ denied). Also, as referenced in the last section, a series of cases held that estoppel applied when the defense did not send specific notice that it was ceasing all medical care. That, too, was based on a defunct regulation, CCR 9859. *Viking Freight Systems v. WCAB (Coutee)* (1997) 62 CCC 123 (writ denied); *Texture Coatings of America v. WCAB (Alaia)* (1984) 49 CCC 707 (writ denied); *Pacific Bell v. WCAB (Bowers)* (1988) 54 CCC 10 (writ denied).

[18] *Meyer v. WCAB* (2010) 75 CCC 1210 (writ denied); *Duarte v. WCAB* (2008) 73 CCC 1447 (writ denied).

[19] *McAfee v. WCAB* (1997) 62 CCC 1395, 1398 (Court of Appeal opinion unpublished in official reports).

[20] (1996) 61 CCC 1228 (writ denied).

[21] *Modesto City Schools v. WCAB (Finch)* (2002) 67 CCC 1647 (writ denied). See also *Santa Barbara County v. WCAB (Santos)* (2009) 75 CCC 56 (writ denied) (employer estopped from asserting statute of limitations because pamphlet was inadequate to provide notice and employer was required to provide specific notices).

NO TOLLING WITHOUT EMPLOYER KNOWLEDGE OF INJURY

An employer is estopped from asserting the statute of limitations defense only if the employer knew that an employee's injury was industrially related, but failed to provide the employee with the required notices.[22] So if the employer does not have notice of an injury sufficient to trigger its duty to notify the employee of his or her rights to workers' compensation benefits, the statute of limitations will not be tolled as a result of an employer's failure to provide the required notices. As a result, an employee's claim may be barred by the statute of limitations even if the employer does not provide the required notices if the employer was under no obligation to provide the requisite notices.[23]

If an employer has no notice that the employee was injured, it would have no duty to provide the required notices. For example, an applicant experienced pain radiating down his left leg within a week of starting an assignment to disassemble and reassemble bottle racks. In October 1981 the applicant went off work because of the injury, but did not file a claim until after consulting an attorney in April 1983. The applicant argued that the claim was not barred by the statute of limitations because the employer failed to comply with its duty to provide the required notices. The court determined that there was no evidence that the employer should have known that the condition was work related. The applicant never informed the employer of any specific injury or accident. Furthermore, the applicant never informed the employer that he believed that he was injured at work. In fact, the applicant told a supervisor that he was injured during a nonindustrial kickboxing episode. Because the evidence did not establish that the employer had knowledge or notice of facts from which it could or should have recognized that the applicant was injured on the job or that his condition might have arisen from the employment, the court found no basis for estopping the employer from asserting the statute of limitations defense.[24]

In another case, an applicant claimed a cumulative trauma injury ending in 1989, but did not file his application for adjudication until 1995. The applicant argued that his claim was not barred by the statute of limitations because he was not advised of his workers' compensation rights by his employer. The applicant

---

[22] *Reynolds v. WCAB* (1974) 39 CCC 768. See *Gustafson v. WCAB* (1976) 41 CCC 737 (writ denied); *Barrett Business Services, Inc. v. WCAB (Hathcock)*, 2012 Cal. Wrk. Comp. LEXIS 151 (writ denied).

[23] *Rowe v. WCAB* (1986) 51 CCC 57 (writ denied).

[24] *Nielsen v. WCAB* (1985) 50 CCC 104. The Court of Appeal noted that the duty of an employer to give the required notice is triggered only when the employer has received "knowledge of an injury to an employee as defined in Labor Code Section 3208 or notice or knowledge of a claimed injury sufficient to afford an opportunity to make an investigation into the facts." But this standard has been limited to actual knowledge of injury by the subsequent Supreme Court case of *Honeywell v. WCAB (Wagner)* (2005) 70 CCC 97, as described in depth in Section 6.5 Post-Injury Notices.

testified that he complained to his supervisor about his injury, but on cross-examination admitted that he believed he told his supervisor that his body was aching but was unsure about what exactly he told him. The appeals board found that there was not sufficient notice of injury given by the applicant to trigger the employer's duty to notify him of his rights to benefits under CCR 9880, to provide notice of denial of liability or to toll the statute of limitations. The appeals board found that *Reynolds* was inapplicable.[25]

In one case, the applicant testified that a doctor told her in 2006 that her neck and back problems were work related, and that she did not return to work after May 2006 because of her injuries. She filed an application for adjudication in 2010, but asserted that the statute of limitations was tolled because she did not know that she was entitled to workers' compensation for her injuries, and that the statute was tolled because the defendant failed to inform her of her rights pursuant to *Reynolds*. The majority, however, concluded that the claim was barred by the statute of limitations. It found that the applicant introduced no evidence that the defendant had knowledge or notice of injury sufficient to trigger its duty to provide the applicant notice of her workers' compensation rights. It also rejected any sweeping proposition that the statute of limitations on a cumulative injury claim does not begin to run until an applicant has his or her full legal rights explained in detail by an attorney.[26]

As discussed in Section 6.5 Post-Injury Notices, not all injuries trigger the duty to provide notice. Per LC 5401(a), an employer's duty to provide a claim form and notice of potential eligibility commences on notice of an injury that results in lost time beyond the employee's work shift or that results in medical treatment beyond first aid. So, even if an employer has notice of an injury, but its duty to provide notice under LC 5401(a) is not triggered, the statute of limitations will not be tolled based on the employer's failure to provide notice.

In one case, it was undisputed that the applicant fell March 8, 2005, and injured her knees. The injury was reported to the employer and an occurrence report form was completed. The applicant described the injury, but reported that she

---

[25] *Forrest v. WCAB* (2004) 69 CCC 271 (writ denied). See also *County of San Bernardino v. WCAB (Schroeder)* (2007) 72 CCC 1365 (Court of Appeal opinion unpublished in official reports) (employer not estopped from raising a statute of limitations defense when it had no knowledge of an applicant's cumulative trauma injury); *Liberty Mutual Insurance Co. v. WCAB (Stanfill)* (1981) 46 CCC 1269 (Court of Appeal opinion unpublished in official reports) (no estoppel when the employer received no knowledge or notice sufficient to trigger its duty to give notice).

[26] *Geren v. WCAB* (2012) 77 CCC 999 (writ denied). The dissent believed that the statute of limitations in a cumulative injury case does not start to run until an injured worker is aware of his or her legal entitlement to workers' compensation benefits.

did not need a doctor at the time. The applicant initially lost no time from work and did not seek medical care for her knees until December 2006, after she voluntarily terminated her employment. The applicant did not file her application until May 8, 2008. The WCJ found that the employer was not required to provide written notice of the applicant's entitlement to workers' compensation benefits pursuant to LC 5401(a), but also found that the defendant was estopped from raising the statute of limitations for failure to investigate. The appeals board rescinded the decision.

It found that the WCJ imposed a duty on the employer that is not required by law. It was not convinced that the employer was required to investigate the injury more than it did. It also found that the applicant was offered medical treatment, and that she declined. So there was no evidence that the employer knew or should have known that the applicant's injury might be serious. Accordingly, the appeals board found that the applicant's claim was barred by the statute of limitations, and ordered that she take nothing.[27]

NO TOLLING WITH ACTUAL KNOWLEDGE OF WORKERS' COMPENSATION RIGHTS

The tolling period may end before the employer provides a claim form to an employee if the employee has "actual" knowledge of his workers' compensation rights. The employer bears the burden of proving actual knowledge.[28] Actual knowledge is knowledge given directly to, or received personally by a party.[29] Constructive knowledge (awareness the employee *should have* possessed) is not sufficient.[30] This is a very difficult burden for the employer. The employee's ignorance is presumed until the employee is given the requisite notice, or otherwise gains actual knowledge that he may be entitled to workers' compensation.[31]

In *Hurwitz v. WCAB (Esposito),*[32] a decision before *Martin,* a legal secretary injured her right leg falling down an unlit stairway in her office building. She hired an attorney, and decided to sue the building owner in tort rather than seek workers'

---

[27] *Wheldon v. Golden Empire Transit,* 2012 Cal. Wrk. Comp. P.D. LEXIS 496.
[28] *Kaiser Foundation Hospitals, Permanente Medical Group v. WCAB (Martin)* (1985) 50 CCC 411, 417.
[29] *CIGA v. WCAB (Carls)* (2008) 73 CCC 771, 779.
[30] *CIGA v. WCAB (Carls)* (2008) 73 CCC 771, 779; *Mitchell v. WCAB* (1987) 52 CCC 520 (Court of Appeal opinion unpublished in official reports); *Dalangin v. WCAB* (1988) 53 CCC 299 (Court of Appeal opinion unpublished in official reports).
[31] *CIGA v. WCAB (Carls)* (2008) 73 CCC 771, 776. See also *Deeny v. WCAB* (1980) 45 CCC 968 (writ denied).
[32] (1979) 44 CCC 983.

compensation benefits from her employer. She later filed her workers' compensation claim almost two years after the injury. At trial, the applicant testified that she was aware that she could file a workers' compensation application and that she had one year within which to file it because of her experience working in an attorney's office. But her attorney did not want to file a workers' compensation claim against her employer, because her attorney had other cases with her employer that would create a conflict. So she did not timely file the claim. The Court of Appeal held that an applicant's claim was barred by the statute of limitations because she retained an attorney and the evidence demonstrated that the applicant knew she had a right to a workers' compensation claim and even knew of the one-year limitations period, but deliberately decided not to file a workers' compensation claim.[33]

Likewise in the case of *Busse v. WCAB,*[34] a union leader filed a claim. The court determined that the leader had extensive knowledge of workers' compensation and was aware of his rights. So even though the notice sent to him was deficient, the claim was barred by the statue of limitations when it was filed more than a year after the last payment of benefits. In another case, a supervisor-level employee was found to be aware of his rights in part because he had helped other employees file their claims. He testified that he knew his rights and had deliberately withheld from reporting or filing a claim for several years.[35]

In a more recent case, *CIGA v. WCAB (Carls),*[36] a painter sustained an industrial injury in 1996 to his left shoulder, filed a workers' compensation claim and received temporary disability benefits. In 1997, the employee injured his back after arriving at work two hours early. He notified his employer of the injury, but the employer did not advise him of his potential eligibility for workers' compensation and did not give him a claim form. In 1999, the employee retained an attorney, who filed an application for adjudication for the 1996 injury, but not for the 1997 injury. In 2002, when the 1996 injury was called for trial, the WCJ took the matter off calendar to allow the applicant to file a new or amended claim for the 1997 injury, but no new application was filed until 2004. At trial, the applicant testified that when he reported the 1997 injury, the supervisor did not give him a claim form and the workers' compensation manager gave him a hard time because he came to work two hours early. The applicant added that he

---

[33] *Hurwitz v. WCAB (Esposito)* (1979) 44 CCC 983. See also *Keeton v. WCAB* (1979) 44 CCC 547 (no estoppel to plead the statute of limitations when the applicant had actual knowledge that he had a compensable injury and was required to file a timely claim).
[34] (1986) 51 CCC 207 (writ denied).
[35] *Escalante v. WCAB* (2000) 66 CCC 173 (writ denied).
[36] (2008) 73 CCC 771.

never received a letter from his employer advising him of his right to file a workers' compensation claim.

The California Insurance Guarantee Association (CIGA), assuming liability for an insolvent insurer, argued that the claim was barred by the statute of limitations because three events showed that the employee had gained the requisite knowledge. First, CIGA argued that the employee knew he might have been entitled to workers' compensation from the moment of his 1997 injury because he had received benefits for the 1996 injury. Second, CIGA argued that the employee had knowledge because he signed an application for adjudication for the 1996 injury and retained counsel in 1999 to represent him for that injury. Third, CIGA argued that the employee was aware no later than 2002, when the WCJ continued the trial as to the 1996 injury to permit the filing of a new or amended application for the 1997 injury.

Despite these arguments, the Court of Appeal agreed with the appeals board that the employer had not met its burden that the employee had actual knowledge of his right to claim workers' compensation benefits for the 1997 injury. Regarding the first event, that is, the employee previously receiving benefits for the 1996 injury, the court stated that general awareness of the workers' compensation system and past experience with the workers' compensation system was not by itself sufficient to prove knowledge of potential eligibility for a particular injury. The court stated that CIGA was required to show that the employee knew the 1997 injury was a potentially compensable injury, and there was no evidence of this. The court added that the employee's testimony suggested that the employer had convinced him that his injury was not work related because he arrived two hours early and the employer gave him a hard time.[37]

Other cases have agreed that just because an employee has had a claim in the past does not necessarily mean that he has actual knowledge when a new injury occurs.[38] But as seen above, a complete knowledge and familiarity of workers' compensation does amount to actual knowledge, and having experience with previous claims can contribute to that knowledge.[39] Ultimately, the decision rests

---

[37] *CIGA v. WCAB (Carls)* (2008) 73 CCC 771, 777-78.

[38] *Galloway v. WCAB* (1998) 63 CCC 532 (the fact that the applicant had two previous claims did not mean that he was acquainted with the time parameters for making a claim); *City of Wasco v. WCAB (Gibson)* (2002) 67 CCC 318 (writ denied); *Allied Sysco Food Services, Inc. v. WCAB (Norris)* (2001) 66 CCC 884 (writ denied); *National Steel and Shipbuilding Co. v. WCAB (Avant)* (1999) 64 CCC 110 (writ denied); *Alpine Recreation v. WCAB (Johnson)* (1996) 61 CCC 1456.

[39] *Morris v. WCAB* (2004) 69 CCC 819 (writ denied) (appeals board holding that an applicant was aware of her right to file a compensation claim because she was involved in ongoing compensation proceedings and therefore the employer was not estopped from asserting the statute of limitations defense for failing to provide a claim form); *Day v. WCAB* (1991) 56 CCC 160 (Court of Appeal opinion unpublished in official reports) (an

on whether the actual knowledge can be demonstrated to the finder of fact — the WCJ.

Returning to the *Carls* case, the second defense argument was that in retaining counsel and filing an application for adjudication for the 1996 injury, the applicant demonstrated actual knowledge of his rights. The court did not accept this argument either, saying that CIGA failed to explain how the employee's signature on the application for the 1996 injury imparted knowledge of his potential eligibility for the 1997 injury. The court added that the retention of legal counsel did not impart the requisite legal knowledge. The court reasoned that although generally an attorney's knowledge is imputed to his client, knowledge is not imputed where actual knowledge is required, because imputed knowledge is constructive knowledge rather than actual knowledge. A long series of cases support the idea that having an attorney in and of itself is not enough to establish actual knowledge on the part of the applicant.[40] But whether the applicant learned of his rights from his attorney is a question of fact for the WCJ, and many courts have been inclined to lean toward the defense in this situation. The *Hurwitz* case described above is a good example.[41] The *Carls* court distinguished *Hurwitz* on the grounds that in that case, there was substantial evidence that the employee had been advised by her attorney, and thus had actual knowledge of her rights and the statute of limitations, but elected not to file a claim on her attorney's advice.[42] In this case, however, there was no evidence of actual knowledge imputed from the attorney.

Finally, with regard to CIGA's last argument, that the employee had knowledge because the WCJ continued adjudication of the 1996 claim to allow the applicant to file a claim for the 1997 injury, the court noted that this was not sufficient

---

applicant's general knowledge of workers' compensation relieved the employer from providing the required notices).

[40] *CIGA v. WCAB (Carls)* (2008) 73 CCC 771, 778-79. See also *Davenport v. WCAB* (2005) 70 CCC 1566 (Court of Appeal opinion unpublished in official reports) (no actual knowledge inferred from speaking with an attorney); *Allied Sysco Food Services, Inc. v. WCAB (Norris)* (2001) 66 CCC 884 (writ denied) and *King, dba Shellys Catering v. WCAB (Pelton)* (1990) 55 CCC 28 (writ denied) (speaking with civil attorney did not confer knowledge); *Dalangin v. WCAB* (1988) 53 CCC 299 (Court of Appeal opinion unpublished in official reports) and *Allstate Insurance Co. v. WCAB (Bishop)* (1979) 44 CCC 455 (no actual knowledge from hiring an attorney for a civil action).

[41] See also *Price v. WCAB* (2007) 72 CCC 1687 (writ denied) (knowledge inferred when employee was represented by an attorney); *Cooke v. WCAB* (2003) 68 CCC 1703 (writ denied) (no estoppel when employee presumably learned of his rights through his attorney); *Darr v. WCAB* (1998) 63 CCC 850 (writ denied) (employee deemed aware of workers' compensation rights after consulting with an attorney); *Loveland v. WCAB* (1987) 52 CCC 401 (writ denied) (applicant is aware of workers' compensation rights after speaking with an attorney); *Rudd v. Oakland Raiders*, 2011 Cal. Wrk. Comp. P.D. LEXIS 243 (applicant had actual knowledge when he had consulted lawyers and previously filed two claims for the same cumulative trauma injury; they were dismissed for applicant's failure to prosecute).

[42] *CIGA v. WCAB (Carls)* (2008) 73 CCC 771, 779, fn. 9.

because the record did not reflect that the employee was present or otherwise knew why the continuance was sought.[43]

In light of these cases, it is very difficult to prove that the employee had actual knowledge of workers' compensation rights without an admission from the employee to that effect. So in most cases, the statute of limitations will be tolled when the employer fails to provide the employee with the statutorily required notices and there is no definitive showing that the employee had actual knowledge of his or her workers' compensation rights. Several cases have borne out this conclusion.[44]

NOTICE FOR MULTIPLE INJURIES

One case illustrates that a claim form must be separately provided for each date of injury. An applicant sustained a specific injury in 1986 that was accepted, and awarded ongoing medical care. He continued his employment, but his pain level gradually increased. On Feb. 17, 1998, the applicant reported his worsening back pain to the personnel department and completed a claim form. An employee from the personnel department filled in the claim form with the date of injury of Feb. 2, 1998. The insurance carrier identified the applicant's injury as a cumulative trauma claim, but listed the date of injury as Feb. 2, 1998. The insurance carrier denied the claim based on medical evidence that there was no new injury in February 1998.

The applicant was referred to QMEs who found that his disability related to both the 1986 injury and a cumulative trauma injury. It was not until Sept. 8, 2000 that an application for adjudication was filed with the WCAB, formally asserting the continuous trauma claim. The employer pointed out that it had provided a claim form to the employee upon knowledge of injury, and argued that the claim was barred by the statute of limitations under LC 5405. But the appeals board found that the employer did not provide the proper notices. Because the employer and the carrier had identified that the applicant had a CT claim, but noted that there was a specific claim — and then denied the specific — it was held that a claim

---

[43] *CIGA v. WCAB (Carls)* (2008) 73 CCC 771, 777-80.

[44] See *City of Sonoma v. WCAB (Cahill)* (2010) 76 CCC 37 (writ denied); *Insurance Co. of the West v. WCAB (Morris)* (2002) 68 CCC 778 (writ denied); *Lumbermens Mutual Casualty Co. v. WCAB (Shouse)* (2001) 66 CCC 535 (writ denied); *County of Los Angeles v. WCAB (Duran-Dingillo)* (1999) 64 CCC 1075 (writ denied); *Nieves, dba Rick-N-Nachos v. WCAB (McZeal)* (1998) 63 CCC 1083 (writ denied); *Ukiah Valley Medical Center v. WCAB (Salmans)* (1997) 62 CCC 999 (writ denied); *CIGNA Insurance Co. v. WCAB (Garza)* (1997) 62 CCC 337 (writ denied); *County of San Bernardino v. WCAB (Sprague)* (1995) 60 CCC 221 (writ denied); *Manhart v. WCAB* (1979) 44 CCC 525 (Court of Appeal opinion unpublished in official reports).

form and notice had not been provided to the applicant for the CT claim. It was held that the employer was estopped from raising the statute of limitations.[45]

TIME TO RAISE THE ISSUE

The appeals board has held that an employer's failure to provide a claim form in accordance with LC 5401 is an issue that may not be raised for the first time on reconsideration.[46] So if the employee does not raise this issue until after trial, a claim may be barred by the statute of limitations, even if the employer fails to demonstrate that it provided a claim or that the employee had actual knowledge of his workers' compensation rights.

APPLICABILITY TO LIEN CLAIMANTS

A lien claimant may initiate workers' compensation proceedings by filing an application. But there is only one statute of limitations period, and that is the period applicable to the injured employee. The statute of limitations will be tolled for a lien claimant if it is tolled for the employee. So regardless of the lien claimant's own prior knowledge of the workers' compensation laws, a lien claimant has one year from the date of the employee's injury plus the period of the employer's breach to file a timely claim if the employee did not previously file one.[47] If the employee gains the requisite actual knowledge of his right to workers' compensation benefits from other sources, a lien claim may be barred even if the employer did not give the employee notice of his right to workers' compensation benefits.[48]

The employer is not required to provide a lien claimant with notice of its workers' compensation rights, as the Legislature has concluded that they do not need notice from the employer to inform them of their rights.[49] Nevertheless, lien claims for medical-legal services are not barred by the statute of limitations even if the underlying claim has been barred by the statute of limitations.[50]

---

[45] *Crown Cork & Seal v. WCAB (Fields)* (2002) 67 CCC 175 (writ denied).
[46] *Cottrell v. WCAB* (1998) 63 CCC 760 (writ denied).
[47] *Kaiser Foundation Hospitals, Permanente Medical Group v. WCAB (Martin)* (1985) 50 CCC 411, 418-19.
[48] *Permanente Medical Group v. WCAB (Taylor)* (1989) 54 CCC 44 (writ denied).
[49] *Permanente Medical Group v. WCAB (Williams)* (1985) 50 CCC 491, 497.
[50] *Anchor Glass Container v. WCAB (Benton)* (1995) 60 CCC 403 (writ denied) citing *Turudich v. IAC (Smale)* (1965) 30 CCC 316; *PERS v. WCAB* (1978) 43 CCC 1291.

6.18 ESTOPPEL BASED ON MISREPRESENTATION OR MISCONDUCT

An employer is also estopped to plead the statute of limitations as a defense when its conduct or representations induce an employee to refrain from filing his claim until after the statute of limitations has run.[1] That is, the employer or insurer may not take actions that influence an employee to delay in filing a workers' compensation claim and then argue that the claim is barred by the statute of limitations. Actual fraud, bad faith or an intent to mislead are not essential to an estoppel. It is sufficient that the employer made misrepresentations or engaged in conduct that misled the employee, who acted on such in good faith and as a result failed to timely file a claim. And any acts or conduct that wrongfully influence an employee to believe that an amicable adjustment of his or her claim will be made may create an estoppel to plead the statute of limitations.[2]

PROVING ESTOPPEL BASED ON MISREPRESENTATION OR MISCONDUCT

To prove estoppel, the employee must show reliance on some act, omission or statement of the employer or insurer.[3] Misrepresentations made by the employer

[1] *Nolan v. WCAB* (1977) 42 CCC 401, 405; *U.S. Casualty Co. v. IAC (Moynahan)* (1954) 19 CCC 8; *Industrial Indemnity Co. v. IAC (Varela)* (1953) 18 CCC 39; *Benner v. IAC* (1945) 10 CCC 110.
[2] *Industrial Indemnity Co. v. IAC (Varela)* (1953) 18 CCC 39, 42.
[3] *McGee Street Productions/Hallmark Entertainment v. WCAB (Peterson)* (2003) 68 CCC 708, 715.

after the statute of limitations has expired do not toll the statute of limitations.[4] Whether estoppel exists, that is, whether the acts, representations or conduct lulled the employee into a sense of security preventing him or her from instituting proceedings before the running of the statute of limitations, and whether the employee relied on that conduct to his prejudice, is a question of fact.[5]

For example, in *Nolan v. WCAB,*[6] an applicant sustained an industrial injury and received voluntary compensation benefits from his employer. The employee was sent to prison approximately one year after his injury and was advised that a medical examination and claim processing would be arranged on his release from prison. A workers' compensation application was filed while the applicant was in prison. More than two years after the incarceration, the insurer filed a motion to dismiss the claim without prejudice for lack of prosecution. The applicant's attorney received the motion to dismiss but did not oppose it because it was without prejudice; he considered that this would allow the applicant to request an adjudication of his claim upon his release from prison. The claim was dismissed without prejudice because no response was made.

The applicant was released from prison more than five years after his date of injury and requested activation of his claim. The insurer advised the applicant that its file was closed. Ten months after being released from prison, and five years and 11 months after the date of injury, the applicant filed a petition to reopen. The Court of Appeal noted that although termed a petition to reopen, the applicant's request was really to have adjudicated the original claim left pending by the dismissal without prejudice. The court then noted that generally a dismissal without prejudice has the effect of holding open an applicant's right to refile his application as long as it was not barred by the statute of limitations. Because the dismissal was more than a year after the last provision of benefits, it would normally terminate the applicant's claim. Nevertheless, the court held that the employer was estopped to assert the statute of limitations because the insurer had represented that the claim was to be processed upon the applicant's release from prison. The court stated, "An employee will not be barred from reopening his claim for benefits after a dismissal thereof when the conduct or representations of the employer's workers' compensation insurance carrier induce the employee not to contest the dismissal of his claim and the result of

---

[4] See *McGee Street Productions/Hallmark Entertainment v. WCAB (Peterson)* (2003) 68 CCC 708, 715; *Royal Globe Insurance Co. v. WCAB (Ulrich)* (1974) 39 CCC 6 (writ denied).

[5] *Industrial Indemnity Co. v. IAC (Varela)* (1953) 18 CCC 39, 42.

[6] (1977) 42 CCC 401.

such dismissal has the effect of barring the refiling of the claim because of the running of the statute of limitations."[7]

In another case, an employee sustained an injury in 1977, and an employer told an applicant that it would provide future medical care and that he did not need an attorney. The applicant also was told that there was no statute of limitations on future medical treatment. The applicant relied on this advice and received various forms but did not read that the claim might be barred by the statute of limitations. He received medical treatment, temporary disability indemnity and permanent disability advances that were paid until 1979. That year, the applicant was sent a form advising him that if he waited too long, he could lose his right to benefits. The applicant did not file his claim until 1985. The appeals board held that the claim was not barred by the statute of limitations because the applicant was "lulled into a false sense of security" by assurances that medical care would be provided and that an attorney was not necessary.[8]

In one case, the appeals board held that an insurer was estopped to assert the statute of limitations when it wrongly informed the applicant that his claim was dead, and the applicant relied on this statement and did not timely file his claim until after consulting with an attorney.[9] In another case, an applicant was told to attend a medical examination, which was to help to determine if her claim was valid. The exam was scheduled after the statute of limitations had expired. It was found that she was misled and the employer was estopped.[10]

In one especially troublesome case, *National Lead Co. v. WCAB (Randolph),*[11] a treating doctor told an applicant that he could return for treatment if he thought he needed to. The applicant did return years later, and the statute of limitations was raised. It was held that the physician "chosen by the petitioner was its agent for the treatment of the applicant." As such, the doctor's words were found to lull the applicant into a false sense of security, and the defense was estopped form raising the statute of limitations defense. This case was decided in 1967, when the defense got to choose the treating doctor. That situation changed in the 1970s, when the employee was allowed free choice of physician. It remains to be

---

[7] *Nolan v. WCAB* (1977) 42 CCC 401, 405.

[8] Furthermore, because the applicant was never informed that there was a one-year statute of limitations, the applicant relied on "some act, omission, or statement of the employer or insurance carrier" and the employer was estopped from asserting the statute of limitations defense. *Times Mirror Co. v. WCAB (Berke)* (1987) 52 CCC 124 (writ denied). See also *American Home Assurance Co. v. WCAB (Morones)* (2002) 67 CCC 822 (writ denied) (employer estopped to assert the statute of limitations when it represented that it would continue to pay medical expenses and never recanted that representation).

[9] *University Mechanical v. WCAB (Doherty)* (1996) 61 CCC 900 (writ denied).

[10] *Foremost Insurance Co. v. WCAB (Strom)* (1979) 44 CCC 182 (writ denied).

[11] (1967) 32 CCC 230 (writ denied).

seen whether the 2004 SB 899 creation of employer-controlled networks will breathe new life into the idea presented by this case. In any case, *Randolph* stands for the principle that a defendant can be held responsible for the statements of its agents.

This concept applies when the employee files the application in the wrong place, the employer knows of the mistake, but does nothing about it. In one case, the applicant thought he had filed with the appropriate state agency, when in fact he had filed the document with the State Compensation Insurance Fund. SCIF did nothing to disabuse him of the misconception, despite the fact that the mistake was obvious from the cover letter. Estoppel applied due to this misconduct.[12]

The appeals board also held that a special employer was estopped to raise the statute of limitations against an employee's attempt to join it in a timely filed action against a general employer. The special employer had instructed the employee to pursue benefits from the general employer, the employee relied on the instructions, proceeding only against the general employer. The applicant suffered as result of his reliance on the special employer's instruction to pursue his compensation claim against the general employer instead of the special employer.[13] (The general and special employment relationship is discussed in depth in Section 4.73 General and Special Employment.)

NO ESTOPPEL WITHOUT MISREPRESENTATION OR MISCONDUCT

A claim of estoppel will not defeat the statute of limitations defense if there are no facts to support it. When the employer and insurer neither said nor did anything to mislead an applicant to preclude him or her from seeking relief through the appeals board, the employer is not estopped to raise the statute of limitations defense.[14] If an employer flatly, completely and consistently denies liability for a claim, estoppel cannot be shown.[15] Moreover, estoppel does not bar an employer from relying upon the statute of limitations if the nature of its conduct or advice was reasonable when given.[16]

---

[12] *SIF and SCIF v. IAC (Fenn)* (1965) 30 CCC 175 (writ denied). See also *City of Anaheim v. WCAB (Hagan)* (1995) 60 CCC 1017 (writ denied).

[13] *Production Framing Systems v. WCAB (Dove)* (2005) 70 CCC 735 (writ denied).

[14] *Royal Indemnity Co. v. IAC (Clutter)* (1966) 31 CCC 47, 52. See also *Kelley v. WCAB* (2002) 68 CCC 84 (writ denied) (appeals board held that a claim was barred by the statute of limitations when the employer had advised the applicant of her rights to compensation, and there was nothing in the record to reflect that the applicant detrimentally relied on any advice given before the statute of limitations had run).

[15] *American Can Co. v. IAC (Wright)* (1962) 27 CCC 137.

[16] *City of Los Angeles v. IAC (Dillin, Catlow)* (1965) 30 CCC 278.

NO ESTOPPEL WITHOUT RELIANCE ON MISREPRESENTATION OR MISCONDUCT

An employer's misrepresentation or misconduct will not warrant estoppel if the employee has actual knowledge of his or her rights, as the conduct only allows for estoppel *because* it misleads the employee.[17] The statute of limitations runs when the employee acquires actual knowledge of his or her workers' compensation rights.[18]

The applicant may have actual knowledge of his or her workers' compensation rights, despite the employer's conduct, but choose not to file a claim for other reasons. For example, an employee may have actual knowledge that he had a compensable injury and was required to file a timely claim, but decline to do so because he believed he would receive good treatment from his private insurance.[19] When this happens, there is no estoppel. Moreover, an employee may be aware of his or her workers' compensation rights, but decline to file a workers' compensation claim on the advice of an attorney.[20] Again, when this happens, there is no estoppel. This means that it may be more difficult for applicants to impose estoppel when they have been represented by counsel.[21] Nevertheless, an applicant must still have actual knowledge, and the attorney's imputed knowledge is not sufficient.[22]

---

[17] *Industrial Indemnity Co. v. IAC (Varela)* (1953) 18 CCC 39, 43.
[18] *Kaiser Foundation Hospitals, Permanente Medical Group v. WCAB (Martin)* (1985) 50 CCC 411, 416.
[19] *Keeton v. WCAB* (1979) 44 CCC 547. See also *SCIF v. WCAB (Murphy)* (1984) 49 CCC 295 (Court of Appeal opinion unpublished in official reports).
[20] See *Hurwitz v. WCAB (Esposito)* (1979) 44 CCC 983.
[21] See *Chichester v. WCAB* (1994) 60 CCC 37 (writ denied).
[22] *CIGA v. WCAB (Carls)* (2008) 73 CCC 771, 778-79.

6.19 TOLLING THE STATUTE OF LIMITATIONS FOR A CIVIL CLAIM

If an employee pursues both a civil claim and a workers' compensation against an employer, the statute of limitations on the action for damages for personal injury is tolled when the workers' compensation action is timely commenced, and for the period in which the workers' compensation remedy is pursued against the employer.[1] The tolling of the statute of limitations in such cases will not frustrate its purpose, which is to "[p]revent surprises through the revival of claims that have been allowed to slumber until evidence is lost, memories have faded, and witnesses have disappeared."[2]

It does not necessarily work the other way around. There is no clear-cut court decision on the issue, but from what we do have, it seems that whether the filing of a civil action tolls the statute of limitations in a related workers' compensation case depends largely on whether the employer is on notice of the action. Civil actions against a third party related to an industrial injury may not toll the statute of limitations, but civil actions filed directly against the employer may.

For example, the appeals board has held in one case that the statute of limitations for an employee's workers' compensation claim was not tolled by the filing of a third-party civil action. The employee never informed his employer of the injury, but before filing the civil action knew of his right to workers' compensation

[1] *Elkins v. Derby* (1974) 39 CCC 624; *Valdez v. Himmelfarb* (2006) 71 CCC 1574.

[2] *Elkins v. Derby* (1974) 39 CCC 624. But the filing of a workers' compensation claim does not toll the statute of limitations for a civil lawsuit allegation of fraudulent concealment resulting in aggravation of the original injury — the harm from fraudulent concealment is distinct from the original injury. *Aerojet General Corp. v. The Superior Court of Sacramento County (Larson)* (1986) 177 Cal. App. 3d 950.

benefits through his attorney. So the statute of limitations on the workers' compensation claim filed more than six years after the injury was not tolled while the civil claim was pending. The court made it a point to recite that the employer was not aware of the civil action, and if it were, things might have been different.[3] In another case, an applicant's widow filed a timely federal action against a third party. The employer did not know of the claim for asbestosis until after more than a year had passed. So the workers' compensation action was barred by the statute of limitations.[4]

In contrast, in another case, a civil suit directly against an uninsured employer was found to toll the statute of limitations, and the filing of the workers' compensation action was timely. In willfully uninsured employer cases, the employer may be sued in both civil court and the WCAB. But the case was decided on the concept that the employer had notice of the suit.[5] Also, the appeals board has held that the filing of a civil suit against a special employer tolled the statute of limitations of LC 5405 for the purposes of joining the special employer in a timely filed workers' compensation claim against a general employer. (The general-special employer relationship is discussed in depth in Section 4.73 General and Special Employment.) The appeals board concluded that joinder of the special employer more than one year after the injury was appropriate when the special employer was aware of the action from the outset.[6]

So the standard seems to center around whether the employer is timely made aware of the civil action. Nevertheless, this area does await a definitive standard from the courts. It should be pointed out that this area often overlaps with the concept of estoppel — the idea that an employer who fails to provide notice of rights and a claim form to an applicant on becoming aware of the injury is not allowed to raise the statute of limitations at all; this is discussed in Section 6.17 Estoppel Based on Failure to Provide Notice. When an employer becomes aware of the civil suit and thus the allegation of work-related injury, it has an obligation to provide the proper notices, and the failure to do so will result in estoppel. Some statute-of-limitation cases have failed for this reason.[7]

---

[3] *Rojas v. WCAB* (1989) 54 CCC 45 (writ denied).
[4] *Derocher v. WCAB* (1986) 51 CCC 8 (writ denied).
[5] *Springer v. WCAB (Cooper)* (1999) 64 CCC 601 (writ denied).
[6] *Production Framing Systems v. WCAB (Dove)* (2005) 70 CCC 735 (writ denied).
[7] *Wyndorf v. WCAB (De Jesus)* (1993) 58 CCC 50 (writ denied); *Gorelik v. Norris Industries* (1991) 20 CWCR 92 (panel decision).

SECTIONS 6.20 THROUGH 6.23 ARE RESERVED FOR FUTURE USE

6.24 FIVE-YEAR STATUTE — ORIGINAL JURISDICTION

REOPENING FOR NEW AND FURTHER DISABILITY

Per LC 5410, an employee who has been furnished workers' compensation benefits either voluntarily by the employer or pursuant to an award from the appeals board has five years after the date of injury to institute proceedings to claim benefits for new and further disability.[1] The five-year period defined in LC 5410 has been called the "five-year statute of limitations."[2]

Under LC 5410, the employee must have a new disability or have additional disability, and the disability must be a result of the original injury. New and further disability does not exist within the meaning of LC 5410 unless workers' compensation benefits have been either voluntarily furnished or awarded.

Most often, this statute comes into play when an applicant has been given an award by a WCJ of a certain amount of permanent disability. That award can be by way of stipulation of the parties or after a trial. It is not unusual for the applicant, within five years from the date of injury, to attempt to increase the award later within the five-year period.

LC 5410 can also come into play when there is no award, but benefits are furnished and the defense attempts to invoke the one-year statute of limitations. Once the employer provides disability or medical benefits, the five-year statute

[1] *Standard Rectifier Corp. v. WCAB (Whiddon)* (1966) 31 CCC 340, 341; *J.T. Thorp, Inc. v. WCAB (Butler)* (1984) 49 CCC 224, 230.

[2] *General Foundry Service v. WCAB (Jackson)* (1986) 51 CCC 375, 378.

of limitations comes into effect. The one-year period is extended until at least five years from the date of injury, as described below, as long as new and further disability can be shown. But if an employer denies a claim after voluntarily furnishing benefits, and there is no award, the five-year statute of limitations under LC 5410 becomes inoperative and the applicant has one year from the date notice was given to commence workers' compensation proceedings.[3]

So a claim for new and further disability filed within five years from the date of injury is timely even though it was filed more than one year from the last furnishing of benefits.[4] LC 5410 states in pertinent part, "Nothing in this chapter shall bar the right of any injured worker to institute proceedings for the collection of compensation ... within five years after the date of the injury upon the ground that the original injury has caused new and further disability. ... The jurisdiction of the appeals board in these cases shall be a continuing jurisdiction within this period." The rationale for this rule is that the "new and further disability" is a disability in addition to that for which the employer previously provided benefits as required by the statute.[5]

If the employer has not voluntarily furnished benefits or there has not been a prior award, LC 5410 does not apply and the claim must filed within one year from the date of injury under LC 5405.[6]

The date of injury for the purposes of LC 5410 is defined in LC 5411 and LC 5412.[7] LC 5411 provides that the date of injury for most injuries "is that date during the employment on which occurred the alleged incident or exposure, for the consequences of which compensation is claim." LC 5412 defines the date of injury in cumulative injury and occupational disease cases.[8] These definitions of injury, and how they relate to the statute of limitations, are discussed in Section 6.14 One Year From Date of Injury.

The purpose of the five-year statute of limitations in LC 5410 is to "foster both certainty and finality in the law."[9] LC 5410 provides assurance to an employer or

---

[3] *Kaiser Foundation Hospitals, Permanente Medical Group v. WCAB (Webb)* (1977) 42 CCC 302; *McDaniel v. WCAB* (1990) 55 CCC 72, 76. See *Barragan v. WCAB* (2011) 76 CCC 356 (writ denied).

[4] *Mercury Die & Container Corp. v. WCAB (Cisneros)* (1988) 53 CCC 556 (writ denied).

[5] *Standard Rectifier Corp. v. WCAB (Whiddon)* (1966) 31 CCC 340, 342.

[6] *Pizza Hut of San Diego, Inc. v. WCAB* (1978) 43 CCC 70, 72.

[7] *J.T. Thorp, Inc. v. WCAB (Butler)* (1984) 49 CCC 224, 231; *Smith v. Johns-Manville Products Corp.* (1981) 46 CCC 557 (appeals board *en banc*).

[8] *J.T. Thorp, Inc. v. WCAB (Butler)* (1984) 49 CCC 224, 231; *Palmer v. WCAB* (1987) 52 CCC 298.

[9] *Barnes v. WCAB* (2000) 65 CCC 780, 788; *Granite Construction Co. v. WCAB (McReynolds)* (2003) 68 CCC 1548, 1555.

insurer that after five years following and industrial injury, they need not worry about further claims.[10]

REOPENING BY ORIGINAL APPLICATION

The manner in which the employee will institute proceedings under LC 5410 depends on whether jurisdiction arises because the employer voluntarily furnished benefits or the appeals board has issued an award. If the applicant is pursuing a claim under the appeals board's original jurisdiction because the employer voluntarily provided benefits — if there has been no award — the employee institutes proceedings by filing an application for adjudication of claim (CCR 10458). Once an application is filed, there is no required time period in which a decision must be rendered by the court. Jurisdiction continues indefinitely.

Remember, it is the application for adjudication that commences proceedings. It is supposed to be filed within one year of the injury or last furnishing of benefits under LC 5405. If not, the claim is barred by the statute of limitations.[11] The situation can and does arise when the application is filed for new and further disability more than one year from the last payment of benefits but within five years from the date of injury. Is this allowed? Is that application barred by the statute of limitations? The application is not in violation of the statute of limitations to the extent that the employee has new and further disability.

The statute of limitations defined in LC 5410 only pertains to the situation in which the "original injury has caused new and further disability." LC 5410 does not nullify the limiting provisions of LC 5405. That is to say, the payment of workers' compensation benefits does not automatically convert the one-year statute of limitations under LC 5405 into the five-year statute in LC 5410. Instead, LC 5410 gives the appeals board jurisdiction for the period between the date of injury and five years thereafter, *but only in the case of new and further disability.* So a claim for an original injury may be barred under LC 5405(b)(c) when the claim is brought more than one year after the last furnishing of benefits, and within five years from the date of injury, but there is no finding of new and further

[10] *Granite Construction Co. v. WCAB (McReynolds)* (2003) 68 CCC 1548, 1555; *Smith v. Johns-Manville Products Corp.* (1981) 46 CCC 557 (appeals board *en banc*).
[11] See *Malloy v. Target*, 2012 Cal. Wrk. Comp. P.D. LEXIS 86.

disability caused by the original injury.[12]

Read together, LC 5405 and LC 5410 contemplate that: (1) an employee must institute proceedings before the appeals board within one year after the date of injury unless there has been voluntary payment of benefits; (2) such voluntary payments will toll the statute of limitations during their provision, but the period commences again when they are stopped; and (3) if there occurs a "new and further disability" resulting from the original injury within five years from the date of injury, the employee may institute proceedings for it and the appeals board has the jurisdiction to hear, determine and make awards based on, and limited to such, "new and further disability."[13]

The employee does not have five years from the date of injury to seek an award of additional benefits under LC 5410 unless there is some change in the employee's previously known condition. Absent a new or further disability, the statute of limitations to commence proceedings is one year from the date of the last provision of benefits. If there is a finding of new and further disability more than one year beyond the three designated points, but within five years of the date of injury, employees are only permitted to recover benefits related to the new and further disability, not for the original injury.[14]

As a practical matter, however, the practitioner must recognize that it is not difficult to successfully allege that new and further disability has occurred. The courts have been notoriously liberal on the issue.[15] The term "new and further disability" has been defined to mean disability resulting from some "demonstrable change in an employee's condition" and includes a new period of temporary disability, a change from temporary disability to permanent

[12] *Royal Indemnity Co. v. IAC (Clutter)* (1966) 31 CCC 47, 50. There is arguably a conflict in the law on this point, as some cases indicate that the five-year statute applies regardless of whether new and further disability can be shown. The decision of *McDaniel v. WCAB* (1990) 55 CCC 72 states, "Once the one-year limitation is tolled by the voluntary furnishing of benefits, the five-year rule of section 5410 is in turn triggered," suggesting that the employee automatically has five years to file a claim upon the furnishing of benefits, regardless of whether there is new and further disability. Likewise, in *Sanchez v. WCAB* (1990) 55 CCC 179, the court stated that "after the voluntary furnishing of benefits, section 5410 extends the period within which an original proceeding may be instituted from one to five years on the ground that the injury has resulted in further disability or a need for vocational rehabilitation." In accord with this interpretation is *Kansas City Chiefs v. WCAB (Allen)* (2002) 67 CCC 1634 (writ denied). But both *McDaniel* and *Sanchez* state only that the applicant has five years from the date of injury to file his claim under LC 5410 following the voluntary furnishing of medical benefits, but do not discuss whether an applicant may recover under LC 5410 in the absence of new and further disability. So the analysis of *McDaniel* and *Sanchez* appear to be incomplete and the holding of *Royal Indemnity Co. v. IAC (Clutter)* (1966) 31 CCC 47, which has not been overturned, should be controlling.

[13] *Royal Indemnity Co. v. IAC (Clutter)* (1966) 31 CCC 47, 50.

[14] See *Lockheed Missiles & Space Co. v. WCAB (Buckman)* (1991) 56 CCC 84 (Court of Appeal opinion unpublished in official reports) (appeals board could not award PD benefits for an injury that was barred by the statute of limitations).

[15] *Armstrong v. IAC* (1934) 20 IAC 193.

disability, a gradual increase in permanent disability or a change in physical condition necessitating further medical treatment whether or not accompanied by time lost from work.[16] It is quite easy for the employee and his physician to allege a new problem, and quite difficult for the defense to disprove it. Employees generally recover the full range of benefits due when new and further disability has been proved. But one can visualize a situation in which some benefits are barred by the statute of limitations, as they are filed more than one year from the date of injury, and are not the result of the new and further disability.[17]

[16] *Nicky Blairs Restaurant v. WCAB (Macias)* (1980) 45 CCC 876.

[17] A possibility here is an early TTD period, or a demonstrable PD that pre-existed the new and further disability.

6.25 FIVE-YEAR STATUTE — CONTINUING JURISDICTION

If workers' compensation benefits were provided under an award, LC 5410 permits an employee to file a claim for new and further disability to request alteration of the terms of that award. The employee does not file an application, because one is on file. The employee institutes proceedings for new and further disability by filing a petition to reopen (CCR 10458). Likewise, if the defense perceives that permanent disability should be reduced, a petition to reopen with the goal of reducing the award may be filed within the same time period. This is less common than petitions filed by applicants, but it does happen, and is examined in a later section.

The term "reopening" has special meaning in workers' compensation, and generally refers to reopening an order, decision or award for new and further disability under LC 5410.[1] When benefits have been awarded in a workers' compensation claim, LC 5410 permits the employee to reopen a previous decision of the appeals board on the grounds of new and further disability upon the filing of a petition to reopen within five years from the date of injury.[2] LC 5410 is jurisdictional and bars the reopening of a workers' compensation case more than five years after the date of injury.[3]

Similarly, an applicant or defendant may file a petition to reopen an award pursuant to LC 5803 and LC 5804. LC 5803 confers power on the appeals board

---

[1] *Green v. WCAB* (2005) 70 CCC 294, 307; *Kleemann v. WCAB* (2005) 70 CCC 133, 142.
[2] *Nicky Blairs Restaurant v. WCAB (Macias)* (1980) 45 CCC 876, 883; *Sarabi v. WCAB* (2007) 72 CCC 778, 781.
[3] *Granite Construction Co. v. WCAB (McReynolds)* (2003) 68 CCC 1548, 1550.

to rescind, alter or amend any order, decisions or award upon showing of good cause. This power includes the right to review, grant or regrant, diminish, increase or terminate any compensation awarded on the grounds that the disability has either recurred, increased, diminished or terminated.[4] That is, evidence of new and further disability under LC 5410 also constitutes good cause to reopen under LC 5803. LC 5804 limits application of LC 5803 to five years from the date of injury.[5] Together, LC 5410 and LC 5803 - LC 5804 provide parallel time limitations.[6] The Legislature has determined that any event or circumstance that would constitute good cause to reopen under LC 5803 or new and further disability under LC 5410 must occur within a five-year period from the date of injury.[7]

Historically, claims of new and further disability have been analyzed under both LC 5410 and LC 5803 - LC 5804. But one court suggested that supplemental claims for new and further disability are governed by LC 5410, rather than LC 5803 - LC 5804, which allows for the reopening of claims for good cause, because LC 5410 is made paramount by its express terms.[8] It really doesn't seem to matter. Claims of new or further disability continue to be analyzed under both statutes and the court has stated that the appeals board has jurisdiction to decide the matter if a petition to reopen under either is filed within the five-year period.[9]

What if the original, underlying award has an appeal pending? Generally, LC 5410 and LC 5803 - LC 5804 apply to orders, decisions or awards that are beyond the reconsideration period under LC 5900 et. seq., or when appeals have been exhausted and a decision is final or no longer pending.[10] When a petition to reopen on the grounds of new and further disability is filed within five years from the date of injury, the appeals board has authority to issue a decision more

---

[4] LC 5803 states in pertinent part, "The appeals board has continuing jurisdiction over all its orders, decisions, and awards made and entered under the provisions of this division. ... At any time, upon notice and after an opportunity to be heard is given to the parties in interest, the appeals board may rescind, alter, or amend any order, decision, or award, good cause appearing therefor. This power includes the right to review, grant or regrant, diminish, increase, or terminate, within the limits prescribed by this division, any compensation awarded, upon the grounds that the disability of the person in whose favor the award was made has either recurred, increased, diminished, or terminated."

[5] LC 5804 states, "No award of compensation shall be rescinded, altered, or amended after five years from the date of the injury except upon a petition by a party in interest filed within such five years and any counterpetition seeking other relief filed by the adverse party within 30 days of the original petition raising issues in addition to those raised by such original petition."

[6] *Beaida v. WCAB* (1968) 33 CCC 345, 347.

[7] *Smith v. Johns-Manville Products Corp.* (1981) 46 CCC 557, 561-62 (appeals board *en banc*).

[8] *J.T. Thorp, Inc. v. WCAB (Butler)* (1984) 49 CCC 224, 230 fn. 12.

[9] *Sarabi v. WCAB* (2007) 72 CCC 778, 781.

[10] *Green v. WCAB* (2005) 70 CCC 294, 307; *Kleemann v. WCAB* (2005) 70 CCC 133, 142.

than five years after the date of injury.[11] But the new and further disability must occur within the five-year period.[12] So in order to file a petition to reopen on the grounds of new and further disability: (1) the petition must be filed within five years of the injury; (2) the applicant must have suffered new and further disability; and (3) the disability must arise within five years of the date of injury.

When an employee is entitled to an increased permanent disability award because he or she has sustained new and further disability, payment of the award commences on the date the employee was first diagnosed as sustaining the increased disability.[13]

PETITION TO REOPEN

Per LC 5410 and LC 5803 - LC 5804, a petition to reopen must be filed within five years from the date of injury. Note that this time limit — five years from the date of injury — is strict; it applies regardless of whether medical or other benefits have continued to be paid.[14] But the relevant statutes do not direct that a petition to reopen take any particular form, and the courts have been liberal in deciding what constitutes a petition to reopen.[15] The only real requirements are that some sort of filing is made with the WCAB within five years, and that the defense is put on notice of the applicant's claim of new and further disability.

CCR 10455 and CCR 10458 provide that petitions to reopen pursuant to LC 5803 and LC 5410, respectively, should enumerate in detail the facts they rely on. The courts have stated that such rules of procedure serve the convenience of the appeals board and facilitate the proceedings, but do not deprive the board of the power to dispense with compliance when the purposes of justice require it, particularly when the violation is formal and does not substantially prejudice the other party.[16]

Petitions lacking detail or that are very broad and general are sufficient.[17] In one case, the Court of Appeal held that a technically deficient petition to reopen that did not specify the facts on which it relied was adequate to preserve the

---

[11] *SIF v. IAC (Pranzitelli)* (1957) 22 CCC 132; *Casualty Insurance Co. of California v. IAC (Felton)* (1964) 29 CCC 95; *Aliano v. WCAB* (1979) 44 CCC 1156; *Nicky Blairs Restaurant v. WCAB (Macias)* (1980) 45 CCC 876, 883; *Sarabi v. WCAB* (2007) 72 CCC 778, 781.

[12] *Sarabi v. WCAB* (2007) 72 CCC 778, 782.

[13] *Sorensen v. WCAB* (1983) 48 CCC 535 (writ denied).

[14] *Robinson v. WCAB* (1997) 62 CCC 825 (writ denied).

[15] *Bekins Moving and Storage Co. v. WCAB* (1982) 47 CCC 1260, 1265.

[16] *Beaida v. WCAB* (1968) 33 CCC 345, 349.

[17] *Sarabi v. WCAB* (2007) 72 CCC 778, 781; *CIGA v. WCAB (Winters)* (2006) 71 CCC 814 (writ denied); *Miles & Sons Trucking/Beazer v. WCAB (Angell)* (1995) 60 CCC 432 (writ denied).

jurisdiction of the appeals board to reopen the case when it was filed within five years and gave notice that the applicant was alleging increased disability.[18] In another case, the Court of Appeal held that a petition to reopen that alleged a "change in condition" without specifying the nature of the change was sufficient for the purposes of LC 5410 and LC 5803 because it informed the employer of the claim.[19] The appeals board may not summarily deny a skeletal petition to reopen without first giving the petitioner the opportunity to append more specific allegations.[20]

An applicant's failure to state the correct case number in a petition to reopen will not deprive him or her of an appeals board decision on the merits of the petition to reopen.[21] Such a petition needn't request any particular classification of compensation in order to vest the appeals board with jurisdiction to reconsider the entire case.[22] For example, the California Supreme Court held that a petition to reopen praying "that the Appeals Board take such steps as may be necessary to a redetermination of this matter and for an increase in the benefits payable to petitioner on account of said permanent disability" also authorized the appeals board to award further temporary disability.[23]

A petition to reopen needn't be supported by medical evidence at the time of filing. An applicant needn't obtain proof of new and further disability within five years of the injury. Medical evidence acquired more than five years after the date of injury may be used to support a timely petition to reopen.[24]

Furthermore, the courts have indicated that a formal petition to reopen doesn't need to be created even if the employer is on notice that the applicant may have new and further disability. In one case, the applicant's treating physician addressed a letter to the appeals board within five years of the injury date calling attention to the applicant's protracted symptoms and enclosing several medical reports. The doctor expressed his opinion that the award did not fairly cover the extent of the applicant's disability and asked whether an adjustment in the disability rating was justified. The Court of Appeal held that the letter expressed

---

[18] *Blanchard v. WCAB* (1975) 40 CCC 784.
[19] *Sarabi v. WCAB* (2007) 72 CCC 778, 781-82.
[20] *Liberty Mutual Insurance Co. v. WCAB (Aprahamian)* (1980) 45 CCC 866 (employer's timely, but skeletal, petition to reopen to reduce benefits could not be summarily denied).
[21] *City of Richmond v. WCAB (Brown)* (1998) 63 CCC 1419 (writ denied).
[22] *Bland v. WCAB* (1970) 35 CCC 513, 517.
[23] *Bland v. WCAB* (1970) 35 CCC 513.
[24] *Continental Baking Co. and Ralston-Purina Co. v. WCAB (Williams)* (1997) 62 CCC 1705 (writ denied); *CIGA v. WCAB (Winters)* (2006) 71 CCC 814 (writ denied).

good cause for an increased award for increased disability under LC 5803 and preserved the appeals board's jurisdiction.[25]

Accordingly, the appeals board determined that a claim was not barred by LC 5410 and LC 5804 when it found that an AME report, which was prepared within five years of the date of injury and addressed to the appeals board, expressed an opinion that the applicant's condition had worsened. The board concluded that the report put it and the defendant on notice that the earlier award was inadequate, and that it could be constructed as a petition to reopen because of new and further disability.[26] Note that the case does not indicate if the report actually was filed with the appeals board within the five-year period.

But the appeals board has also held that the timely filing of medical reports with evidence of new and further disability but without any accompanying request that the board reopen the case or award further benefits did not qualify as a petition for new and further disability.[27] Also, a routine medical report filed with the appeals board what was not a request for action would not be a substitute for a petition to reopen.[28]

The appeals board has held that an amended application could be treated as a petition to reopen under LC 5410.[29] The appeals board has also held that the filing of a declaration of readiness to proceed (DOR) within five years of the date of injury that listed good cause to reopen as an issue served as the functional equivalent of a petition to reopen. The appeals board reasoned that the DOR provided the employer with adequate notice that the applicant's condition had deteriorated and resulted in an additional need for temporary disability and probable permanent disability.[30] But the appeals board held that a DOR requesting an expedited hearing on the issue of entitlement to medical treatment was not equivalent to a petition to reopen for new and further disability. A DOR addressing only the applicant's entitlement to further medical treatment involves the enforcement of an award and does not raise the issue of new and further disability to alter an award.[31]

---

[25] *Beaida v. WCAB* (1968) 33 CCC 345. See also *CMIS/Springfield Insurance Co. v. WCAB (Guillen)* (2006) 71 CCC 274 (writ denied).
[26] *Saldana v. Mike Thompson's RV Superstore*, 2012 Cal. Wrk. Comp. P.D. LEXIS 384.
[27] *Mayes v. WCAB* (1998) 63 CCC 462 (writ denied); *Mancillas v. WCAB* (1983) 48 CCC 303 (writ denied).
[28] *Chavez v. River Ranch Fresh Foods, Inc.*, 2011 Cal. Wrk. Comp. P.D. LEXIS 307.
[29] *County of San Bernardino v. WCAB (Spencer)* (1996) 61 CCC 860 (writ denied).
[30] *Southern California Permanente Medical Group v. WCAB (Phillips)* (1999) 64 CCC 485 (writ denied). See also *Helms v. Everest Nat'l. Ins. Co.* (2011) 39 CWCR 119 [*Helms v. El Cajon Ford*, 2011 Cal. Wrk. Comp. P.D. LEXIS 25].
[31] *Lobos v. WCAB* (2003) 68 CCC 261 (writ denied); *Chavez v. River Ranch Fresh Foods, Inc.*, 2011 Cal. Wrk. Comp. P.D. LEXIS 307.

In an unpublished opinion, the court held that a letter requesting an advisory PD rating on two medical reports filed before the expiration of the five-year period qualified as a petition to reopen.[32] In another unpublished opinion, the court held that a letter from a *pro per* applicant to the appeals board within five years of the date of injury sent after the appeals board had dismissed the claim for lack of prosecution was a timely petition to reopen.[33] The appeals board has also held that an untimely petition for reconsideration could be treated as a petition to reopen if good cause was shown.[34]

In yet another unpublished opinion, an applicant's claim was resolved by way of stipulated award, and she attempted vocational rehabilitation (VR). But a VR report stated that she would not benefit from additional vocational rehabilitation services. So the applicant's treating physician reported that she was permanently and totally disabled. The report was served on the employer within five years of the date of injury. In response to the report, the employer had the applicant examined by its own physician who found additional permanent disability. Based on this report, the employer offered to increase the previous PD rating. The applicant filed a DOR and attached the treating physician's report before the expiration of the five-year period, but did not file a formal petition to reopen. When the case went to a settlement conference, the five-year period had expired. Nevertheless, the court noted that within the five-year period, the applicant presented the employer with evidence of total permanent disability, the employer had her examined by its own expert, offered to raise her disability rating and the applicant filed a DOR to which she attached her treating physician's report. The court found that the employer was not prejudiced by the applicant's failure to file a formal petition to reopen, as it knew that the applicant believed she was entitled to new and further permanent disability and had an opportunity to fully investigate the claim before the five-year period expired. The court concluded that the DOR served as a petition to reopen.[35]

The Court of Appeal held that a request for vocational rehabilitation benefits filed with the Rehabilitation Bureau subsequent to an award of disability benefits was to be construed as a petition to the appeals board to reopen the award under

[32] *Custard v. WCAB* (1992) 57 CCC 545 (Court of Appeal opinion unpublished in official reports).
[33] *San Diego Unified School District v. WCAB (Hayslett)* (1996) 61 CCC 1421 (Court of Appeal opinion unpublished in official reports).
[34] *Formica Corp. v. WCAB (Stobbe)* (1999) 64 CCC 1398 (writ denied). See also *U.S. Pipe and Foundry Co. v. IAC (Hinojoza)* (1962) 27 CCC 73 (Court of Appeal found that the process of the reopening of the case is not identical with the process of reconsideration, but commission could reopen the case upon a finding of good cause).
[35] *County of San Diego v. WCAB (Rojas-Melzer)* (2005) 70 CCC 126 (Court of Appeal opinion unpublished in official reports).

LC 5803 and LC 5804. The court noted that those statutes do not direct that a petition to reopen be filed before the board itself and that it was appropriate that the request be made first before the bureau, as it is given the initial dispute resolution assignment.[36]

The appeals board may also reopen a case on its own motion within five years of the date of injury. In one case, within five years of an award, the WCJ issued a notice of intention to increase compensation awarded, but no petition to reopen was ever filed by the applicant. The California Supreme Court *en banc* held that the WCJ's notice should be treated as a petition to reopen because it did not prejudice the employer and the applicant could have been lulled by the WCJ's action into thinking that there was no necessity for him to file a petition.[37] So if the appeals board issues a notice of intention to increase an award of compensation, filing a petition to reopen is unnecessary.

In contrast, the California Supreme Court has held that a petition for further medical treatment that did not indicate that the applicant sought increased disability did not qualify as a timely petition to reopen.[38] Likewise, the Court of Appeal held that a letter by the applicant to the appeals board complaining that the insurer was refusing to pay for medical treatment did not constitute a petition to reopen.[39] In that case, the Court of Appeal held that the letter was insufficient because it did not claim further disability, but instead sought enforcement of the original requirement that the insurer provide medical care. The court added that the attached medical report was also insufficient because although the doctor opined that the applicant was not responding to physical therapy and further treatment would be necessary, it did not specify that this was due to a new and further disability or that the original award was inadequate. The court also recognized that there was nothing in the record to suggest that the insurer was aware of the letter or attached report until after the five-year limitations period had expired.[40]

In another case, the Court of Appeal held that a timely filed petition to reopen to reduce benefits filed by the defendant did not qualify as a petition to reopen to

---

[36] *Bekins Moving and Storage Co. v. WCAB* (1982) 47 CCC 1260, 1265.
[37] *Zurich Insurance Co. v. WCAB (Cairo)* (1973) 38 CCC 500, 502-03.
[38] *Sprague v. IAC* (1956) 21 CCC 173. See also *Mercado v. WCAB* (1988) 53 CCC 140 (writ denied) (petition to reopen only requesting enforcement of a medical care award was found not to request new and further disability and therefore was not a petition to reopen).
[39] *Granite Construction Co. v. WCAB (McReynolds)* (2003) 68 CCC 1548, 1554-55.
[40] *Granite Construction Co. v. WCAB (McReynolds)* (2003) 68 CCC 1548, 1554-55.

increase benefits by the applicant.[41] (These kinds of petitions are discussed in the next sections; basically, the defense may petition to reduce a permanent disability award just as the applicant may petition to increase it.) That works both ways – if an applicant files a timely petition to reopen, the defense may not use that to establish a timely petition to reduce the award.[42] In one case though, the defense filed an unsuccessful petition to reopen, and within the five-year period the applicant raised the issue of new and further disability on the framed issues for trial. This was held to be a timely petition on the part of the applicant.[43]

Of course, an employer and its insurance carrier are estopped to plead the statute of limitations if the conduct or representations of either induces the employee to refrain from filing his claim until after the statute of limitations has run.[44] But an employer is not estopped to assert the statute of limitations in LC 5410 if the applicant has failed to demonstrate conduct from the employer inducing the applicant to refrain from filing his claim.[45] In one case, the appeals board held that an agreement of the parties to refer the applicant to an agreed medical examiner (AME) did not toll the five-year statute of limitations under LC 5410 and LC 5804. The appeals board noted that the applicant was represented by an attorney and suggested that the argument might have been persuasive if applied to an unrepresented worker.[46]

In contrast, another applicant's petition to reopen was dismissed when it was filed before a stipulated award was signed and before any award was made. The petition was barred by statute of limitations under LC 5410 even though it was filed two days before statute ran out but was not served on the employer within the statutory period. The appeals board concluded that the applicant failed to act in good faith by not informing defendant that he had filed a petition to reopen for new and further disability at the time the parties signed stipulated award, and the applicant was not denied due process by WCJ's dismissal of his petition to reopen requesting an increase in his PD award.[47]

---

[41] *Selden v. WCAB* (1986) 51 CCC 28. See also *Boeing Services v. WCAB (Higgerson)* (1992) 57 CCC 307 (Court of Appeal opinion unpublished in official reports).

[42] *A.C. Transit v. WCAB (Stewart)* (1992) 57 CCC 114 (writ denied); *SCIF v. WCAB (Romero)* (2011) 76 CCC 399 (Court of Appeal opinion unpublished in official reports). But compare *Korff v. WCAB* (1997) 63 CCC 88 (writ denied), in which the applicant filed an unsuccessful petition to reopen. The defense did not file a petition to reduce, but was allowed a "credit" of a small amount once the AME came in lower than he did in the original case. *Korff*, in our opinion, is wrongly decided.

[43] *Tolmasov v. WCAB* (1974) 39 CCC 554 (writ denied).

[44] *Nolan v. WCAB* (1977) 42 CCC 401.

[45] *White v. WCAB* (2005) 70 CCC 170 (Court of Appeal opinion unpublished in official reports).

[46] *Chichester v. WCAB* (1994) 60 CCC 37 (writ denied).

[47] *Bowman v. WCAB* (1996) 61 CCC 140 (writ denied).

NEW AND FURTHER DISABILITY

Applicants who file petitions to reopen within five years of the date of injury must demonstrate that they have sustained "new and further disability" within the meaning of LC 5410. The term is not defined by statute.[48] But as explained by the Court of Appeal in *Nicky Blairs Restaurant v. WCAB (Macias),*[49] "The term 'new and further disability' has been defined to mean disability which results from some demonstrable change in an employee's condition."[50] These include a new period of temporary disability or a change from temporary disability to permanent disability, a gradual increase in permanent disability and a change in physical condition necessitating further medical treatment whether or not accompanied by time lost from work. "Thus, [c]ommonly, new and further disability refers to a recurrence of temporary disability, a new need for medical treatment, or the change of a temporary disability into a permanent disability."[51]

The claim for new and further disability must be real, and it must be proved. It is not enough to rehash the allegations and evidence that were presented in the original claim — authentic new and further disability must be shown with new evidence. Absent a change in the applicant's condition, there is no new and further disability.[52] A petition to reopen is not appropriate if the arguments it presents should have been asserted in a petition for reconsideration.[53] It is not permitted to use the concept of new and further disability to re-litigate a period of indemnity that has been decided against the applicant[54] or to re-litigate a body part that should have been decided at the time of the initial stipulated award.[55] The petition to reopen is not an excuse to extend the statute of limitations for the original claim and try the case over again.[56] Rather, reopening an award for new and further disability requires that the new and further disability occurred after

---

[48] *Pizza Hut of San Diego, Inc. v. WCAB* (1978) 43 CCC 70, 74; *Nicky Blairs Restaurant v. WCAB (Macias)* (1980) 45 CCC 876, 883.

[49] (1980) 45 CCC 876.

[50] *Nicky Blairs Restaurant v. WCAB (Macias)* (1980) 45 CCC 876, 884.

[51] *Nicky Blairs Restaurant v. WCAB (Macias)* (1980) 45 CCC 876, 884-84 (citations and quotations omitted); *Pizza Hut of San Diego, Inc. v. WCAB* (1978) 43 CCC 70, 74.

[52] *Smith v. WCAB* (1978) 43 CCC 834 (writ denied).

[53] *Matook v. WCAB* (2012) 77 CCC 576, 577 (writ denied) (applicant could not reopen psyche claim when claim and treatment previously were denied in a decision that was not appealed, and WCAB did not believe that the psychiatric condition developed after the original decision).

[54] *Lopez v. WCAB* (1989) 54 CCC 454 (writ denied).

[55] *Vargas v. UCLA Department of Nutrition,* 2010 Cal. Wrk. Comp. P.D. LEXIS 550.

[56] *Burris v. Southern California Rapid Transit District* (1968) 33 CCC 419 (*Burris* was later overturned on other grounds).

the original award.[57] If an applicant's condition is unchanged from the time of the original decision, there is no new and further disability within the meaning of LC 5410 to permit reopening of the case.

Medical evidence especially must be gathered to show that the applicant is worse off than at the conclusion of the underlying original claim. Facts that are known and events that occur during the pendency of an original claim may not be used to support a claim of new and further disability.[58] A doctor's report that recites no new facts and merely re-evaluates the applicant's condition as it was at the time of the original condition does not prove new and further disability.[59]

The fact that an applicant's condition may be worse than at the time of the original decision, standing alone, does not justify the reopening of a case upon the theory of "new and further disability."[60] The new and further disability must be caused by the industrial injury. Conditions completely unrelated to the industrial injury are not "new and further disability." Naturally, if the underlying industrial disability worsens, or helps to cause a new condition, the new and further disability is industrial.[61] But unrelated conditions are not sufficient.[62]

Generally, whether or not an applicant has suffered new and further disability will be a medical question. The applicant may return to the same QME in connection with a petition to reopen. Often the parties find it convenient to use the same doctor, and the WCJ also may order an applicant to return to the same doctor.[63] If there is no testimony or medical evidence supporting a change in the applicant's condition, a petition to reopen on the grounds of new and further disability will be rejected.[64] When there is conflicting medical evidence as to whether an applicant has sustained new and further disability, the conflict is to

---

[57] *Edgar v. WCAB* (1966) 31 CCC 376, 380. In *Delaware North Cos., Inc., dba Yosemite Concession Services Corp. v. WCAB (Sanders)* (1997) 62 CCC 1451 (writ denied), stipulations were signed, new and further disability was incurred and only afterward the WCJ signed the award. Later a petition to reopen was filed, and the court held in the applicant's favor — it was the signature on the stipulation and not the WCJ's approval that counted as the original award.
[58] *Edgar v. WCAB* (1966) 31 CCC 376, 380; *SCIF v. WCAB (Romero)* (2011) 76 CCC 399 (Court of Appeal opinion unpublished in official reports).
[59] *Nicky Blairs Restaurant v. WCAB (Macias)* (1980) 45 CCC 876, 885. See also *Grenfell v. WCAB* (1968) 33 CCC 632 (writ denied) (no good cause to reopen when applicant has not shown his condition has changed); *Clark v. WCAB* (1980) 45 CCC 499 (writ denied); *Magana v. WCAB* (1981) 46 CCC 308 (writ denied).
[60] *Aliano v. WCAB* (1979) 44 CCC 1156.
[61] *City of Los Angeles v. WCAB (Jones)* (1979) 44 CCC 162.
[62] *Johnson v. WCAB* (1978) 43 CCC 237 (writ denied).
[63] See *Batavia, Inc. v. WCAB (Alcantar)* (1997) 62 CCC 1134 (writ denied); *Cassidy v. Envel Design Corp.*, 2011 Cal. Wrk. Comp. P.D. LEXIS 468.
[64] *Cook v. WCAB* (1982) 47 CCC 1258 (writ denied).

be resolved by the appeals board, and the board's decision will be upheld by the appellate court if supported by substantial evidence.[65]

The finding of new and further disability is common and not difficult to achieve if the evidence is assembled properly. In one case, an applicant testified that since her injury, "her back had worsened, that she could no longer lift objects weighing more than 25 pounds nor sit longer than 5 or 10 minutes or stoop or bend over without feeling intense pain." The treating doctor also reported the applicant had increased pain and therefore increased the applicant's work restrictions. The Court of Appeal held that the applicant's testimony and the treating physician's report constituted substantial evidence of an increase in subjective complaints and additional objective factors of impairment that supported her claim for new and further disability.[66] There are many examples of successful petitions.[67]

But proving new and further disability does not always go smoothly. In *Nicky Blairs Restaurant v. WCAB (Macias),*[68] there was conflicting medical evidence as to whether the applicant had sustained new and further disability. One doctor, Dr. Rose, reported that the applicant's condition had deteriorated, noting an increase in back pain and the development of headaches and neck pain, which he related to the applicant's industrial injury. Another doctor, Dr. Patzakis, reported that there was no objective evidence of deterioration, that the applicant's increased symptoms were unrelated to the industrial injury and that the applicant had the same permanent disability that he had at the time he was originally declared permanent and stationary. The appeals board granted the petition to reopen based on Dr. Patzakis' report. The Court of Appeal annulled the appeals board's

---

[65] *Liberty Mutual Insurance Co. v. IAC (Walden)* (1964) 29 CCC 293. See *Michigan Mutual Liability Co. v. WCAB (Diaz)* (1970) 35 CCC 576 (writ denied) (applicant's testimony and reporting of two doctors supported finding of new and further disability, despite AME report indicating applicant's condition was unchanged); *Stijakovich v. WCAB* (1972) 37 CCC 319 (Court of Appeal opinion unpublished in official reports) (court denied petition to reopen when two doctors reported applicant's condition was unchanged despite conflicting evidence).

[66] *County of San Bernardino v. WCAB (Ramirez)* (1981) 46 CCC 1200.

[67] See, e.g., *Chabot-Las Positas Community College v. WCAB (Sultan)* (2012) 77 CCC 435 (writ denied) (positive straight-leg raising on the left, weakness in muscles related to the L5 level, diminished sensation in the same distribution and calf atrophy not previously reported was new and further disability); *Detjen v. WCAB* (1974) 39 CCC 707 (new and further disability established by medical report that applicant could no longer function adequately in the labor market); *County of Sonoma v. WCAB (Segobiano)* (2003) 68 CCC 1856 (writ denied) (new and further disability based on AME report); *Jonas v. WCAB* (1973) 38 CCC 125 (Court of Appeal opinion unpublished in official reports) (doctor's report stated that the applicant's disability had increased from slight neurosis to moderate supported a petition to reopen); *Safeway Stores, Inc. v. WCAB (James)* (1982) 47 CCC 955 (Court of Appeal opinion unpublished in official reports) (doctor's failure to include work restrictions in original medical report because of upcoming surgery was good cause to reopen); *Ryan v. WCAB* (1968) 33 CCC 548; *Walton v. Hartford Ins. Co.* (1993) 21 CWCR 293 (panel decision); *Hart v. WCAB* (2012) 77 CCC 693 (Court of Appeal opinion unpublished in official reports) (new and further injury to neck).

[68] (1980) 45 CCC 876.

order because Dr. Patzakis' report did not constitute substantial evidence of new and further disability. The court stated that had the board relied on Dr. Rose's report in reopening the case, new and further disability would clearly exist. But because the appeals board relied on Dr. Patzakis' report, the evidence relied on by the board did not support the award of new and further disability.[69]

In one case, an applicant sustained a back injury that was acknowledged by a stipulated award, which provided further medical treatment. At the time of the award, the applicant was wearing a lace-up lumbosacral corset, but the doctor subsequently recommended a stronger back brace. Based on this recommendation, the applicant filed a petition to reopen for new and further disability. The appeals board denied the petition to reopen because the doctor found the applicant's condition had not changed. The board stated that a change in the prescription for a back support, without a change in physical findings, was not a new and further disability that would support granting a petition to reopen. The appeals board noted that the applicant was entitled to enforce the award of further medical care to obtain the new brace, but that there was no justification to reopen the award.[70]

In contrast, the Court of Appeal held that an applicant sustained new and further disability when he underwent heart surgery after entering into a stipulated award. He testified to various changes in his condition and increased symptoms following surgery, and the testimony was supported by a doctor's report. In that case, the parties had stipulated to 90 percent permanent disability and the applicant argued that he had total permanent disability following the surgery. The appeals board incorrectly denied the petition to reopen, because it said there was evidence of the applicant's total disability before the award. It was theorized that, because the board had considered the possibility that the applicant was 100 percent totally permanently disabled at the time of the original injury, that issue was forever settled. But the Court of Appeal awarded new and further disability because the applicant's testimony and medical reporting were unrebutted. Actual evidence of new and further disability had been introduced. The appeals board missed the point. Just because the applicant's complete disability had been at issue beforehand did not make this new evidence a rehashing of the old evidence.[71]

---

[69] *Nicky Blairs Restaurant v. WCAB (Macias)* (1980) 45 CCC 876, 887-88. See also *Martinez v. WCAB* (2000) 65 CCC 939 (writ denied) (no good cause to reopen when a medical report was merely cumulative and based on an unreliable history given by the applicant); *Baghoomian v. WCAB* (2012) 77 CCC 288 (writ denied) (no substantial evidence of new and further disability).
[70] *Mathis v. WCAB* (1998) 63 CCC 1296 (writ denied).
[71] *Draper v. WCAB* (1983) 48 CCC 748. See also *Santillan v. Ultimate Staffing* 2010 Cal. Wrk. Comp. P.D. LEXIS 447.

NEW AND FURTHER DISABILITY MUST ARISE WITHIN FIVE YEARS

In addition to filing a petition to reopen within five years of the date of injury, an applicant must have suffered new and further disability within five years in order to recover additional disability benefits.[72] An injured worker may not confer jurisdiction on the appeals board by filing a petition to reopen an award before the five-year period has expired for anticipated new and further disability occurring thereafter.[73] The appeals board has stated that an award for additional benefits beyond the five-year period when the new and further disability did not occur within that period "would be nothing more than a subterfuge to avoid the limitation of jurisdiction contained in Labor Code Sections 5410 and 5804."[74] But the appeals board has jurisdiction over a petition to reopen if the new and further disability occurred after the filing of the petition but before the expiration of the five-year period.[75] Furthermore, the appeals board may award additional benefits beginning more than five years after the date of injury if the new and further disability occurred within five years and is continuous.[76]

For example, an applicant sustained an industrial injury Aug. 28, 1999 and a findings and award was issued Dec. 15, 2000. The applicant underwent right shoulder surgery Jan. 18, 2002 and filed a petition to reopen Nov. 15, 2002. On May 26, 2004, a doctor found the applicant temporarily disabled and recommended further right shoulder surgery. The applicant was later evaluated by an AME Aug. 17, 2004 who confirmed that the applicant was temporarily totally disabled and needed right shoulder surgery. In a supplemental report, the AME added that the applicant would be considered permanent and stationary Aug. 17, 2005 if he were not medically cleared for right shoulder surgery. The employer, who was voluntarily paying TTD benefits, informed the applicant that it was terminating benefits upon receiving the AME's supplemental report. The matter came before the appeals board and the issue to be decided was whether the applicant was entitled to additional TTD benefits beginning Aug. 17, 2005. The appeals board ultimately determined that the applicant was not entitled to TTD benefits beginning Aug. 17, 2005, as it was more than five years after the date of injury.

---

[72] *Sarabi v. WCAB* (2007) 72 CCC 778, 782. See also *Ruffin v. Olson Glass Co., Inc.* (1987) 52 CCC 335 (appeals board *en banc*). But see *City of Santa Rosa v. WCAB (Scolieri)* (1997) 62 CCC 1703 (writ denied) (appeals board holding there is no requirement that the applicant actually have proof of new and further disability within five years from the date of injury).

[73] *Sarabi v. WCAB* (2007) 72 CCC 778, 782.

[74] *Ruffin v. Olson Glass Co., Inc.* (1987) 52 CCC 335, 343 (appeals board *en banc*); *Sarabi v. WCAB* (2007) 72 CCC 778, 782 fn. 5.

[75] *Sarabi v. WCAB* (2007) 72 CCC 778, 783 fn. 6.

[76] *Sarabi v. WCAB* (2007) 72 CCC 778; *Hartsuiker v. WCAB* (1993) 58 CCC 19.

The Court of Appeal, however, held that the appeals board had jurisdiction to award additional temporary disability because the petition to reopen was timely filed, and the new and further disability began within five years. The court noted that the applicant suffered new and further disability as early as May 26, 2004 or at the latest by Aug. 17, 2004, as his condition worsened and further medical treatment in the form of right shoulder surgery became necessary. The court added that the appeals board could award TTD benefits commencing Aug. 17, 2005, even though it was more than five years after the date of injury, because the new and further disability occurred within five years.[77]

If, in contrast, the new and further disability does not arise within five years from the date of injury, the applicant may not recover additional disability benefits, even if he or she timely filed a petition to reopen. An applicant sustained an injury Aug. 7, 2000 and received a stipulated award April 25, 2005. She filed a petition to reopen for new and further disability July 6, 2005, within five years from the date of injury, but her temporary disability did not begin until Nov. 11, 2005, more than five years after the date of injury. The WCJ awarded additional TTD benefits, stating that a timely filed petition to reopen conferred jurisdiction on the appeals board to award new and further disability, even if the disability occurred more than five years from the date of injury. The appeals board rescinded the award and denied the petition to reopen. The appeals board noted that the five-year limitations period of LC 5410 bars any claim for "new and further disability" arising more than five years after the date of injury, regardless of whether a petition to reopen was timely filed. The appeals board stated, "Allowing compensation for new and further ... disability commencing more than five years from the date of injury would render the limitations of LC 5410 meaningless, since, if such a rule were adopted, any applicant could avoid the prescriptions of LC 5410 and indefinitely extend the limitations period by simply

[77] The court recognized that the TTD benefits after that time became an issue only because the employer voluntarily paid TTD benefits until Aug. 17, 2005. The court concluded that it would be unjust to deny benefits because doing so would allow an employer, knowing that an applicant has filed a timely petition to reopen and has suffered new and further disability within the five-year period, to make voluntary payments until after the five-year period has elapsed, so that an award for additional benefits would be jurisdictionally barred as commencing more than five years after the date of injury. *Sarabi v. WCAB* (2007) 72 CCC 778, 782-83. See also *Franchise Tax Board, State of California v. WCAB (Schultz)* (2004) 69 CCC 277 (writ denied) (appeals board had jurisdiction to award additional disability benefits when a timely petition to reopen was filed and the medical evidence indicated that the applicant had new and further disability at the time the petition was filed, even though the applicant's surgery and TTD status arose beyond the five-year period); *Kelly Staff Leasing, Inc. v. WCAB (Druebert)* (2008) 73 CCC 1097 (writ denied) (appeals board had jurisdiction to award TD more than five years after shoulder injury when evidence indicated the needed surgery within five years from the date of injury and a petition for new and further disability was filed within five years, but the employer denied authorization until after the five-year period); *Connecticut Indemnity Insurance Co. v. WCAB (Barnett)* (2011) 76 CCC 1204 (writ denied) (applicant's condition deteriorated and became TD within five years from the date of injury).

filing a skeletal petition to reopen on the eve of the expiration of the five-year period."[78]

There must be a causal connection between the alleged new and further disability and the original industrial injury.[79] The appeals board may award additional disability benefits for consequential injuries occurring within five years of the industrial injury.[80] But the appeals board has barred disability resulting from consequential injuries more than five years after the date of injury. In one case, the appeals board held that it did not have jurisdiction to award further TD benefits for injuries to an applicant's bilateral hands resulting from a compensable consequence of falls related to her original industrial lower extremity injuries because they occurred more than five years after the date of injury.[81]

Similarly, in another case, an applicant sustained an injury Aug. 5, 1998 to his back. He was awarded 30 percent PD and lifetime medical care for the injury. On April 26, 2003, the applicant fell and injured his left shoulder. The applicant alleged that the shoulder injury was a compensable consequence of his earlier back injury and filed a petition to reopen May 19, 2003. On Aug. 14, 2003, the treating physician reported that the applicant was P&S from the shoulder injury but indicated that surgery would be required if his symptoms worsened. Then, on June 11, 2004, the treating physician reported that the applicant required surgery and changed his status to temporarily totally disabled. The WCJ awarded 34 percent PD and new and further TD from June 11, 2004 to June 4, 2006. The appeals board upheld the additional PD, but changed the amount of the award to reflect the amount due for the injury. The appeals board also deleted the finding of a new period of compensable TD based on its finding that a period of "new and further" TD commencing more than five years from the date of injury is not compensable.[82] So the appeals board allowed new and further PD because it occurred within five years of the date of injury, but denied new and further TD because it did not. Compensable consequence injuries are handled in depth in Section 5.65 Compensable Consequence Injuries.

---

[78] *Duran v. WCAB* (2007) 72 CCC 488 (writ denied). See also *Gomez v. WCAB* (2006) 71 CCC 1721 (Court of Appeal opinion unpublished in official reports); *Borba v. WCAB* (2004) 69 CCC 605 (writ denied); *Berry v. WCAB* (2004) 69 CCC 1320 (writ denied); *Fekkers v. WCAB* (2001) 67 CCC 92 (writ denied); *Beck (Hambrick) v. WCAB* (2000) 65 CCC 845 (writ denied); *Mart v. WCAB* (2011) 76 CCC 578 (writ denied); *Cohen v. Morton's Steakhouse*, 2011 Cal. Wrk. Comp. P.D. LEXIS 207; *McBee v. WCAB* (2011) 76 CCC 1230 (writ denied).

[79] See *SCIF v. WCAB (Hancock)* (2010) 75 CCC 1336 (Court of Appeal opinion unpublished in official reports).

[80] *City of Richmond v. WCAB (Brown)* (1998) 63 CCC 1419 (writ denied).

[81] *Parker v. WCAB* (2005) 70 CCC 1187 (writ denied).

[82] *Briggs v. WCAB* (2007) 72 CCC 1647 (writ denied).

Note, however, that the question centers on the issue of when the new and further disability occurred, not the form of the petition to reopen. That is, as long as a proper petition to reopen is timely filed, it need not specify the particular type of increased disability if it occurred within the five-year time period. In one case, an applicant filed a timely petition to reopen after there had been a prior award of orthopedic disability. Before the petition was adjudicated, but after five years had passed, the application and the petition were amended to allege psychological injury. The recommendation was not on its face invalid simply because it happened outside the five-year time frame, and the applicant was allowed to argue that the psyche had been injured as a compensable consequence within the five-year period.[83]

REOPENING OF MULTIPLE INJURIES

If an applicant has sustained multiple industrial injuries that were acknowledged by a findings and award or a stipulated award, a timely filed petition to reopen one of the claims will not reopen a claim for which the petition is untimely.[84] For example, an applicant sustained two industrial injuries, one Sept. 12, 1990 while working for Granite Construction Co. (Granite) and one Aug. 28, 1991 while working for D.S.S. Engineering (DSS). RSKCo administered the earlier injury and Liberty Mutual insured the later. The cases were consolidated and settled by stipulation of the parties March 26, 1993. On May 9, 1996, the applicant filed a petition to reopen both cases, although only DSS and Liberty Mutual were named as defendants. DSS and Liberty Mutual filed a petition to join Granite and RSKCo on Feb. 26, 1998 that was granted.

Ultimately, the WCJ found that the applicant had sustained new and further disability, and allocated 62 percent of the additional disability to Granite by RSKCo and 38 percent to DSS and Liberty Mutual. This decision was upheld by the appeals board. The Court of Appeal found that the appeals board acted in excess of its jurisdiction, because the applicant did not timely petition to reopen the case against Granite and RSKCo. The court concluded that because the applicant did not file a claim for additional disability within the five-year period for the earlier injury, the appeals board acted beyond its jurisdiction by imposing further liability on Granite and RSKCo.[85]

---

[83] *Metropolitan Transportation Authority (Los Angeles County) v. WCAB (Gonzalez)* (2000) 65 CCC 944 (writ denied).

[84] See *Department of Education, Division of State Special Schools, California School for the Deaf v. WCAB (Gill)* (1993) 58 CCC 195.

[85] *Granite Construction Co. v. WCAB (McReynolds)* (2003) 68 CCC 1548, 1555. But see *Fisher Farms v. WCAB (Paniagua)* (2007) 72 CCC 666 (writ denied) (appeals board allowed amended timely filed petition to reopen specific injury claim to include a CT after the time for filing had ended).

6.26 DISABILITY AWARDED AFTER FIVE YEARS

When there is an award, if the petition to reopen is not filed on time, further indemnity benefits may not be sought more than five years from the date of injury. (Note that if there is a new injury from the same event, it might be filed as a new application; see Section 5.6 Defining Multiple Injury Dates.) Also, after the petition to reopen results in an award, the right to seek further indemnity benefits ends, as long as the second award is outside the five-year period. There can be exceptions to the five-year limitation in general, but only under very limited, specific circumstances. For exceptions to the five-year period for petitions to reopen in cases of fraud, see Section 6.29 Reopening for Fraud after Five Years and Section 6.30 Estoppel and the Five-Year Statute.

It is important to realize that the appeals board retains jurisdiction over the original claim. If the original claim is not adjudicated within five years, the appeals board still has jurisdiction to issue an award for indemnity benefits. In this way, the workers' compensation system is different from the civil law system, which requires trial within five years. If the case is delayed long enough, the applicant may claim indemnity benefits incurred after the five-year period under the original jurisdiction of the claim.

Normally neither a judge nor the parties may, by agreement or order, extend the five-year statute of limitations. That is, an award or order may not issue that decides to hold jurisdiction in abeyance — to reserve it for a later decision. The jurisdiction of the appeals board is set by statute, and may not be disturbed by judges. But in limited circumstances as described below, jurisdiction can be reserved past the five years.

ADJUDICATION OF ORIGINAL CLAIM

The five-year statute does not prevent adjudication of the original, underlying claim, even if it contains issues or claims that arose more than five years from the date of injury. The appeals board's "original jurisdiction" — jurisdiction over the original claim — remains. This is distinct from the board's continuing jurisdiction over claims for which an award has issued.

No Time Limit for Original Jurisdiction

Sometimes the case does not come to trial or stipulation within the five-year period. This is not uncommon. The cases dealing with the appeals board's original jurisdiction suggest that the board may award disability benefits even if they come to be more than five years after the date of injury. That is, if there is not an award within five years, either after trial or by stipulation, the WCAB retains jurisdiction over all issues that exist at the time of the trial. That original jurisdiction remains until an award issues.

So, an employer may have greater total liability for indemnity benefits if an award is delayed than if the applicant moves the case along efficiently. For example, a case may be set for trial more than five years from the date of injury. The WCJ may decide that the applicant has become worse since he last saw the reporting physicians, and order the case off calendar for additional medical examination. The applicant again may lose permanent and stationary status, and eventually, years later, become permanent and stationary again. In this way, an applicant may receive much more permanent disability than he would have if the case had proceeded to an award earlier.

There really is no time limit here. In an older case, the Court of Appeal explicitly stated that the power of original decision invested in the appeals board is unrestricted by any limitations of time other than that established by LC 5400 - LC 5412, and that the appeals board could make a valid decision on an original claim several years after the injury if the original proceedings are commenced within the time prescribed by LC 5405.[1] And so, benefits that might be denied as too late when there was an award and a petition to reopen might be allowed if

[1] *SIF v. IAC (Busch)* (1962) 27 CCC 14, 20.

the case is being heard by a WCJ for the first time; this is not an illegal reservation of the issue by the WCJ or parties. In the California system, there are plenty of cases without an award that are 10 years old and even much older.

Original Jurisdiction and Temporary Disability

In some cases, the original jurisdiction of the appeals board is more circumscribed for temporary disability benefits (LC 4656). As discussed in depth in Section 9.13 Time Limits on Payments before April 19, 2004, LC 4656 contains limits for temporary disability indemnity based on the date of injury. This is an independent statutory ground, beyond the jurisdictional statutes, that may limit the time periods within which an applicant may receive temporary disability benefits. So there are limits for temporary disability that do not exist for permanent disability.

As discussed in that section, the California Supreme Court has held that LC 4656(b) does not provide the appeals board with unlimited authority to award TTD following an award. Because the appeals board's authority in that case is subject to the five-year limits of LC 5410 and LC 5804,[2] there is some dispute as to whether the appeals board may award TD under its original jurisdiction more than five years after the date of injury unless the temporary disability began within the five-year period and was continuous.[3] Many cases from the appeals board have held that the appeals board may, under its original jurisdiction, award temporary disability benefits, even for a period of temporary disability commencing more than five years after date of injury if there has been no prior award.[4] But one unpublished opinion holds that LC 4656 authorizes temporary disability to extend beyond five years from the date of injury only when the period of temporary total disability commences within five years from the date of injury and is continuous.[5] This issue has not been resolved by an appellate court.

---

[2] *Nickelsberg v. WCAB* (1991) 56 CCC 476.

[3] See *Hartsuiker v. WCAB* (1993) 58 CCC 19, 27, which interpreted LC 4656 "to allow temporary total disability payments to extend beyond five years from the date of injury only when the period of such disability commences in the five-year period and is continuous."

[4] See *Unigard Insurance Co. v. WCAB (Acosta)* (1994) 59 CCC 966 (writ denied); *Denny's, Inc. v. WCAB (Kakudo)* (2006) 71 CCC 831 (writ denied); *Central Wholesale Electric Supplies v. WCAB (Laudenbach)* (2008) 73 CCC 255 (writ denied); *New Hope Community Church v. WCAB (Burke)* (2009) 74 CCC 1194 (writ denied); *Oakland Unified School District v. WCAB (Little)* (2009) 74 CCC 1399 (writ denied); *CIGA v. WCAB (Carrigan)* (2010) 75 CCC 292 (writ denied).

[5] *Los Angeles County Department of Parks and Recreation v. WCAB (Calvillo)* (2008) 73 CCC 798, 810 (Court of Appeal opinion unpublished in official reports).

But for injuries occurring on or after April 19, 2004, LC 4656(c) limits an applicant to 104 weeks of temporary disability within a period of two years from the commencement of TD payment for injuries occurring before Jan. 1, 2008, and to 104 weeks of temporary disability within a period of five years from the date of injury for injuries on or after Jan. 1, 2008 (see 9.14 Time Limits on Payments on or After April 19, 2004). There is little doubt that if the limits of LC 4656(c) have been reached, the appeals board does not have authority under either its original or continuing jurisdiction to award additional temporary disability benefits.

For example, an applicant was injured July 14, 2004 and the first payment of temporary disability was Aug. 19, 2004. On Sept. 7, 2004, the employer notified that it stopped paying temporary disability indemnity as of Sept. 2, 2004 because he returned to work. On March 15, 2007, the applicant received a stipulated award of temporary disability indemnity for the period from Aug. 6, 2004 through Dec. 24, 2004, further medical treatment and 15 percent permanent disability. Two months later, on May 14, 2007, the applicant filed a petition to reopen his award on the grounds of new and further disability. The employer notified the applicant that he was not entitled to additional TD indemnity because of the limitations in LC 4656(c)(1). The appeals board agreed that the applicant was not entitled to any additional TD indemnity because he was first paid Aug. 19, 2004, and because LC 4656(c)(1) limited TD indemnity to two years from the commencement of temporary disability payment, he was not entitled to TD indemnity after Aug. 19, 2006.[6]

Original Jurisdiction Survives Some Awards

It is clear that an award of both temporary and permanent disability benefits within the five-year period ends the original jurisdiction of the appeals board. The applicant is then obliged, if he or she desires more temporary or permanent disability than what is awarded, to file the petition to reopen within five years of the date of injury. If not, he or she is out of luck. In *Nickelsberg v. WCAB,*[7] the California Supreme Court held that an employee who was awarded temporary disability, permanent disability and future medical treatment, and received surgery more than five years after the date of injury, was not entitled to receive temporary disability benefits based on the jurisdictional limits of LC 5410 and LC 5804. The court held that just because the appeals board has continuing jurisdiction over an award of medical care that goes on indefinitely, the applicant

---

[6] *Medina v. Utility Tree Services, Inc.*, 2008 Cal. Wrk. Comp. P.D. LEXIS 435.

[7] (1991) 56 CCC 476.

is not also entitled to indefinite temporary disability.[8] Furthermore, generally neither a judge nor the parties may, by agreement or order, reserve jurisdiction over permanent disability.[9] That rule and the exceptions to it are discussed below. But the original jurisdiction of the appeals board may survive some sorts of awards or orders of a WCJ.

This is because it can and does happen that some issues are tried separately. If no benefits are directly given by an order or award, the original jurisdiction of the appeals board is not disturbed. For example, there might be a dispute over a discovery issue that goes to hearing and results in a judicial order. That order would not be an "award" sufficient to divest the board of its original jurisdiction. Or a case might be denied and go to trial just on the issue of whether the applicant was injured on the job. Suppose the case is appealed and takes several years to reach a final verdict. A finding that the applicant was injured on the job does not stop him from prosecuting issues of entitlement to permanent or temporary disability later on, even more than five years from the date of injury.

Also, an award issued in one case does not affect the original jurisdiction of an award in other cases. So if an applicant files claims for multiple injuries, and only some of them are resolved in an award, the appeals board would retain original jurisdiction over the unresolved claim(s). For example, in one case an applicant claimed three injuries while working for the same employer — a specific injury in 1999; a specific injury in 2000; and a CT injury. A stipulated award was issued in 2007 listing all three case numbers, but the facts indicated that it was signed only by the applicant's attorney and the attorney for the 1999 injury. The applicant claimed new and further TD beginning in 2011. The appeals board held that it still had jurisdiction to award TD because there was no final resolution on the issue of TD with respect to the 2000 injury and the CT injury. So it concluded that the issue of entitlement to TD remained pending, and that it had jurisdiction to make a TD award for a period incurred more than five years from the date of injury.[10]

What happens if there is an award of TD but not PD benefits? Does the original jurisdiction of the appeals board survive? It is not uncommon for disputes to arise over temporary disability as the case moves along, and often well before the

---

[8] *Nickelsberg v. WCAB* (1991) 56 CCC 476. See also *Melton v. WCAB* (1996) 61 CCC 625 (writ denied) (applicant not entitled to TD beyond the five-year statute of limitations even though timely petition to reopen filed when applicant delayed surgery for more than five years due to her own fears); *Brockman v. Ukiah Valley Medical Center*, 2010 Cal. Wrk. Comp. P.D. LEXIS 514 (no jurisdiction over TD when defendant's liability for that benefit was earlier terminated even though there has not yet been an award of permanent disability).

[9] *Hartsuiker v. WCAB* (1993) 58 CCC 19.

[10] *Insurance Co. of the State of Pennsylvania v. WCAB (Sepulveda)* (2012) 77 CCC 734 (writ denied).

applicant is permanent and stationary. The parties may disagree, for example, on the applicant's weekly wage and the resulting TD rate that should be paid. Or the parties may disagree simply on whether temporary disability is owed at all. Such cases often come to trial and result in awards of continuing temporary disability. Only later is the applicant declared P&S and the issue of permanent disability is adjudicated. Can the applicant in these cases be awarded permanent disability and more temporary disability after the five-year period, without a petition to reopen? The answer is that the appeals board retains original jurisdiction over benefits that were not previously reduced to a final judgment.

As a general principle, an award that renders a final judgment on one species of benefit but does not decide another will not divest the appeals board of original jurisdiction over the undecided benefit. In one case, a trial was held, the WCJ found that the applicant was permanent and stationary, and made a finding of what the permanent disability was. But the judge also refused at that time to decide what the temporary disability periods were, and what the Employment Development Department (EDD), which paid the applicant in lieu of temporary disability and then filed a lien, should be paid. These issues were deferred by the WCJ at the time of trial. The defense later argued that LC 5410 applied as to the issues of the EDD lien and the periods of temporary disability. But it was held that these issues had never been decided. So they were under the original jurisdiction of the appeals board and could be heard more than five years from the date of injury.[11]

In contrast, an award that renders a final judgment on one species of benefit will require an applicant to file the petition to reopen within five years of the date of injury in order to receive more of the decided benefit. For example, in one case, an applicant sustained a CT injury through 2003. There were broken periods of time off, treatment and multiple permanent and stationary dates. The applicant was returned to work in June 2008. The parties stipulated and the WCJ issued an order that the defendant would pay retroactive TD through June 2, 2008 and that "[t]his resolves all retro TD issues through 6/2/08." Thereafter, the applicant underwent additional surgery, and claimed further TD, arguing that there had been no final award. The appeals board found that there was an award of temporary disability and that it was not a continuing award. Even though there had been no final award resolving all issues and closing the case, the board concluded that because a temporary disability award issued and no timely

[11] *Central Wholesale Electric Supplies v. WCAB (Laudenbach)* (2008) 73 CCC 255 (writ denied).

petition to reopen was filed, it had no jurisdiction to award temporary disability benefits for a period commencing more than five years from the date of injury.[12]

In another case, an applicant sustained multiple injuries, the last occurring in 2001, and received an award of continuing temporary disability in 2007. In 2010, however, the defendant filed a petition to terminate liability for the temporary disability indemnity that was granted, and the defendant was relieved of its obligation to pay TD under the prior award. Later the WCJ concluded that the applicant was entitled to TD from March 30, 2011 and continuing. The WCAB found that the WCJ erred in awarding the additional TD. It explained that even though it still had original jurisdiction over permanent disability, because there was a prior award on the issue of TD, the new award of TD was clearly new and further disability within the meaning of LC 5410. The WCAB concluded that a new award of TD subsequent to an order terminating a prior award of temporary disability is a "new and further" award, and the limitations of LC 5410 apply to a new period of TD apply even in an "actively litigated" case in which there has been no adjudication of permanent disability.[13]

If there is a continuing award, it may be deemed not to be a final disposition of entitlement to a particular benefit, and therefore original jurisdiction is retained. So, a continuing award of temporary disability benefits and medical care that was never terminated will not completely divest the appeals board of its original jurisdiction over those issues. In one case, the appeals board held that it had original jurisdiction over temporary disability more than five years after applicant's date of injury, even though the applicant was not continuously temporarily disabled from the date of injury. The applicant had received a prior award of continuing TD and medical care that had never been legally terminated, and there had never been a finding or award of permanent disability.[14] So in this case, there was an award. But it was for a continuing benefit and did not find the applicant to be permanent and stationary, nor did it make a finding of permanent disability. The decision was made under the appeals board's original jurisdiction, and LC 5410 did not operate to bar indemnity benefits beyond the five years.

We are left with some gray area. What if the award was the subject of a petition by the defense to end it within the five-year period? Or what if an award resolves

---

[12] *Trinidad v. Albertson's*, 2011 Cal. Wrk. Comp. P.D. LEXIS 251.

[13] *Duncan v. Town of Scotia Pacific Lumber*, 2011 Cal. Wrk. Comp. P.D. LEXIS 571 citing *Brierly v. WCAB* (2003) 68 CCC 1289 (writ denied); *Shannon v. Chief Auto Parts*, 2007 Cal. Wrk. Comp. P.D. LEXIS 88.

[14] *Denny's, Inc. v. WCAB (Kakudo)* (2006) 71 CCC 831 (writ denied).

one aspect of a certain benefit, but is not a final order regarding the benefit? For example, suppose the WCJ issues an award finding the applicant to be permanent and stationary, but defers the issue of what exactly the permanent disability is? The law gives insufficient guidance in all of these situations to allow a firm conclusion as to whether original jurisdiction continues. Nevertheless, it is a good bet that an award that is incomplete in regard to indemnity issues will not be deemed to foreclose original jurisdiction.

For example, in one unpublished decision, the Court of Appeal decided that an order by a WCJ approving a stipulation of the parties as to the rate of TD constituted an interim order rather than an award. The court determined that a petition for continuing jurisdiction under LC 5410 and LC 5804 was not required. The appeals board retained its original jurisdiction over temporary disability more than five years after the date of injury.[15] For a full discussion on the nature of stipulations between parties and the nature of an award, see Section 15.60 Evidence at Trial — Effect of a Stipulation.

Also, in one case, an applicant sustained industrial esophageal cancer. More than five years after the date of injury, the WCJ found that the cancer caused TD and the need for further medical treatment. The WCJ also found that the applicant sustained PD, but was unable to find ratable factors of disability in the medical record and therefore reserved jurisdiction over PD. Subsequently, the WCJ determined that the medical record required further development on the issue of PD and requested a supplemental report from the AME. The AME issued a supplemental report finding PD referable to the esophageal injury as well as pulmonary/respiratory disability stemming from the esophageal injury. The WCJ found that the applicant was entitled to a claim for the pulmonary/respiratory disability. The WCJ reasoned that she was not deprived of jurisdiction over the PD claim because PD was reserved and a final PD award had never been issued. This decision was upheld by the appeals board.[16] So this case was decided on the grounds that the WCJ had not rendered a final decision on the PD issue, and therefore a petition to reopen under LC 5410 or LC 5803 was not necessary because the appeals board decided the issue under its original jurisdiction.

But in another case, an award was issued that found that the applicant was permanent and stationary, but added that "if and when the applicant undergoes

[15] *Los Angeles County Department of Parks and Recreation v. WCAB (Calvillo)* (2008) 73 CCC 798 (Court of Appeal opinion unpublished in official reports). *Calvillo*, however, held that the appeals board did not have jurisdiction to award temporary disability that began more than five years from the date of injury because the TD was required to begin within the five-year period and be continuous under *Nickelsberg* and *Hartsuiker*.
[16] *Continental Airlines v. WCAB (Younger)* (2009) 75 CCC 52 (writ denied).

orthopedic surgery, he may be entitled to a further period of temporary disability and a new permanent and stationary date." The applicant ultimately underwent surgery and claimed additional temporary disability and an increase in permanent disability. It was held that this was not a "provisional award" that preserved the appeals board's original jurisdiction. The claim was dismissed because it was more than five years after the injury and the applicant did not timely file a petition to reopen.[17]

INSIDIOUS, PROGRESSIVE DISEASE

Neither a judge nor the parties may, by agreement or order, extend the five-year statute of limitations. In *Hartsuiker v. WCAB,*[18] the Court of Appeal held that the appeals board may not reserve jurisdiction to award additional disability benefits more than five years from the date of injury following an award.[19] Even if parties stipulate to reserve jurisdiction, the stipulation is not valid as it violates the law.[20]

But in *General Foundry Service v. WCAB (Jackson),*[21] the California Supreme Court created an exception to the five-year limitation of LC 5410 in cases involving insidious, progressive diseases such as asbestosis. In *Jackson,* the court noted that the concept of permanent disability could not adequately apply to these diseases because of their progressive nature. The court held that in such cases, the appeals board may reserve jurisdiction on the question of permanent disability and continue its jurisdiction beyond the five-year period. In doing so, the appeals board may tentatively rate an applicant's known permanent disability and order advances based on that tentative rating, and reserve jurisdiction for a final determination of permanent disability when either (1) the applicant's condition becomes permanent and stationary, or (2) the permanent disability is total (100 percent) and further deterioration would be irrelevant for ratings purposes.[22] The court concluded that "the Board's reservation of jurisdiction on the issue of permanent disability in the case of insidious, progressive diseases serves to

---

[17] *Garibay v. WCAB* (1997) 62 CCC 806 (writ denied).
[18] (1993) 58 CCC 19.
[19] See also *Loewenthal v. WCAB* (1993) 58 CCC 63 (Court of Appeal opinion unpublished in official reports); *Corbett v. WCAB* (1993) 58 CCC 60 (Court of Appeal opinion unpublished in official reports); *Rosso v. WCAB* (2003) 68 CCC 1255 (writ denied).
[20] *Finley v. WCAB* (2006) 71 CCC 361 (Court of Appeal opinion unpublished in official reports).
[21] (1986) 51 CCC 375.
[22] *General Foundry Service v. WCAB (Jackson)* (1986) 51 CCC 375, 380.

further the compensatory goals of the workers' compensation system."[23]

So for the special and narrow circumstances of insidious, progressive diseases, the court held that the appeals board is allowed to reserve jurisdiction on the issue of permanent disability irrespective of the limitations contained in LC 5804 and LC 5410.[24] In a footnote, the court further indicated that due to the uncertain progression of insidious, progressive diseases, it may be necessary for the appeals board to rate PD in stages at several subsequent proceedings, and if the appeals board determines at the conclusion of each proceeding that the condition is not either (1) permanent and stationary or (2) a total (100 percent) permanent disability, it may continue to reserve its jurisdiction for a future final determination of permanent disability.[25] It has even been held that the appeals board in this type of case may refuse to find permanent disability at all, but only injury and the need for medical care; if there is no disability as yet, the court is not even required to define the date of injury under LC 5412. This truly is an open-ended award.[26]

Naturally, once this doctrine was promulgated, parties began to try to expand it into other areas. In a subsequent *en banc* decision, the appeals board articulated what an insidious, progressive disease is: (1) it is caused by "remote" and "undramatic" work exposure — one that is unlikely to be detected at the time, or if detected, the significance is unlikely to be appreciated; (2) the disease worsens over time, but at a rate so gradual that it is well established before becoming apparent; and (3) it has a long latency period between exposure to the risk and the onset of symptoms. In that case, the appeals board held specifically that injuries such as a chronic lumbosacral sprain or a degenerative knee condition are not insidious, progressive diseases.[27] So orthopedic injuries are not insidious, progressive diseases for purposes of the appeals board's authority to reserve jurisdiction beyond the five-year limit, even though they might require

[23] *General Foundry Service v. WCAB (Jackson)* (1986) 51 CCC 375, 380. The *Jackson* case validated previous opinions that had allowed the appeals board to delay determining the date of injury of occupational disease cases, as described in Section 5.9 Occupational Disease. It also validated prior writ-denied cases that had allowed for awards of permanent disability that could be revisited — *Los Angeles Unified School District v. WCAB (Reed)* (1984) 49 CCC 17 (writ denied) and *Los Angeles Unified School District v. WCAB (Anicich)* (1983) 48 CCC 880 (writ denied).

[24] *Ruffin v. Olson Glass Co., Inc.* (1987) 52 CCC 335, 341 (appeals board *en banc*).

[25] *General Foundry Service v. WCAB (Jackson)* (1986) 51 CCC 375, 380 fn. 4.

[26] *Piedemonte v. Western Asbestos* (1981) 46 CCC 691 (appeals board *en banc*).

[27] *Ruffin v. Olson Glass Co., Inc.* (1987) 52 CCC 335, 342 (appeals board *en banc*).

additional surgery over time.[28]

But the appeals board has held that hepatitis C is an insidious, progressive disease for which the appeals board could reserve jurisdiction to award additional disability beyond the five-year period of LC 5804.[29] The appeals board has also held that thyroid cancer constitutes an insidious, progressive disease.[30]

The appeals board, however, found no grounds to justify reservation of jurisdiction over an applicant's skin cancer, even though the AME stated that the condition was insidious. It found no evidence that the applicant's condition was progressive as the AME did not state that the disability was likely to deteriorate because of the insidiousness of the disease process.[31] In another case, the appeals board found that an applicant's skin cancer was not an insidious, progressive disease when it had been excised completely and the AME reported that it was likelier than not that the applicant's cancer would not recur.[32]

A finding that a condition is insidious and progressive requires a clear medical opinion. A WCJ finding that hairy cell leukemia was an insidious, progressive disease based on Internet research was not sustained. In that case, the appeals board remanded the matter to the WCJ for further development on the record as to whether hairy cell leukemia was an insidious, progressive disease.[33]

The appeals board has held that an express reservation of jurisdiction is unnecessary, and that the appeals board may impliedly reserve jurisdiction to determine the extent of an applicant's permanent disability beyond the five-year limit. In that case, the appeals board held that the WCJ implicitly reserved jurisdiction by using phrases such as "unable to establish at this juncture what

[28] *Finley v. WCAB* (2006) 71 CCC 361, 367 (Court of Appeal opinion unpublished in official reports). See also *Hartsuiker v. WCAB* (1993) 58 CCC 19 (specific injury to the back not an insidious progressive disease); *Rosso v. WCAB* (2003) 68 CCC 1255 (writ denied) (WCAB held it could not reserve jurisdiction to award permanent disability more than five years after date of injury for applicant's orthopedic injuries); *Gray v. WCAB* (1996) 61 CCC 393 (writ denied) (no authority to reserve jurisdiction for an ankle injury); *Green v. WCAB* (1988) 53 CCC 88 (writ denied) (chronic lumbosacral sprain is not an insidious progressive disease).

[29] *City of Calexio v. WCAB (Valdez)* (2006) 71 CCC 817 (writ denied); *City of Santa Rosa v. WCAB (Bertolucci)* (2003) 68 CCC 248 (writ denied); *County of Marin v. WCAB (Carter)* (2001) 66 CCC 1533 (writ denied); *Tenet/Garfield Medical Center v. WCAB (Laughran)* (2000) 65 CCC 1343 (writ denied).

[30] *Lockheed Martin Corp./Lockheed Martin Skunk Works v. WCAB (DeSoto)* (2003) 68 CCC 1878 (writ denied). But see *Continental Airlines v. WCAB (Younger)* (2009) 75 CCC 52 (writ denied) (WCJ found esophageal cancer was not an insidious progressive disease).

[31] *Bean v. City of Chula Vista*, 2012 Cal. Wrk. Comp. P.D. LEXIS 8.

[32] *Seavello v. WCAB* (2012) 77 CCC 596 (writ denied). See also *Murphy v. California Highway Patrol*, 2012 Cal. Wrk. Comp. P.D. LEXIS 374; *O'Brien v. County of San Diego*, 2012 Cal. Wrk. Comp. P.D. LEXIS 375; *Croucher v. Orange County Fire Authority*, 2012 Cal. Wrk. Comp. P.D. LEXIS 508.

[33] *City of Los Angeles, Police Department v. WCAB (Warren)* (2007) 72 CCC 244 (writ denied). See also *Gregoryk v. State of California/California Highway Patrol Officers*, 2012 Cal. Wrk. Comp. P.D. LEXIS 412 (remand to determine whether myeloid leukemia/cancer was an insidious progressive disease).

the ultimate disability is," further stating that the "medical evidence does not assist the Court," and by making "a precautionary permanent disability award."[34]

What works for the applicant in this area does not, it seems, work for the defense. In one case, the applicant submitted a series of petitions to reopen after being diagnosed with hepatitis C. Eventually, she was found to be 100 percent totally permanently disabled. The enterprising defense attorney asked the court to leave the permanent disability award open, in case she got better. The Court of Appeal denied the request, finding the *Jackson* case to be "inapposite."[35]

Another question that may arise: In cases of insidious, progressive disease, does the appeals board have authority to reserve jurisdiction to award *temporary* disability benefits beyond the limitations period? Or may it do so only for permanent disability?

In one case, an applicant filed an application for hepatitis C. In 2002, the parties entered into a stipulation that she had not yet suffered either temporary or permanent disability as a result of the injury. In 2009, the applicant filed a petition to reopen, seeking an award of temporary disability. The appeals board found that it could not reserve jurisdiction over provision of temporary disability. But this finding was reversed by the Court of Appeal. It found that, because the five-year limitations period did not begin to run until the applicant suffered disability, and because that did not occur until 2009, the petition to reopen was timely.[36] Because this decision was unpublished, though, there is no current citable case law on this point.

---

[34] *Lockheed Martin Corp./Lockheed Martin Skunk Works v. WCAB (DeSoto)* (2003) 68 CCC 1878 (writ denied).

[35] *Kaiser Foundation Hospital v. WCAB (Yturralde)* (1996) 61 CCC 876, 879 (writ denied).

[36] *Popovich v. WCAB* (2011) 76 CCC 1050 (Court of Appeal opinion unpublished in official reports) reversing *Popovich v. Folsom State Prison, State of California Department of Corrections,* 2010 Cal. Wrk. Comp. P.D. LEXIS 498.

6.27 FIVE-YEAR STATUTE — REOPENING FOR GOOD CAUSE

As discussed, the concepts of good cause and new and further disability often intertwine in petitions to reopen, and good cause includes new and further disability.[1] But under LC 5803, good cause is also a separate and distinct ground for reopening.[2] An award may be reopened if an applicant has timely filed a petition to reopen and did not suffer new and further disability, but there are reasons other than that to justify reopening a case after an award.[3] Absent a new and further disability within the meaning of LC 5410, an appeals board action to reopen is governed by the provisions of LC 5803 and LC 5804.[4]

Again, LC 5804 limits application of LC 5803 to five years from the date of injury, and any event or circumstance that would constitute good cause to reopen under LC 5803 must occur within a five-year period from the date of injury.[5] A petition to reopen must be filed before the expiration of the five-year period. Beyond that, a previous award may not be altered, and the prior decision will remain in effect.[6] Under LC 5803 a "counter petition" may be filed by the adverse party

[1] *Detjen v. WCAB* (1974) 33 CCC 707; *Nicky Blairs Restaurant v. WCAB (Macias)* (1980) 45 CCC 876, 886; *Draper v. WCAB* (1983) 48 CCC 748, 750; *County of San Bernardino v. WCAB (Ramirez)* (1981) 46 CCC 1200, 1203.

[2] *Nicky Blairs Restaurant v. WCAB (Macias)* (1980) 45 CCC 876, 886; *Draper v. WCAB* (1983) 48 CCC 748, 750.

[3] *Sarabi v. WCAB* (2007) 72 CCC 778, 782.

[4] *Argonaut Insurance Co. v. WCAB (Helm)* (1967) 32 CCC 14, 17.

[5] *Smith v. Johns-Manville Products Corp.* (1981) 46 CCC 557, 561-62 (appeals board *en banc*).

[6] See *Priest v. WCAB (Housepian)* (2008) 73 CCC 1556 (Court of Appeal opinion unpublished in official reports) (no jurisdiction under LC 5803 even though WCJ used "faulty" math to calculate average weekly wage, but there was no record of a petition to reopen for good cause).

within 30 days of the petition. In practice, this usually does little but answer the petition.

If the original decision held that there was no connection between the industrial injury and the employee's disability, the applicant may not attempt to retry the issue of work connection through the device of a reopening on the grounds of "new and further" disability. The applicant must petition to reopen the award for "good cause" pursuant to LC 5803. The idea here is not that the applicant has gotten worse and more disability is established, but that new conditions have appeared — in the form of a worsening progressive condition — that now show the original award to have been wrongly decided. So there is good cause to reopen the award and reconsider the issue of industrial injury.[7]

LC 5410 allows an applicant to petition for new and further disability following either an award or the voluntary furnishing of benefits. A petition to reopen under LC 5803, however, always requires a prior order, decision or award. The payment of benefits is not enough to allow for a petition to reopen under LC 5803. Unlike petitions to reopen for new and further disability, those under LC 5803 typically seek to attack the underlying award in some way — to invalidate it and set it aside for good reason, such as fraud or error. LC 5803 essentially provides a five-year window for the appeals board and the parties to rescind, alter or supplement an award. Good cause is required, but a certain flexibility is allowed within this fixed period.

PETITION TO REDUCE

LC 5803 allows for reopening a case by either the employee or the employer — the statute does not contemplate that good cause for reopening must exist only in favor of the employee.[8] Unlike LC 5410, which limits the right to reopen to "any injured worker" on the grounds of "new and further disability," LC 5803 allows any party in interest to petition to reopen an award with a showing of good cause, including grounds that the "disability of the person in whose favor the award was made has either recurred, increased, diminished or terminated." Therefore, LC 5803 also allows an employer to petition to reduce benefits on the

[7] *Aliano v. WCAB* (1979) 44 CCC 1156. See also *SCIF v. WCAB (Soper)* (1970) 35 CCC 100 (Court of Appeal opinion unpublished in official reports) (LC 5410 cannot be used to redetermine the question of industrial causation).

[8] *SCIF v. IAC (Dean)* (1946) 11 CCC 30, 37.

grounds that the disability has diminished or terminated. An employer seeking to reopen an award must do so under LC 5803 rather than LC 5410.[9]

There are a couple of potential pitfalls here for employers. Often the petition is filed when there is a continuing order or award in place for the defendant to pay permanent disability benefits biweekly. (Payment of PD benefits is discussed in depth in Chapter 10.) A failure to make these payments may result in penalties and sanctions if not done in good faith and with substantial evidence in hand.[10] Caution on this point may be a hard pill to swallow for an employer that feels it has discovered new evidence that should deprive the applicant of further payments. To that end it has been found permissible to ask the appeals board for a quick finding that permanent disability payments be suspended until it can rule on the petition to reduce.[11]

Also, it should be noted that if the employer fails to prove the petition to reduce, the appeals board is entitled to order the payment of applicant's attorney's fees in defending it (LC 5410.1). So a second thought before filing is warranted.

SCOPE OF THE APPEALS BOARD'S AUTHORITY TO REOPEN AN AWARD

A distinction must be made between the appeals process once a case or issue is lost, and the right of the losing party to petition to reopen an award under LC 5803. The appeals process, starting with the right of reconsideration of a final order, and moving through the appeals courts and finally to the California Supreme Court, is discussed in depth in Chapter 16. That process allows for a direct challenge to the validity of the award, and essentially asks a higher court to reverse all or a portion of it.

A petition to reopen for good cause, in contrast, assumes that the award has issued and the appeals process has been exhausted.[12] If the appellate process has not been exhausted, there is no final judgment and there is nothing to reopen, rescind, alter or amend.[13] A petition to reopen under LC 5803 is not an argument that the original award is subject to grounds for appeal, but rather an assertion

---

[9] *Sutton v. IAC* (1956) 46 Cal. 2d 791, 796. (*Sutton* was superseded by statute on other grounds as stated in *City and County of San Francisco v. WCAB (Powell)* (1967) 32 CCC 86.)
[10] *County of Los Angeles v. WCAB (King)* (1980) 45 CCC 248.
[11] *Sachak v. WCAB* (1982) 47 CCC 1049 (writ denied).
[12] *Green v. WCAB* (2005) 70 CCC 294, 307; *Kleemann v. WCAB* (2005) 70 CCC 133, 142.
[13] *Green v. WCAB* (2005) 70 CCC 294, 307.

that there is good cause to rescind or modify it, often because circumstances have changed or new facts have been discovered.

Not all awards are subject to a petition to reopen — some topics are off-limits. LC 5803 provides that the appeals board has continuing jurisdiction only over orders, decisions and awards made and entered under the provisions of Division 4 of the Labor Code, and decisions of the Rehabilitation Unit under LC 139.5. This includes continuing jurisdiction over a timely filed serious and willful proceeding.[14] But the appeals board does not have authority under LC 5803 to reopen contempt proceedings under LC 134[15] or claims of discrimination under LC 132a because both are covered under Division 1 of the Labor Code.

LC 5804 also limits the power to reopen an award on a finding of employment. Specifically, LC 5804 states, in pertinent part, "[A]fter an award has been made finding that there was employment ... the appeals board upon a petition to reopen shall not have the power to find that there was no employment." So if there is an award finding employment, after the time in which to file a petition for reconsideration and any subsequent appeals has passed, the appeals board does not have the power, upon a petition to reopen, to find that there was no employment.

In *Solari v. Atlas-Universal Service, Inc.*,[16] the Court of Appeal stated in dicta that the opposite is not true. That is, "a finding of no employment, it is not res judicata in a subsequent proceeding brought before the [appeals board] on this issue as long as the petition to reopen is made within the five-year period."[17] But a recent appeals board decision noted that the issue in *Solari* was not reopening, but rather the application of *res judicata* in a civil action for damages against a third party based on a prior finding by the IAC that the applicant did not suffer injuries in an accident. Instead, the appeals board concluded that when the foundational issue is employment and employment is not found, the WCAB loses jurisdiction after the statutory time for seeking reconsideration has expired.[18] It has been held, however, that the portion of LC 5804 that limits the power of the appeals board to revisit an award regarding employment does not

---

[14] *Western Pipe & Steel Co. v. IAC (Huston)* (1932) 126 Cal. App. 225.
[15] See *Quintero v. WCAB* (1982) 47 CCC 592 (writ denied).
[16] (1963) 28 CCC 277.
[17] *Solari v. Atlas-Universal Service, Inc.* (1963) 28 CCC 277, 280. See also *Edwards v. City of Chico* (1972) 37 CCC 792 (appeals board decision that an injured person was not an employee was not binding on a civil court when: (1) the decision was rendered after judgment was filed in the civil action; and (2) there was a five-year period in which the board's decision could be rescinded, altered or amended).
[18] *Yang v. WCAB* (2011) 76 CCC 607 (writ denied).

bar it from addressing the issue of coverage for one of several employers involved as co-defendants.[19]

The power to reopen an award may not be predicated upon a mere change of opinion by the appeals board as to the correctness of its original decision.[20] The appeals board may not direct the taking of additional evidence in support of a petition to reopen without first determining whether good cause to reopen the case exists pursuant to LC 5803.[21] For example, an applicant sought to reopen an order approving a compromise and release agreement on grounds that his previous counsel purported to be an attorney admitted to practice law in California but was not so qualified. The appeals board then referred the parties to an independent physician to determine the merits of the applicant's petition. The court stated that such action violated the procedural requirements of LC 5803 and of due process of law.[22] Whether the nonattorney made the representations and whether that would constitute good cause should have been determined first, as a threshold issue.

The standard for reopening a claim under LC 5803 is "good cause." That standard will be looked at regardless of the form of the petition to reopen. In one case, a petition to reopen indicated that it was based on the "new and further disability" provision of LC 5410. It was not, but the court found that the petition disclosed the possible existence of good cause under LC 5803, and allowed it.[23]

Good cause requires something new. The standard is not as loose as to allow a re-examination of every decided issue without a good reason; the principle of reopening an award for good cause does not permit a party to attempt to simply re-litigate the original award.[24] And a petition to reopen may not be used to litigate issues that should have been raised by a timely petition for reconsideration.[25] If the grounds urged as justification for reopening an award

---

[19] *Republic Indemnity Co. of America v. WCAB (Hunter)* (2008) 73 CCC 414 (writ denied).

[20] *Merritt-Chapman & Scott Corp. v. IAC (Smith)* (1936) 1 CCC 144, 146; *Consolidated Western Steel Division, U.S. Steel Corp. v. IAC (Williams)* (1962) 27 CCC 159, 161.

[21] *Fidelity & Casualty Co. of New York v. WCAB (Harris)* (1980) 45 CCC 381.

[22] *Fidelity & Casualty Co. of New York v. WCAB (Harris)* (1980) 45 CCC 381. But see *Formica Corp. v. WCAB (Stobbe)* (1999) 64 CCC 1398 (writ denied) (appeals board allowed applicant to obtain a supplemental report on a petition to reopen without making a finding as to whether there was good cause to reopen).

[23] *Stiles v. WCAB* (1971) 36 CCC 554, 558 (Court of Appeal opinion unpublished in official reports).

[24] *Nicky Blairs Restaurant v. WCAB (Macias)* (1980) 45 CCC 876, 886. See also *County of San Bernardino v. WCAB (Ramirez)* (1981) 46 CCC 1200 (Court of Appeal stating, "Neither the desire by one of the parties to re-litigate the original decision nor a change of mind on the part of the WCAB constitutes 'good cause' for reopening").

[25] *Young v. IAC* (1944) 9 CCC 79; *Royster v. WCAB* (1974) 39 CCC 513, 515-16; *Nicky Blairs Restaurant v. WCAB (Macias)* (1980) 45 CCC 876, 886.

existed at the time a petition for reconsideration should have been filed, the petition to reopen will be denied.[26]

GOOD CAUSE — GENERALLY

A petitioner is not entitled to have his or her case reopened as a matter of right upon the filing of a petition to reopen.[27] LC 5803 vests broad powers in the appeals board to "rescind, alter, or amend" an order, but only upon a showing of "good cause" pursuant to a petition filed by a real party in interest within five years of the date of injury.[28] The existence of good cause is essential to the exercise of continuing jurisdiction vested in the appeals board by LC 5803.[29] The good cause requirement is a limitation on the powers of the appeals board. Without good cause, the appeals board is powerless to act, and the former award or orders are final and invulnerable.[30] What constitutes good cause depends largely on the circumstances of each case. The appeals board's determination of what constitutes good cause is accorded great weight in appellate proceedings, but it is not conclusive."[31]

Mere discontent with the appeals board's original decision does not constitute good cause to reopen.[32] In order to have good cause, "[T]he existence of some fact or circumstance which warrants the conclusion that the challenged award is inequitable is a necessary element to the exercise of the continuing jurisdiction of the [appeals board] under the authority of [LC 5803]."[33] Furthermore, to reopen for good cause there must exist some ground, not within the knowledge of the appeals board at the time of making the former award or orders, that renders said original award or orders inequitable.[34] This means that the appeals board may not rely on circumstances existing and known to it when it made its findings and award to support a petition to reopen.[35] The appeals board can only rescind, alter or amend a prior award if there is some circumstance unknown to

---

[26] *Royster v. WCAB* (1974) 39 CCC 513, 515-16; *Polach v. American Smelting & Refining Co.* (1969) 34 CCC 511, 515 (appeals board *en banc*).
[27] *Clendaniel v. IAC* (1941) 6 CCC 85, 661; *Nicky Blairs Restaurant v. WCAB (Macias)* (1980) 45 CCC 876, 886.
[28] *Fidelity & Casualty Co. of New York v. WCAB (Harris)* (1980) 45 CCC 381, 387.
[29] *Azadigian v. WCAB* (1992) 57 CCC 391, 406.
[30] *Merritt-Chapman & Scott Corp. v. IAC (Smith)* (1936) 1 CCC 144, 146; *Fidelity & Casualty Co. of New York v. WCAB (Harris)* (1980) 45 CCC 381, 388.
[31] *Bartlett Haywood Co. v. IAC (Slate)* (1928) 203 Cal. 522, 532; *Merritt-Chapman & Scott Corp. v. IAC (Smith)* (1936) 1 CCC 144, 146; *Clendaniel v. IAC* (1941) 6 CCC 85; *Nicky Blairs Restaurant v. WCAB (Macias)* (1980) 45 CCC 876, 885.
[32] *Polach v. American Smelting & Refining Co.* (1969) 34 CCC 511, 515 (appeals board *en banc*).
[33] *Merritt-Chapman & Scott Corp. v. IAC (Smith)* (1936) 1 CCC 144, 146; *Fidelity & Casualty Co. of New York v. WCAB (Harris)* (1980) 45 CCC 381, 388.
[34] *Aliano v. WCAB* (1979) 44 CCC 1156; *Nicky Blairs Restaurant v. WCAB (Macias)* (1980) 45 CCC 876, 885.
[35] *Young v. IAC* (1944) 9 CCC 79, 81.

it at the time it made the original award that renders the original award inequitable.[36]

LC 5803 specifically provides that good cause for reopening includes evidence that the applicant's disability has either recurred, increased, diminished or terminated. Good cause may also be commonly found in: (1) mistake of fact; (2) mistake of law; (3) inadvertence; (4) newly discovered evidence; (5) fraud;[37] or (6) any factor or circumstance unknown at the time the original award or order was made that renders the previous award inequitable.[38]

So, "in order to constitute 'good cause' for reopening, new evidence (a) must present some good ground, not previously known to the Appeals Board, which renders the original award inequitable, (b) must be more than merely cumulative or a restatement of the original evidence or contentions, and (c) must be accompanied by a showing that such evidence could not with reasonable diligence have been discovered and produced at the original hearing."[39]

Mistake of Fact

A mistake of fact, occasioned by the failure or inability to produce certain evidence at a previous hearing, may be good cause to reopen an award.[40] The reopening of a case based on a mistake of fact generally involves evidence discovered subsequent to the previous hearing that demonstrates that the earlier decision was incorrect. This will not work if the moving party did know or should have known of the vital fact at the hearing, but it will if hidden facts or evidence are revealed only after the hearing is done.

In one case, the Court of Appeal found good cause to reopen an award based on an insurer's failure to adequately and fairly investigate an applicant's injury that rendered the medical reports, and the appeals board decision relying on same, insubstantial. In that case, an applicant sustained an industrial injury to the head, but the appeals board concluded that the applicant's disability was the result of nonindustrial viral encephalitis, not the industrial injury. Following a petition to reopen, the applicant introduced laboratory tests done at the time of the injury that indicated negative results for virus and for encephalitis. This evidence was not before the WCJ at the time of the original decision. The Court of Appeal

---

36 *The Pullman Co. v. IAC (Mira)* (1946) 11 CCC 155, 161.
37 *Nicky Blairs Restaurant v. WCAB (Macias)* (1980) 45 CCC 876, 886.
38 *LeBoeuf v. WCAB* (1983) 48 CCC 587, 592-93.
39 *Nicky Blairs Restaurant v. WCAB (Macias)* (1980) 45 CCC 876, 886 (citations omitted).
40 *Nicky Blairs Restaurant v. WCAB (Macias)* (1980) 45 CCC 876, 886.

noted that the insurer authorized the testing and diagnosis, and stated that if the employer had possession and control of the tests results, its failure to bring the results to the attention of the doctors and the appeals board would constitute good cause to reopen. The court added there was no evidence of willful suppression of the laboratory test results, but instead found that the insurer negligently presented medical facts to the original proceedings. The court concluded there was good cause to reopen the award.[41]

In another case, the court held that there was good cause to reopen an award when the Industrial Accident Commission (IAC — now the Workers' Compensation Appeals Board) awarded benefits based on the wages actually received by the applicant during the preceding year, rather than the "average weekly earning capacity of the injured employee at the time of injury" as required by LC 4453. The court concluded that because the original award was based on an illegal rule of computation, it was within the power of the commission to reopen the proceeding on that ground.[42]

Mistake of Law

A mistake of law may also constitute good cause for reopening an award. This occurs when the appeals board issues an award that becomes final, and the appellate court subsequently issues a decision demonstrating that the award was made in error. The Court of Appeal has stated, "[A] subsequent judicial interpretation of the compensation statutes contrary to a prior administrative interpretation is 'good cause' to reopen a case under LC 5803, if the request to reopen is made within five years of the date of injury."[43] The California Supreme Court has also stated, "A subsequent clarification of the applicable law by a reviewing court which indicates that an employee was originally entitled to a different award than that given is 'good cause' to reopen a case and amend an award."[44]

---

[41] *Aliano v. WCAB* (1979) 44 CCC 1156. See also *Stiles v. WCAB* (1971) 36 CCC 554 (Court of Appeal opinion unpublished in official reports) (court held that subsequent objective medical evidence confirming the existence of a ruptured disk was good cause to reopen when the original award was based on opinion that applicant's complaints were psychosomatic overlay and chronic pelvic inflammatory disease); *Walker v. WCAB* (2006) 71 CCC 1077 (Court of Appeal opinion unpublished in official reports) (subsequent MRI revealed findings in the applicant's back established good cause to reopen an award that previously only awarded benefits for internal injury); *Woodward v. WCAB* (1976) 41 CCC 468 (Court of Appeal opinion unpublished in official reports) (subsequent medical evidence of a herniated cervical nucleus pulposis and a recommended fusion constituted good cause).

[42] *Colonial Mutual Compensation Insurance Co. v. IAC (Miller)* (1941) 6 CCC 266. See also *Knudsen Frozen Foods v. WCAB (Ostos)* (1979) 44 CCC 999 (Court of Appeal opinion unpublished in official reports) (stipulation to incorrect TD rate was potentially a mutual mistake of fact that could be good cause to reopen an award).

[43] *Knowles v. WCAB* (1970) 35 CCC 411, 412.

[44] *LeBoeuf v. WCAB* (1983) 48 CCC 587, 592-93.

For example, an applicant lost his right eye in an industrial accident. He had previously lost sight in his left eye, and was therefore blind following the accident. The IAC awarded the applicant 25 percent permanent disability for the loss of one eye. The applicant did not file a petition for reconsideration. Subsequently, the California Supreme Court issued a decision in a different case that under such circumstances, an employee was entitled to permanent total disability.[45] The applicant later petitioned to reopen the award. The Court of Appeal held that there was good cause to reopen the award because the applicant was awarded 25 percent PD when, as a matter of law, he was 100 percent permanently disabled.[46]

The Court of Appeal held that the erroneous construction of the law as shown by a subsequent decision of the court was good cause to reopen the award. In that case, two employers, a general and special employer, were joined in claim. (The relationship between general and special employers is discussed in depth in Section 4.73 General and Special Employment.) The special employer asserted that the claim against it was untimely, as it did not provide any workers' compensation benefits, although benefits were provided by the general employer. The IAC determined that the claim against the special employer was barred by the statute of limitations. The general employer filed a petition for rehearing, but did nothing after the findings and award (F&A) was affirmed. The order became final. Subsequently, the California Supreme Court held that in cases involving multiple employers, the statute of limitations runs from the last payment of any compensation and not from the last payment by the party sought to be joined.[47] The general employer filed a petition to reopen the proceedings. The Court of Appeal held that this was permissible because of the erroneous construction of the law by the IAC.[48]

In an unpublished opinion, the court held that the changes to apportionment in SB 899 invalidated the *Fuentes* rule for apportionment and held that the applicant was entitled to the monetary difference between the previous award and his current disability. The Supreme Court denied review in that case, but later decided in *Brodie v. WCAB*[49] that the *Fuentes* rule had not been altered by

---

[45] *Liptak v. IAC* (1926) 200 Cal. 39.

[46] *Bartlett Haywood Co. v. IAC (Slate)* (1928) 203 Cal. 522. See also *Tran v. Tran*, 2012 Cal. Wrk. Comp. P.D. LEXIS 444 (*Almaraz/Guzman* good cause to reopen PD award).

[47] *SCIF v. IAC (Rodgers)* (1945) 10 CCC 96.

[48] *SCIF v. IAC (Dean)* (1946) 11 CCC 30. See also *Knowles v. WCAB* (1970) 35 CCC 411 (subsequent interpretation of heart trouble presumption in LC 3212.5 constituted good cause to reopen an award); *Ryerson Concrete Co. v. WCAB (Pena)* (1973) 38 CCC 649 (subsequent interpretation of penalties under LC 5814 good cause to reopen); *County of Sonoma v. WCAB (Byrne)* (1990) 55 CCC 286 (when the law changed by way of judicial interpretation, granting the petition to reopen was mandatory).

[49] (2007) 72 CCC 565.

SB 899.[50] The employer sought to reopen the award. The appeals board did so, and applied the *Brodie* decision. The court held that the Supreme Court's decision in *Brodie* constituted good cause to reopen the previous award, even after it has been affirmed by the Court of Appeal and the Supreme Court denied review. This was because the employer timely petitioned to reopen within five years of the date of injury.[51]

The appeals board has held that a subsequent *en banc* opinion of the appeals board could be a change of law that would constitute good cause to support a petition to reopen.[52] The WCJ in that case found that an applicant's permanent disability should be rated based on the 1997 PD schedule. This was based upon the appeals board's *en banc* decision, holding that the 1997 Schedule applied if the first payment of temporary disability was made before Jan. 1, 2005.[53] But one day after the WCJ's decision, a reformed appeals board determined *en banc* that the 1997 Schedule applied if the last payment of temporary disability indemnity was made for any period of ending before Jan. 1, 2005.[54] The employer filed a petition arguing that the 2005 Schedule applied to rate the applicant's permanent disability under the new law. The WCJ denied the petition finding that a change of law sufficient to constitute good cause requires a subsequent appellate decision, and therefore the appeals board *en banc* decision did not constitute good cause. The appeals board, however, held that the change of law announced by the appeals board *en banc* constituted good cause to reopen.[55]

The appeals board has also held that change in case law altering a binding rule to a situation in which the appeals board could choose which rule to follow constitutes good cause to reopen. That case went to trial on the issue of whether the 1997 Permanent Disability Rating Schedule (PDRS) or 2005 PDRS applied to determine an applicant's permanent disability. Based on the decision of *Vera v. WCAB*,[56] the WCJ held that the 2005 PDRS applied because the applicant was not permanent and stationary before Jan. 1, 2005. Subsequently, in *Genlyte Group, L.L.C. v. WCAB (Zavala)*,[57] the 2nd District Court of Appeal held that a report

[50] See Section 10.36 Fuentes Rule and Brodie for a more thorough discussion of these ideas.
[51] *Dykes v. WCAB* (2008) 73 CCC 1535 (Court of Appeal opinion unpublished in official reports).
[52] *Gonzalez v. WCAB* (2008) 73 CCC 284 (writ denied).
[53] *Pendergrass v. Duggan Plumbing* (2007) 72 CCC 95 (appeals board *en banc*).
[54] *Pendergrass v. Duggan Plumbing* (2007) 72 CCC 456 (appeals board *en banc*). See Section 10.13 Exception to Application of the 2005 Schedule for Notice Under LC 4061 for a more thorough discussion of these cases.
[55] *Gonzalez v. WCAB* (2008) 73 CCC 284 (writ denied). See also *Jenkins v. Family Practice Medical Associates*, 2011 Cal. Wrk. Comp. P.D. LEXIS 167; *Burnham v. WCAB* (2008) 73 CCC 579 (Court of Appeal opinion unpublished in official reports).
[56] (2007) 72 CCC 1115.
[57] (2008) 73 CCC 6.

indicating the existence of permanent disability was not limited to a permanent and stationary report. The applicant then timely moved to reopen the issue of which schedule applied in light of the change in law. The appeals board held there was no good cause to reopen because *Vera* had not been overruled by the Supreme Court.

The Court of Appeal reversed and allowed the petition to reopen. The court stated that "the case law interpreting section 4660(d) changed from a binding rule (under *Vera*) to a situation in which a WCJ or Board panel may choose to follow *Vera* or *Genlyte*," and that "[t]his development constituted a significant change in the law governing this issue, and it constituted good cause to reopen under section 5803."[58] The court remanded the case to determine which PDRS applied. The appeals board then concluded that the 1997 PDRS applied to determine the applicant's permanent disability.[59]

Note that if a party wishes to reopen a previous award based on a mistake of law, the party must first file a petition to reopen with the appeals board. If the party files a petition for writ of review before filing a petition to reopen, it will be dismissed.[60] In any event, an appellate decision will not be good cause to reopen an award if the decision existed at the time a petition for reconsideration should have been filed.[61] And an appellate decision will not be good cause to reopen an award if it merely restates the existing decisional law.[62] There must be a change in the law after the award is final. In addition, when parties knowingly take the risk of unsettled law, and their settlement reflects such basis for their settlement, there would not be good cause to reopen.[63]

Inadvertence

Inadvertence on the part of the court may constitute good cause to reopen an award pursuant to LC 5803. In one case, the appeals board found an employer liable while under the mistaken impression that the employer had been joined as a party and noticed of the same. In fact, the employer had never been noticed of

---

[58] *Avila-Gonzalez v. WCAB* (2010) 75 CCC 1069 (Court of Appeal opinion unpublished in official reports).

[59] *Avila-Gonzalez v. Barrett Business Services, Inc.*, 2011 Cal. Wrk. Comp. P.D. LEXIS 4. For a discussion on the conflict between *Vera* and *Zavala*, see Section 10.12 Exceptions for Medical Reports Indicating the Existence of Permanent Disability.

[60] *Howell v. WCAB* (1984) 49 CCC 93 (writ denied).

[61] *Royster v. WCAB* (1974) 39 CCC 513, 515.

[62] *General Insurance Co. of America v. WCAB (Sale)* (1980) 45 CCC 403, 408.

[63] *Fireman's Fund Insurance Co. v. WCAB (Allen)* (2010) 75 CCC 1. See also *Cerda v. Jacoby Landscape Management*, 2010 Cal. Wrk. Comp. P.D. LEXIS 340; *Adams v. State of California, California Youth Authority*, 2012 Cal. Wrk. Comp. P.D. LEXIS 449.

the joinder, and never even received the award against him. The employer filed a petition to reopen under LC 5803 when it learned of the mistake.

The employer had appeared in court in response to a subpoena without an attorney and without notice that he was a defendant in the action. The employer was not treated as a party at the hearing, only as a witness. Nevertheless, the WCJ found him to be the liable employer. The court found good cause to reopen as a matter of law. It noted that the facts established either mistake of fact, mistake of law, inadvertence or a combination thereof, because an order was issued making the employer a party, but he was not treated as a party and was not permitted to participate in the proceedings as a party. The court noted that with the assistance of counsel, the employer might very well have adduced evidence that would have affected the determination of whose employee the applicant was at the time of injury.[64]

Newly Discovered Evidence

Newly discovered evidence may constitute good cause to reopen an award pursuant to LC 5803. But to show good cause, it must be shown that the evidence is discovered after the decision is made.[65] Newly discovered evidence does not include evidence that a party knew of and was in possession of before the hearing.[66] Furthermore, newly discovered evidence that is merely cumulative of that on which the earlier order was based does not establish good cause.[67] A finding and conclusion of the appeals board that the newly discovered evidence is cumulative and insufficient to reopen an award is generally upheld by the appellate courts.[68]

The newly discovered evidence must be evidence that could not have been discovered or produced at the original hearing with reasonable diligence.[69] In cases invoking newly discovered evidence, the court has instructed that the

---

[64] *Arias v. WCAB* (1983) 48 CCC 659, 665-66.

[65] *Nicky Blairs Restaurant v. WCAB (Macias)* (1980) 45 CCC 876, 886.

[66] *Royal Globe Insurance Co. v. WCAB (Faulkner)* (1978) 43 CCC 895 (employer's diary that did not come to the attention of his attorney until after the hearing before the appeals board was not newly discovered evidence because the employer knew of it at all times, created it and was a party to the proceeding before the board). See also *Robinson v. WCAB* (1988) 53 CCC 142 (writ denied) (applicant's Social Security records were not newly discovered evidence because the applicant knew of them during trial, even though his attorney did not).

[67] *Clendaniel v. IAC* (1941) 6 CCC 85; *Walters v. IAC* (1962) 27 CCC 67, 72; *Consolidated Western Steel Division, U.S. Steel Corp. v. IAC (Williams)* (1962) 27 CCC 159, 160; *Nicky Blairs Restaurant v. WCAB (Macias)* (1980) 45 CCC 876, 885; *La Barre v. WCAB* (1969) 34 CCC 551 (writ denied); *McFarland v. IAC* (1965) 30 CCC 165 (writ denied).

[68] *Clendaniel v. IAC* (1941) 6 CCC 85.

[69] *Mantyla v. IAC (Stoneson)* (1933) 130 Cal. App. 139, 141; *Merritt-Chapman & Scott Corp. v. IAC (Smith)* (1936) 1 CCC 144, 151; *LeBoeuf v. WCAB* (1983) 48 CCC 587, 592-93.

appeals board's power to reopen a case "should be exercised with great caution and when fraud, inadvertence, mistake or excusable neglect are clearly shown. Otherwise, the process of introducing evidence before the [WCAB] would be interminable and the [WCAB] might be held to abuse its discretion in the exercise of its power."[70] If a party files a petition to reopen based on newly discovered evidence, the party must present the alleged new evidence, detail its materiality and relevance in a manner that shows that the evidence is not merely cumulative of evidence earlier received and must demonstrate that it could not have been discovered earlier because of fraud, excusable neglect, inadvertence or mistake.[71]

Good cause to reopen does not consist of medical evidence obtained subsequent to the original decision that merely disagrees with the medical opinion relied upon by the WCAB at the time of the original decision.[72] For example, one applicant alleged an industrial injury to his back. Following a hearing, the appeals board issued a take nothing award because "[t]here [was] no convincing evidence that the employee sustained any injury as alleged" and "[h]is testimony [was] not credible." The applicant later filed a petition to reopen that was denied by the WCJ. The appeals board, however, overruled the WCJ and appointed an independent medical examiner (IME) who found medical corroboration of the applicant's claim, and the appeals board awarded benefits.

The Court of Appeal, however, held that there was no good cause to reopen the award. The court noted that the IME's medical opinion was based on the same medical evidence and testimony introduced at the previous hearing. The court further noted that the WCJ had earlier found the applicant to be not credible and the IME's finding that the applicant was credible did not constitute new, noncumulative evidence, as it was merely a different appraisal of the applicant's veracity. The court held that because the case had been determined adversely to the applicant on conflicting evidence covering all of the same ground on which the appeals board purported to act, the appeals board's award was annulled and

[70] *Ingram v. DIR (Stoolfire)* (1930) 208 Cal. 633, 637; *Clendaniel v. IAC* (1941) 6 CCC 85; *Nicky Blairs Restaurant v. WCAB (Macias)* (1980) 45 CCC 876, 886 (citations omitted).

[71] *Polach v. American Smelting & Refining Co.* (1969) 34 CCC 511, 516 (appeals board *en banc*). See also *Young v. WCAB* (2003) 68 CCC 1325 (Court of Appeal opinion unpublished in official reports) (MRI obtained after an award finding no injury AOE/COE was not good cause to reopen an award when the applicant did not show that the award was inequitable, or that the MRI could not have been obtained before the award); *Harrell v. WCAB* (1995) 60 CCC 339 (writ denied) (applicant's petition to reopen denied when there was no showing as to why witnesses were not available at the original trial).

[72] *Nicky Blairs Restaurant v. WCAB (Macias)* (1980) 45 CCC 876, 885.

the original award was reinstated.[73]

In another case, an applicant claimed injury to his back, neck and left shoulder. The agreed medical examiner found that the applicant sustained industrial injury to his low back and left shoulder, but found injury to the neck to be nonindustrial. The parties entered into a stipulated award providing that the applicant sustained injury to his back and left shoulder, but did not include a stipulation to the neck as an injured body part. Subsequently, the applicant filed a petition to reopen alleging his neck condition had worsened.

The applicant was subsequently examined by three AMEs, who disagreed with the original AME regarding industrial causation of the neck. Their opinions were based on the same information available to the original AME. The appeals board found no good cause to reopen. The appeals board acknowledged that good cause may not be premised merely on a change of opinion based on the same facts, and that a party cannot re-litigate the original award based on facts or evidence that were in existence at the time of the original award. The board then noted that none of the new AMEs identified any new or unknown information in forming the basis for their opinions. The appeals board concluded that the petition to reopen was not allowed, because the applicant did not rely on any newly discovered facts or evidence that were unknown at the time of the original award. Rather, the applicant was seeking to re-litigate the issue of industrial causation of injury.[74]

The court has found good cause to reopen an award based on a previously unavailable disinterested witness whose testimony impeached the testimony of other witnesses during the original hearing regarding the issue of injury arising out of employment or in the course of employment.[75] But good cause was not found based on a witness who was previously unavailable during the earlier hearing when the testimony of the witness and other evidence produced on the hearing to reopen was cumulative of evidence introduced at the original hearing.[76]

---

[73] *Consolidated Western Steel Division, U.S. Steel Corp. v. IAC (Williams)* (1962) 27 CCC 159. See also *County of Los Angeles v. WCAB (Johnson)* (2003) 68 CCC 69 (writ denied) (AME's subsequent report finding an injury nonindustrial was not good cause to reopen an award when it was merely a re-interpretation of his earlier opinion); *SCIF v. WCAB (Soper)* (1970) 35 CCC 100 (Court of Appeal opinion unpublished in official reports) (cumulative evidence insufficient to reopen a claim); *Brannen v. WCAB* (1996) 61 CCC 554; *Dill v. WCAB* (1971) 36 CCC 355.

[74] *Brown v. WCAB* (2006) 72 CCC 118 (writ denied).

[75] *Walters v. IAC* (1962) 27 CCC 67. See also *Ford Motor Co. v. WCAB (McCuien)* (1967) 32 CCC 313 (writ denied) (good cause included previously unknown witness whose testimony tends to impeach earlier testimony).

[76] *Clendaniel v. IAC* (1941) 6 CCC 85.

The court has held that uncontroverted evidence in the form of surveillance film depicting the applicant engaging in physical activities inconsistent with the permanent disability previously awarded, as well as a medical report commenting on same, could support an employer's petition to reopen to reduce benefits.[77]

The California Supreme Court has held that a determination by the Rehabilitation Bureau that an applicant was not qualified to receive any rehabilitation benefits constituted "new evidence" not previously available, which might render the previous award inequitable. The court found that such evidence constituted good cause to reopen a permanent disability award. The applicant had tried to complete vocational rehabilitation but could not; this was evidence of total permanent disability. Because this benefit was being provided after the award, it could not have been discovered before.[78]

The Court of Appeal has also held that good caused existed to reopen an award that did not provide rehabilitation benefits when the applicant initially sought to rehabilitate himself. The court noted that the circumstances changed when the applicant's attempt at self-rehabilitation failed, and that it would be inequitable to bar the applicant from seeking rehabilitation benefits under those circumstances.[79] It was held that an applicant should be permitted to make his choice to enroll in a rehabilitation program at any time during the first five years after the injury and that, as a matter of law, his exercise of that choice constituted "good cause" to reopen the award for a possible addition of rehabilitation benefits.[80]

In an unpublished case, an applicant settled a variety of claims by way of stipulated award. The applicant experienced symptoms to the left hand and heart. The appeals board found that industrial injury to those body parts developed during employment but each manifested after the issuance of the stipulated award. The court found that the applicant could not have produced evidence of those injuries at the original proceedings. It concluded that this

---

[77] *Sully-Miller Contracting Co. v. WCAB (Sommer)* (1980) 45 CCC 683. See also *Weishaar v. WCAB* (2004) 69 CCC 151 (writ denied) (petition to reopen granted when *sub rosa* tapes showed the applicant engaging in activities inconsistent with disability awarded, and on opinion of AME and WCJ that applicant was not credible). But see *Cunningham v. WCAB* (1973) 38 CCC 313 (Court of Appeal opinion unpublished in official reports) (film of an applicant showing improvement in his condition did not constitute good cause when the employer failed to show that similar evidence would not have been available at earlier hearings, and the employee testified that the nature of his activities had not changed and there had been earlier surveillance).

[78] *LeBoeuf v. WCAB* (1983) 48 CCC 587. See also *C&C Industries v. WCAB (Fraga)* (2001) 66 CCC 1186 (writ denied).

[79] *Bekins Moving and Storage Co. v. WCAB (Hansen)* (1982) 47 CCC 1260.

[80] *Armodia v. WCAB* (1987) 53 CCC 151, 153.

constituted good cause to reopen under LC 5803 because that statute does not require a causal connection to the original injury.[81]

But in another unpublished opinion, the court found that there was no good cause when the employer sought to reopen the award based upon a report from a vocational counselor that "technological advances" in the form of voice-activated software might allow the applicant to perform some limited work. The court noted that the vocational counselor had previously advised the applicant of the possibility of using voice-activated software at the time of her original evaluation, and because the employer failed to explain why the evidence was unavailable before entering into the stipulated award, there was no good cause to reopen.[82]

Excusable Neglect

Excusable neglect is one listed ground for a petition to reopen.[83] No case to date explicitly allows for a reopening based on this ground. But there is a sense through the series of cases in this area that fairness should play a part — if a party has been responsible in prosecuting its case, the chances of a petition to reopen succeeding are increased.

A good example of this is *Dunlap v. WCAB*.[84] In *Dunlap*, the applicant, based on an IME report, was found to have an industrial injury with a very small amount of permanent disability. The matter was submitted for reconsideration, and the appeals board found that the report was ambiguous on the AOE/COE issue. The finding of injury was shakily confirmed based upon that ambiguity. The defense then deposed the IME and obtained testimony clarifying the ambiguity. One normally would think that this evidence obtained after trial and appeal would not constitute newly discovered evidence, as the issue could have been identified and the deposition done before or during the trial process. But in this case, the petition to reopen was allowed. The appeals board held that the defense could not have reasonably identified the ambiguity before the record was closed at trial.

---

[81] *California Highway Patrol v. WCAB (Griffin)* (2010) 75 CCC 1241 (Court of Appeal opinion unpublished in official reports).
[82] *Wal-Mart Stores, Inc. v. WCAB (Collier)* (2007) 72 CCC 210 (Court of Appeal opinion unpublished in official reports).
[83] *Ingram v. DIR (Stoolfire)* (1930) 208 Cal. 633, 637; *Clendaniel v. IAC* (1941) 6 CCC 85; *Nicky Blairs Restaurant v. WCAB (Macias)* (1980) 45 CCC 876, 886 (citations omitted).
[84] (1986) 51 CCC 354 (writ denied).

But negligence of counsel has not been sufficient to allow a finding of excusable neglect. In another case, a newly hired attorney dictated a letter during the trial process that requested a cross-examination of an IME. The letter was never transcribed or submitted to the court. The applicant attorney discovered this only after the award issued. It was held that negligence on the part of the applicant attorney was not good cause to reopen the case.[85] There are multiple writ-denied cases supporting the idea that negligence by counsel shall not be afforded relief.[86]

Fraud

A finding that a party committed fraud during a prior hearing may be good cause to reopen an award.[87] For example, one applicant sustained an injury when he jumped off a rail car. On the date of injury, the applicant had been drinking and decided to imitate a stunt he had seen earlier in the day. He climbed onto the rail car, jumped off onto a pile of boxes and injured himself. On the way to the hospital, the applicant, his wife and a co-worker agreed to say that the applicant was performing work duties when he accidentally fell and was injured. Based on these statements, the employer entered into stipulations with the applicant accepting the injury and waiving affirmative defenses such as intoxication (See Section 5.22 Intoxication) and horseplay (See Section 5.62 Horseplay – Skylarking). Several months after the stipulations, the applicant and his wife separated. She then contacted the employer and told the truth. The co-worker confirmed the true circumstances of the injury. Although the WCJ found that the employer entered into the stipulations because of a lack of due diligence, the appeals board found there was good cause to withdraw from the stipulated award.

The appeals board observed that a showing that an agreement had been procured by fraud had long been recognized as good cause to set it aside. The appeals board found that at the time of the stipulation, the employer was not aware that the applicant jumped off a rail car while trying to imitate a stuntman, because the three eyewitnesses conspired to conceal that material fact. It found that if the employer was aware of the facts it would not have entered into the

[85] *Jwaideh v. WCAB* (1983) 48 CCC 461.

[86] See also *Azadigian v. WCAB* (1992) 57 CCC 391 (applicant attorney's negligence in dismissing part of a case was not grounds for a petition to reopen); *Interplay Productions v. WCAB (Fisher)* (2000) 65 CCC 411 (writ denied) (appeals board found no good cause to allow defense from a stipulation to pay an agreed settlement of lien); *The Home Depot v. WCAB (Bryden)* (2008) 73 CCC 744 (writ denied) (no relief from stipulation when parties agreed on jurisdiction, despite attorney not having authority to make the stipulation); *Rocha v. TTX Co.*, 2008 Cal. Wrk. Comp. P.D. LEXIS 348.

[87] *Brunski v. IAC* (1928) 203 Cal. 761 (discovery of perjury and false statements after the original settlement by the applicant to the appeals board and doctors regarding his history of physical injury was found to be good cause to reopen an award).

stipulation. It also found that the employer was not at fault because the employer obtained statements from the eyewitnesses who provided false information. The appeals board stated that it would not condone the applicant's wrongdoing by denying the employer relief from the stipulations that were fraudulently entered into.[88]

In another case, an applicant was awarded 100 percent PD. The employer later filed a petition to reopen requesting a reduction of the award. At trial, the employer submitted into evidence a video tape of the applicant engaging in activities that were inconsistent with her level of disability. The tape showed several hours of activity including lifting and pulling, pushing, scrubbing a boat deck, freely standing, walking, bending, lifting and squatting. Following the trial, the WCJ reduced the award from 100 percent to 49.5 percent PD, based on a semi-sedentary work restriction. The WCJ found that the applicant was not credible and exaggerated her level of disability to medical evaluators. The WCJ also found that the evidence was not cumulative of the original evidence presented to support the 100 percent award, and there was no evidence that the film evidence could have been discovered by the exercise of due diligence before the award. This decision was upheld by the appeals board.[89]

Other Grounds for Good Cause

The grounds outlined above are not the only ones that are considered good cause for reopening under LC 5803. It has been stated that "any factor or circumstance unknown at the time the original award or order was made which renders the previous Findings and Award 'inequitable,' will justify the reopening of a case and amendment of the Findings and Award."[90]

The appeals board in one case held that an applicant's release from prison constituted good cause under LC 5803. The applicant filed a timely application for an industrial injury but was imprisoned shortly thereafter. The application was dismissed without prejudice for failure to prosecute. After being released from prison, but within five years of the industrial injury, the applicant filed a petition to reopen indicating he was ready to proceed with prosecution of his case. Although recognizing that the applicant could have prosecuted his case

[88] *Edgington v. WCAB* (2007) 72 CCC 1153 (writ denied)

[89] *Weishaar v. WCAB* (2004) 69 CCC 151 (writ denied). See also *California Indemnity Insurance Co. v. WCAB (Whiteley)* (2011) 76 CCC 1332 (writ denied) (WCAB set aside an earlier stipulated award of 18 percent; carrier's failure to adequately assess the applicant's disability and to provide appropriate treatment along with the rush to settlement, which was meaningless in describing injury, was so egregious that it found knowing and material misrepresentation, fraud and overreaching).

[90] *LeBoeuf v. WCAB* (1983) 48 CCC 587, 592-93.

while in prison, the appeals board found good cause to reopen under LC 5803 because the reason for the dismissal without prejudice, the incarceration, had been removed.[91]

DUE PROCESS

LC 5803 precludes the rescinding of any order except "upon notice and after an opportunity to be heard is given the parties in interest." If the appeals board fails to give notice to the parties, it violates the procedural requirements of LC 5803 and of due process of law. The appellate court may then issue a writ of mandate directing the appeals board not to proceed to reopen a claim except for good cause, to inform the parties of the ground of good cause on which it seeks to take or consider additional evidence and to afford the parties the opportunity to cross-examine witnesses and present rebuttal evidence on the noticed grounds.[92]

[91] *California Contractors Network, Inc. v. WCAB (Hanss)* (2009) 74 CCC 780 (writ denied). Note this decision appears to contradict the law that good cause must be something that was not known to the WCJ at the time of the original award.
[92] *Fidelity & Casualty Co. of New York v. WCAB (Harris)* (1980) 45 CCC 381, 389-91.

6.28 REOPENING A COMPROMISE AND RELEASE

A compromise and release settlement is an agreement by the parties to resolve a claim. It must be approved by the appeals board and has "the same force and effect as an award made after a full hearing."[1] Payment of a C&R approved by the appeals board terminates the liability of the employer and its insurance carrier on account of the involved injury, including any liability for increased disability, unless the order approving the C&R becomes vacated for legal reasons.[2] For a full discussion of the Compromse & Release, see section 14.74 Resolution by Compromise and Release.

As with other orders, decisions and awards of the WCAB, when an order approving a C&R is final (that is, after the time for reconsideration and appeal has passed), it may only be rescinded, altered or amended pursuant to LC 5803 by the board in response to a petition filed within five years of the date of injury.[3] Such a petition is generally labeled as a petition to set aside a compromise and release and is, in effect, a petition to reopen a closed case that, likewise, requires a showing of good cause to reopen.[4]

GOOD CAUSE TO SET ASIDE A COMPROMISE AND RELEASE

Generally, setting aside an award resulting from a C&R is difficult. These agreements are to be respected, or there will be little incentive to resolve cases. In

---

[1] *Johnson v. WCAB* (1970) 35 CCC 362, 368; *Silva v. IAC* (1924) 68 Cal. App. 510, 515.
[2] *City of Anaheim v. WCAB (Davis)* (1982) 47 CCC 52, 55.
[3] *Smith v. WCAB* (1985) 50 CCC 311, 318.
[4] *Fidelity & Casualty Co. of New York v. WCAB (Harris)* (1980) 45 CCC 381.

addition to being an award, a C&R is a contract between the parties, and the law of contracts in general can apply. And so, unlike a stipulated award or findings and award, a C&R is generally not subject to reopening when based on evidence of new and further disability.[5]

Negligence of a party to the agreement is not good cause to set aside a C&R.[6] A party may not set aside a C&R simply because he or she changes her mind.[7] Also, dissatisfaction with the C&R alone certainly does not constitute good cause to set aside the award.[8]

Good cause to rescind an order approving a compromise and release may be found if the release was secured by fraud, mistake, duress or undue influence.[9] A C&R may also be set aside on the grounds of procedural irregularities,[10] or incompetency.[11] These grounds do not exhaust all possible equitable grounds for rescinding an order approving a compromise and release. Like a petition to reopen, good cause to set aside a C&R depends upon the facts and circumstances of each case.[12]

Mutual Mistake

A C&R may be set aside on the grounds of mistake, but only if it was a mutual, not unilateral, mistake.[13] A mutual mistake occurs when both parties misapprehend the same material fact(s) in the C&R; a unilateral mistake occurs when only one party makes a mistake to the meaning of the agreement.

A mutual mistake of fact may exist if there is legitimate confusion over who will pay disputed medical-legal costs[14] or outstanding liens.[15] A mutual mistake regarding liability for future medical care may also be grounds to set aside a

---

[5] *Draper v. WCAB* (1983) 48 CCC 748, 751; *Buck v. WCAB* (1990) 55 CCC 308 (writ denied); *Coleman v. WCAB* (1980) 45 CCC 805 (writ denied).

[6] *Smith v. WCAB* (1985) 50 CCC 311, 316.

[7] *Brightwell v. IAC* (1964) 29 CCC 26 (writ denied).

[8] *Schroedel v. WCAB* (1997) 62 CCC 1173 (writ denied); *Moyles v. WCAB* (1982) 47 CCC 328 (Court of Appeal opinion unpublished in official reports).

[9] *Draper v. WCAB* (1983) 48 CCC 748, 751; *Fidelity & Casualty Co. of New York v. WCAB (Harris)* (1980) 45 CCC 381; *Silva v. IAC* (1924) 68 Cal. App. 510, 515; *Johnson v. WCAB* (1970) 35 CCC 362, 368.

[10] *Smith v. WCAB* (1985) 50 CCC 311, 320-21.

[11] *Sun Indemnity Co. of New York v. IAC (McKinney)* (1948) 13 CCC 82, 85.

[12] *Bartlett Haywood Co. v. IAC (Slate)* (1928) 203 Cal. 522, 532.

[13] *Smith v. WCAB* (1985) 50 CCC 311, 319; *Buck v. WCAB* (1990) 55 CCC 308 (writ denied); *Rollins v. County of Solano*, 2012 Cal. Wrk. Comp. P.D. LEXIS 155; *Miller v. Dispatch Transportation*, 2012 Cal. Wrk. Comp. P.D. LEXIS 372.

[14] *Gooch v. WCAB* (1977) 42 CCC 521 (writ denied).

[15] *GTE Data Services v. WCAB (Hannaford)* (1989) 54 CCC 41 (writ denied); *William Bolthouse Farms, Inc. v. WCAB (Alvarez)* (2001) 66 CCC 685 (writ denied).

C&R. For example, both parties in one case believed that private health insurance would pick up the cost of future medical treatment; the C&R was rescinded due to mutual mistake of fact when it was learned that the health insurer did not afford coverage.[16] In another case, the appeals board found that a misunderstanding about whether Medicare would cover the applicant's future medical care constituted good cause to set aside the C&R.[17]

The most common situation that leads to a petition to set aside a C&R is a dispute over the amount of permanent disability advances credited against the settlement. One of the parties may argue that the amount in the C&R did not contemplate deduction of PD advances, or that it inaccurately reflects the amount of PD advanced. Whether a mutual mistake has been made in such situations depends on the facts of the case, but case law reflects that the appeals board is reluctant to set aside a C&R on these grounds.[18]

For example, in one case, the parties executed a C&R settling a claim for $56,950, minus $22,377.50 in PD advances, $8,400 in TD overpayment and $6,834.00 in attorney's fees. Later, the insurer informed the defense counsel that there had been an omission of $9,470 PD previously advanced. The defense counsel filed a petition to set aside the C&R, arguing that the claims examiner did not tell him about the $9,470 in payments, and that the failure to include in the C&R the proper amount of credit constituted a mutual mistake of fact. The appeals board concluded that this was solely the defendant's unilateral mistake in drafting the documents, and that the defendant had not established good cause to set aside the C&R.[19]

In one case, the parties agreed to a C&R workers' compensation claim in which the employer waived all subrogation and credit rights in the employee's third-party case. Once the C&R was approved, the employee proceeded with the civil case. She was unsuccessful and received nothing. The employee then petitioned to set aside the C&R based on mutual mistake of fact and inadequacy of

---

[16] *City of Beverly Hills v. WCAB (Dowdle)* (1997) 62 CCC 1691 (writ denied).
[17] *Santa Maria Bonita School District v. WCAB (Recinos)* (2002) 67 CCC 848 (writ denied).
[18] See *World Mark Resorts v. WCAB (Ramsey)* (2005) 70 CCC 1616 (writ denied) (C&R not set aside when it indicated $4,060 had been advanced but employer argued that $20,471.08 had been advanced); *Blanpea v. WCAB* (2004) 69 CCC 1351 (writ denied) (applicant's argument that C&R did not contemplate deduction for PD advances rejected when appeals board found no mutual mistake of fact about deduction of PD advances); *Armendariz v. WCAB* (1999) 65 CCC 108 (writ denied) (C&R providing credit for PD advances "according to proof" not set aside); *Shull v. WCAB* (1999) 64 CCC 619 (writ denied) (C&R that provided a deduction for all PD advanced was not set aside despite applicant's contention that it provided for only one PD advance); *Lee v. San Diego Superior Court, County of San Diego,* 2011 Cal. Wrk. Comp. P.D. LEXIS 79 (failing to provide provision indicating that permanent disability advances would be deducted from total settlement amount was a unilateral mistake and the C&R was not set aside).
[19] *County of San Joaquin (Sheriff's Department) v. WCAB (Oaks)* (2011) 76 CCC 169 (writ denied).

settlement. The WCJ opined that without a third-party recovery the settlement was inadequate, and the C&R was set aside on the grounds that a third-party settlement was a "condition subsequent" to the C&R, thus invalidating it. The board reversed on appeal because the parties and the judge neglected to mention in the C&R that the settlement would be adequate only if the employee received a third-party recovery.[20]

In a case in which the mistake was made by the civil court, rather than the parties, the appeals board refused to set aside a C&R. The employee's civil suit against the employer for sexual harassment was improperly dismissed on the grounds that the civil action was resolved and included in the employee's workers' compensation settlement. The civil court had misconstrued the terms and conditions of the C&R, which contained specific language that the agreement was intended to settle the applicant's workers' compensation case only. The applicant attempted to have the C&R set aside on the grounds of fraud, mistake of fact and inadequacy. The WCJ found inadequate grounds to rescind the settlement, and said that the applicant should pursue a civil remedy rather than seek rescission of the C&R.[21]

Duress

Duress is one of the stated grounds for setting aside a C&R. But the case law suggests that it is generally difficult to establish duress. For example, one applicant petitioned to set aside a C&R on the grounds of duress and undue influence. At trial, she testified that during settlement negotiations, her attorney mentioned theft allegations would be raised if the case went to trial and told her that it would be in her best interest to settle. The appeals board found that the C&R was not signed under duress or undue influence because the applicant's attorney did not focus, pressure or intimidate the applicant. Moreover, the appeals board noted that the applicant had prior experience with workers' compensation cases, had knowledge of and was given her options in the case. The board did not find good cause to set aside the C&R.[22]

In another case, the appeals board refused to grant a petition to set aside a C&R on the grounds that it required the applicant's resignation. The appeals board reasoned that the agreement was not signed by the applicant under "duress" and

---

[20] *Hilt v. WCAB* (1994) 59 CCC 937 (writ denied).

[21] *Kohler v. WCAB* (2002) 67 CCC 670 (writ denied).

[22] *Jenkins v. WCAB* (2000) 65 CCC 1323 (writ denied). See also *Morales v. WCAB* (2006) 71 CCC 335 (writ denied) (no duress when applicant alleged that attorney told her she would go to jail if she did not sign the C&R, but the appeals board found no showing of duress).

that the settlement was therefore lawful.[23] Also, in a different case, the appeals board refused to set aside a C&R when the applicant alleged fraud, undue influence and duress on the part of his attorney, but the appeals board found no evidence of such conduct.[24]

Fraud

A C&R may be set aside on the grounds of fraud. Intrinsic fraud will suffice to set aside a C&R if the petition to reopen is filed within five years from the date of injury.[25] Intrinsic fraud is a deception that pertains to the original action, and includes perjury.[26]

In one case, the appeals board set aside a C&R on the grounds of fraud when a deputy sheriff resolved claims for his psyche and back through a C&R. After the settlement, the employer learned that the applicant had been working during the period he claimed temporary disability and had concealed his employment. The employer filed a petition to reopen under LC 5803 and sought to have the C&R set aside on the grounds of fraud. The WCJ granted the petition to reopen. The WCJ found that the applicant made fraudulent statements at deposition and concealed his active involvement in his own business while claiming TD. The WCJ then ordered the C&R to be set aside and the applicant take nothing for his workers' compensation claims. The appeals board upheld the decision because the applicant engaged in deception to obtain workers' compensation benefits. But the appeals board noted that the WCJ's order that the applicant take nothing was insufficient, and awarded restitution to the employer in the sum of $14,400.[27]

Incompetency

An applicant's incompetency may be grounds to set aside a C&R. Incompetency, for purposes of workers' compensation, has been defined as the "inability to properly manage or take care of oneself or property without assistance."[28]

---

[23] *Branom v. WCAB* (1988) 54 CCC 3 (writ denied).
[24] *Maloney v. WCAB* (1997) 62 CCC 815 (writ denied). See also *Cook v. Singapore Airlines*, 2011 Cal. Wrk. Comp. P.D. LEXIS 309 (applicant alleged that due to her attorney's misrepresentations, she was misled or forced to sign a C&R, but WCAB found that she did not disclose the supposed impropriety). But see *Nationwide Insurance Co. v. WCAB (Forrest)* (1996) 61 CCC 1496 (writ denied) (C&R set aside for mutual mistake, coercion and duress when language in agreement did not accurately reflect the medical evidence, and when applicant was not fully advised of her rights and felt coerced into signing release based on defendants' representations that they had evidence her injury was not work related).
[25] *Johnson v. WCAB* (1970) 35 CCC 362, 369; *Brunski v. IAC* (1928) 203 Cal. 761, 764-66.
[26] *Home Insurance Co. v. Zurich Insurance Co.* (2002) 96 Cal. App. 4th 17, 26.
[27] *Plass v. WCAB* (1997) 62 CCC 705 (writ denied).
[28] *County of Santa Clara v. WCAB (McMonagle)* (1992) 57 CCC 377 (writ denied).

Obviously, this is a very broad definition in need of interpretation. There is little direct guidance in workers' compensation case law.

In one case, an applicant entered into a C&R agreement with the employer, which was approved by the Industrial Accident Commission (now the WCAB). Two months later, the applicant was declared incompetent. A guardian was appointed who asserted that the C&R should be set aside because the applicant was incompetent at the time she executed the document. The commission found that the applicant was incompetent when she executed the document and set aside the C&R. The Court of Appeal upheld the decision because it was supported by substantial evidence.[29]

In another case, however, the appeals board refused to set aside a C&R when the applicant did not establish incompetency at trial by substantial evidence. The applicant offered visit summaries and progress notes, but the appeals board found that they did not constitute substantial medical evidence on the issue of incompetency, because they did not address her competency at all.[30]

Mistake of Law

In an unpublished opinion, the court held that a mistake of law about the applicant's proper employer was good cause to set aside a C&R. In that case, an applicant municipal judge named the County of Sonoma as his employer. The county settled the claim by way of C&R. Subsequently, the Court of Appeal issued an opinion that municipal court judges were employees of the state rather than the county.[31] The county sought reimbursement from the state, adjusted by SCIF. The court concluded that there was a mutual mistake of law and fact, and therefore the appeals board had jurisdiction and authority to remedy the mistake because of equitable considerations.[32]

Estoppel and Procedural Irregularities

In another unpublished opinion, the court found good cause to set aside a C&R in a *pro per* applicant's case when the adjuster made statements to the applicant

---

[29] *Sun Indemnity Co. of New York v. IAC (McKinney)* (1948) 13 CCC 82, 85.

[30] *Rollins v. County of Solano*, 2012 Cal. Wrk. Comp. P.D. LEXIS 155; *Rollins v. County of Solano*, 2012 Cal. Wrk. Comp. P.D. LEXIS 254. See also *Garcia v. WCAB* (2011) 76 CCC 205 (writ denied) (C&R not set aside when applicant did not meet burden of proving incompetence because there was no medical evidence that applicant was incompetent).

[31] *County of Sonoma v. WCAB (Byrne)* (1990) 55 CCC 286.

[32] *County of Los Angeles v. WCAB (Burke)* (1994) 59 CCC 312 (Court of Appeal opinion unpublished in official reports).

indicating that further adjustment of his claim would be made after a C&R was executed if it were demonstrated that the applicant was entitled to a higher indemnity rate. There were also procedural irregularities that included the WCJ having an ex parte communication with the information and assistance officer and then having an "off the record" conversation with the applicant and defendant regarding the conversation.[33]

Medical Evidence Subsequent to Settlement

In a couple of cases, the appeals board has proved that it is reluctant to set aside a C&R based on medical evidence obtained after the settlement. In one case, the appeals board held that an MRI performed after an applicant entered into a C&R did not constitute good cause to set aside the C&R. The applicant sustained injury to his right lower leg; no back complaints were mentioned in the medical reports. A chiropractor suggested an MRI of the back, but the applicant settled his claim and did not undergo the MRI until two months after the settlement. The applicant filed his petition to set aside the C&R after undergoing the MRI. The appeals board refused to set aside the agreement, noting that the applicant had knowledge of the imminent diagnostic procedure at the time the C&R was executed and could have waited to settle his claim until after the procedure. The board also noted that the employer had no knowledge of the impending scan or of the applicant's possible back injury, so there was only unilateral and not mutual mistake.[34]

In another case, the appeals board held that it did not have the authority to set aside a compromise and release on the ground of mistake pursuant to LC 5803 based on scientific literature obtained following the settlement. That applicant had sustained an orthopedic injury and claimed that he suffered hearing loss as a result of taking Vicodin. The hearing-loss claim was disputed and the doctors had conflicting opinions as to whether the condition was industrial. After the settlement, the applicant obtained new evidence, consisting of a study co-authored by his evaluating physician, that the overuse of Vicodin causes hearing loss. The appeals board noted that at the time of the C&R, at least two physicians concluded there was a connection between the Vicodin and the applicant's hearing loss, and stated that good cause to reopen an award required more than merely cumulative evidence or a restatement of the original evidence or contentions. The appeals board added that the subsequent publication of the

---

[33] *Phillips v. WCAB* (2007) 72 CCC 406 (Court of Appeal unpublished in official reports).

[34] *Buck v. WCAB* (1990) 55 CCC 308 (writ denied). See also *Ledesma v. WCAB* (1984) 49 CCC 743 (writ denied) (C&R was not set aside based on evidence obtain afterward that the applicant's injury was more severe than the original medical indicated).

scientific paper by the applicant's physician did not constitute fraud or concealment of a medical opinion because the physician rendered the same opinion in his subsequent paper as he rendered at the time of applicant's settlement. The appeals board noted that in C&R settlements, the parties have agreed to accept calculated risks negotiated on the basis of the evidence available at the time of settlement. It concluded that if the C&R were set aside, the precedent would be that any C&R might be set aside when subsequent developments in medical science prove or disprove a causal connection that was disputed or compromised at the time of settlement.[35]

TIME FOR FILING A PETITION TO REOPEN A COMPROMISE AND RELEASE

A petition to reopen a C&R must be filed within five years from the date of injury under LC 5410. A petition to set aside a compromise and release filed within the five-year period grants jurisdiction to the appeals board to decide the petition more than five years after the date of injury.[36] If a petition to reopen a C&R is filed more than five years after the date of injury, the appeals board has jurisdiction to set aside a C&R only on a showing of fraud or mistake of the kind generally referred to as "extrinsic" fraud or mistake, but not "intrinsic."[37] Petitions to reopen more five years after an injury and the definitions of these terms are further discussed in Section 6.29 Reopening for Fraud After Five Years.

[35] *Smith v. WCAB* (2000) 66 CCC 187 (writ denied).
[36] *Smith v. WCAB* (1985) 50 CCC 311, 318.
[37] *Smith v. WCAB* (1985) 50 CCC 311, 319.

6.29 REOPENING FOR FRAUD AFTER FIVE YEARS

LC 5804 limits the appeals board's authority to rescind, alter or amend an award to five years from the date of injury. Beyond that, the appeals board generally does not have jurisdiction to reopen an award.[1] But the courts have crafted a limited exception to the five-year rule: A party is to be protected when it is defrauded and could not have known about it. An award may be set aside after the appeals board's jurisdiction has expired upon a showing of fraud or mistake of the kind generally referred to as "extrinsic," but not if it is "intrinsic."[2]

Extrinsic fraud is one a party could not have known about. It is fraud "extrinsic" to, or outside of, the power of the party to identify it. The courts are protective of the five-year limit. So if the defrauded party, given its ability to do discovery, with due diligence could have found it was being defrauded, there is no extrinsic fraud. That would be considered "intrinsic" fraud. Even though the party may in fact have been defrauded, the five years has passed and the chance is missed. Parties who could have found out about being misled but did not are out of luck. In determining whether a case involves intrinsic or extrinsic fraud or mistake, "It is necessary to examine the facts in light of the policy that a party who failed to assemble all of his evidence at the trial should not be privileged to re-litigate a case, as well as the policy permitting a party to seek relief from a judgment entered into in a proceeding in which he was deprived of a fair opportunity to fully present his case."[3]

---

[1] *Sapp v. WCAB* (1971) 36 CCC 484 (writ denied); *Kachaturian v. WCAB* (1976) 41 CCC 422 (writ denied).
[2] *Smith v. WCAB* (1985) 50 CCC 311, 319.
[3] *Kulchar v. Kulchar* (1969) 1 Cal. 3d 467, 473.

"Extrinsic fraud usually arises when a party is denied a fair adversary hearing because he has been 'deliberately kept in ignorance of the action or proceeding, or in some other way fraudulently prevented from presenting his claim or defense.'"[4] "In demonstrating extrinsic fraud, it is insufficient for a party to come into court and simply assert that the judgment was premised upon false facts. The party must show that such facts could not reasonably have been discovered prior to the entry of judgment."[5] "By contrast, fraud is intrinsic and not valid grounds for setting aside a judgment when the party has been given notice of the action and has had an opportunity to present his case and to protect himself from any mistake or fraud of his adversary but has unreasonably neglected to do so. Such a claim of fraud goes to the merits of the prior proceedings which the moving party should have guarded against at the time. Where the defrauded party has failed to take advantage of liberal discovery policies to fully investigate his claim, any fraud is intrinsic fraud."[6] Generally, the introduction of perjured testimony or false documents, or the concealment or suppression of material evidence is deemed intrinsic fraud.[7]

Extrinsic mistakes occur when there is an excusable neglect by the moving party to appear and present his claim or defense.[8] An extrinsic mistake may occur when a party becomes incompetent but no guardian *ad litem* is appointed or when there is reliance on an attorney who becomes incapacitated to act.[9] A mutual mistake that might be sufficient to set aside a contract or one party's unilateral mistake are not sufficient to set aside a final judgment.[10]

In light of this standard, it is generally very difficult to reopen an award more than five years after the date of injury. For example, the appeals board held that it did not have jurisdiction to reopen an award more than five years after the date of injury, despite the employers' allegation that the award was based on fraudulent trial testimony. The appeals board found that the perjured testimony was intrinsic, not extrinsic fraud, which was insufficient to reopen the award after the five-year period had elapsed.[11]

---

[4] *Kulchar v. Kulchar* (1969) 1 Cal. 3d 467, 471; *Home Insurance Co. v. Zurich Insurance Co.* (2002) 96 Cal. App. 4th 17, 26.

[5] *City and County of San Francisco v. Cartagena* (1995) 35 Cal. App. 4th 1061, 1068. See also *Perez v. Leon* (2000) 28 CWCR 139 (panel decision).

[6] *City and County of San Francisco v. Cartagena* (1995) 35 Cal. App. 4th 1061, 1067-68; *Home Insurance Co. v. Zurich Insurance Co.* (2002) 96 Cal. App. 4th 17, 26.

[7] *Home Insurance Co. v. Zurich Insurance Co.* (2002) 96 Cal. App. 4th 17, 26.

[8] *Kulchar v. Kulchar* (1969) 1 Cal. 3d 467, 471.

[9] *Kulchar v. Kulchar* (1969) 1 Cal. 3d 467, 471-72.

[10] *Kulchar v. Kulchar* (1969) 1 Cal. 3d 467, 472; *Smith v. WCAB* (1985) 50 CCC 311, 319-320.

[11] *Rodgers, dba Rodgers Solar Service v. WCAB (Clark)* (2003) 68 CCC 975 (writ denied). See also *Luckey v. WCAB* (2003) 68 CCC 1454 (Court of Appeal opinion unpublished in official reports) (C&R could not be reopened more than five years after the date of injury without a showing of extrinsic fraud or mistake).

In an unpublished opinion, the court held that an employer's act of deliberately underestimating the applicant's earnings and knowingly submitting a false wage certification so that SCIF would calculate lower disability benefits was an act of intrinsic fraud, rather than extrinsic fraud, So it provided insufficient grounds for the appeals board to set aside a prior award based on a petition filed more than five years after the date of injury.[12]

But in one case, the Court of Appeal has held that a conviction of workers' compensation fraud pursuant to IC 1871.4 and IC 1871.5 provides the appeals board with discretion to reopen an award normally barred by LC 5803. The court noted that LC 5803.5 specifically provides that a conviction pursuant to IC 1871.4 that materially affects the basis of any order, decision or award of the board is sufficient grounds for reconsideration of that order, decision or award.[13]

---

[12] *Burnett v. WCAB* (2003) 68 CCC 1439 (Court of Appeal opinion unpublished in official reports).
[13] *Farmers Insurance Group of Cos. v. WCAB (Sanchez)* (2002) 67 CCC 1545, 1550. Note that the *Sanchez* decision suggests that the appeals board may reopen an award more than five years after the date of injury on a showing of good cause, which is inconsistent with other cases. That decision fails to discuss whether there was intrinsic or extrinsic fraud, so *Sanchez* may be of limited precedential value.

6.30 ESTOPPEL AND THE FIVE-YEAR STATUTE

The concept of estoppel can operate to toll the one-year statute of limitations. The employer may fail to inform the applicant of his statutory rights, and in those cases, the statute of limitations is tolled until it becomes aware of those rights. The employer may also mislead the applicant, and cause him or her to believe that filing an application is unnecessary or that there is more time to do so than there legally is. Do these concepts apply to the five-year statute of limitations?

It would seem that the employer could mislead the applicant into thinking that he or she does not have to file a petition to reopen within five years from the date of injury. In at least one case, an employer advanced permanent disability money beyond what was owed as dictated by the award. It was held that by doing so, the applicant was misled into thinking that he did not have to file a petition to reopen. When the petition was filed more than five years from the date of injury, the employer was estopped from raising LC 5410.[1] But there is no obligation to notice the applicant of his right to reopen a case for new and further disability within five years from the date of injury, so there is no estoppel for failure to provide notice.[2]

---

[1] *El Monte Union School District v. WCAB (Deffenderfer)* (1990) 55 CCC 57 (writ denied). See also *Chichester v. WCAB* (1994) 60 CCC 37 (writ denied). But see *Young v. WCAB* (2006) 71 CCC 1350 (writ denied) (estoppel not established when employer provided at least three letters of the right to file a petition to reopen within five years and paid no benefits, other than medical treatment, beyond the five years).

[2] See *Duarte v. WCAB* (2008) 73 CCC 1447 (writ denied); *Berchtold v. WCAB* (1992) 57 CCC 535 (Court of Appeal opinion unpublished in official reports).

In an unpublished case, the Court of Appeal also concluded that the five year period is jurisdictional, and that the appeals board is without jurisdiction after that.[3] In contrast, in another unpublished opinion, the court concluded that the five-year statute pursuant to LC 5410 was not jurisdictional and could be waived.[4] So at this point, the issue remains open.

---

[3] *Berchtold v. WCAB* (1992) 57 CCC 535 (Court of Appeal opinion unpublished in official reports) citing *Sprague v. IAC* (1956) 21 CCC 173 and *Westvaco Chlorine Products Corp. v. IAC (Johnson)* (1955) 20 CCC 248.

[4] *City of Los Angeles v. WCAB (Johnson)* (2009) 74 CCC 1 (Court of Appeal opinion unpublished in official reports).

6.31 CONTINUING JURISDICTION TO ENFORCE

Per LC 5803, the appeals board has continuing jurisdiction to enforce its orders, decisions and awards. LC 5804 does not change this, but only limits the appeals board's jurisdiction to rescind, alter or amend an award within five years from the date of injury.[1] So the appeals board has jurisdiction to enforce its orders, decisions and awards more than five years after the date of injury.

ENFORCEMENT OF INDEMNITY AWARDS

After the award issues, and the five years have passed, indemnity issues are rarely the subject of litigation. Rather, the appeals board usually finds itself adjudicating cases when a dispute arises during the administration of the open-ended award of future medical care. In regard to indemnity, the appeals board can and does take action that does not rescind, alter or amend the award, but does handle issues about how the award is paid.

After five years from the date of injury, the appeals board will hear a petition from the applicant to commute permanent disability payments due to financial hardship.[2] Also, when disputes occur in a medical care award, the board retains jurisdiction to levy penalties[3] and attorney's fees.[4]

---

[1] *Barnes v. WCAB* (2000) 65 CCC 780, 786; *Kauffman v. WCAB* (1969) 34 CCC 373, 380.
[2] *Norwich Union Indemnity v. IAC* (1934) 20 IAC 261.
[3] *City & County of San Francisco v. WCAB (Little)* (2000) 65 CCC 544 (writ denied); *Crawford & Co., Air Terminal Services, Inc. v. WCAB (Babcock)* (2002) 67 CCC 1490 (writ denied).
[4] *Garcia v. IAC* (1958) 23 CCC 149.

In one case, when the applicant received monies from a third-party action more than five years after the date of injury that were the proper subject of credit against indemnity payments, the credit was allowed. The court noted that before the determination of the third party's responsibility, the employer was not entitled to seek any credit. It stated, "It is axiomatic that statutes of limitation should not be interpreted in a fashion resulting in the right to be lost before it accrues."[5] The court also made a key distinction that " ... the Board's order did not affect the merits of the basic decision determining the injured employee's right to benefits or the amount of those benefits. Rather, the Board's order involved issues collateral to the amount of the award."[6]

ENFORCEMENT OF MEDICAL CARE AWARDS

It is not unusual for the WCAB to preside over disputes over medical treatment years, even decades, after the award is made. If the appeals board has awarded further medical treatment, an employer or insurer can be required to furnish treatment more than five years from the date of injury, unless the appeals board terminates liability pursuant to a petition to do so filed within the five-year period.[7] An order by the appeals board enforcing medical treatment is neither a rescission, an alteration nor an amendment of the award.[8]

Normally, the award itself uses language to circumscribe or allow for the scope of medical care. (For a detailed discussion of awards and the scope of medical treatment, see Section 7.23 Judicial Awards.) But sometimes an applicant asks for medical treatment to a body part that was not part of the original award. For example, an applicant with a back injury may stipulate to that and an award may issue. Years later, the applicant and his or her doctor may allege a need for treatment for depression over the severity of the back pain. Is the applicant then entitled to treatment for the psyche problems? Is he or she too late — more than five years after the date of injury — to modify the award? Or is treatment to a body part not recited in the award simply enforcement of an existing award?

A series of writ-denied cases would allow the treatment in this situation. The idea here is that the applicant may not seek further indemnity monies by adding or attempting to re-litigate body part issues more than five years from the date of injury. But medical treatment is a different matter — the restrictions of LC 5410 and its ilk do not apply to this area, as the award allows for medical care as

[5] *Hodge v. WCAB* (1981) 46 CCC 1034, 1040.
[6] *Hodge v. WCAB* (1981) 46 CCC 1034, 1039.
[7] *Barnes v. WCAB* (2000) 65 CCC 780, 787.
[8] *Barnes v. WCAB* (2000) 65 CCC 780, 786; *Kauffman v. WCAB* (1969) 34 CCC 373, 380.

needed to treat the effects of the industrial injury. So there is jurisdiction to award treatment for a condition that is a compensable consequence of the initial industrial injury — even if the condition was not part of the original award, and even if the employee first requests treatment for the condition more than five years after the date of injury.[9]

For example, the appeals board held that an employer was liable for treatment of an applicant's lower back condition and hepatitis C condition even though they were different from the body parts subject to the original award, and even though the applicant did not seek enforcement of the award until more than 25 years after the date of injury. The appeals board noted that the employer was liable for treatment of the hepatitis C even though it was a nonindustrial condition, because treatment of the condition was reasonably required to cure or relieve the effects of the underlying industrial injury. With regard to the back problems, the appeals board found the employer liable because the original injury was a contributing cause of the condition.[10] Note that of course no further indemnity — no benefits other than medical treatment — could be awarded for these additional body parts.

In another case, the appeals board held that an employer was liable for treatment of an applicant's psychiatric condition that was a compensable consequence of the applicant's orthopedic injuries. This was so despite the fact that the need for the new treatment occurred 10 years after the stipulated award. This case was notable mostly because the original award had dismissed all psychiatric claims with prejudice. It was decided by a panel majority that the claim for psychiatric injury had been dismissed at the time of the award, but that the future medical care award had been open-ended to include all medical treatment needed to address the effects of the industrial injury. Therefore, the future medical care award allowed for treatment needed resulting from the industrial injury; there may well have been a connection with the nonindustrial psychiatric problem at the time of the award, but treatment cannot be apportioned. So all that was

[9] *Testa Enterprises v. WCAB (De La Garza)* (2003) 68 CCC 1626 (writ denied); *Pirelli Armstrong Tire Co. v. WCAB (Van Zant)* (2003) 68 CCC 970 (writ denied); *Gardner v. WCAB* (1992) 57 CCC 670 (Court of Appeal decision unpublished in official reports); *Bidwell v. WCAB* (1993) 58 CCC 237 (Court of Appeal decision unpublished in official reports); *Allar v. Fullerton School District*, 2010 Cal. Wrk. Comp. P.D. LEXIS 455; *Del Rosario v. City of Oakland*, 2010 Cal. Wrk. Comp. P.D. LEXIS 574; *City of Los Altos (Police Department) v. WCAB (Verna)* (2012) 77 CCC 640 (writ denied).

[10] *Testa Enterprises v. WCAB (De La Garza)* (2003) 68 CCC 1626 (writ denied). See also *Pirelli Armstrong Tire Co. v. WCAB (Van Zant)* (2003) 68 CCC 970 (writ denied) (appeals board had continuing jurisdiction to award medical treatment to right knee that was a compensable consequence of injury to left knee, even though more than five years had passed since the date of injury); *Liberty Mutual Insurance Co. v. WCAB (Griffin)* (1983) 48 CCC 36 (writ denied) (applicant's cancer derived from lung disorder and thus medical treatment had to be paid for); *City of San Jose v. WCAB* (1985) 50 CCC 79 (writ denied) (medications for sexual dysfunction allowed where they resulted from industrial hypertension).

needed was a showing of some causal link between the back injury and the need for psychiatric treatment at the later date.[11]

The defense should come away from these cases with an understanding that open-ended future medical care awards do not preclude treatment for body parts that are not part of the award. It does seem from these cases that if the language regarding future medical care were carefully circumscribed in the stipulated award, there would be a limiting effect. A practitioner might insist on language in an award that allows for treatment only to the recited body parts or only in accordance with the approval of a given doctor or AME. The California Supreme Court, however, has also indicated that the appeals board also has jurisdiction more than five years from the date of injury to hear an employer's claim that a particular treatment is unnecessary or otherwise unjustified by the terms of the original award.[12] So there is, in any case, no carte blanche.

If there are multiple insurers, the appeals board may continue to enforce the prior stipulated award in which both insurers are liable for an award of future medical care.[13] The appeals board also may order a change of administrator more than five years after the date of injury, as such an order is not considered to be a rescission, alteration or amendment of the prior award, but is considered enforcement of the award.[14]

---

[11] *San Juan Unified School District v. WCAB (Flannery)* (1999) 64 CCC 1181 (writ denied). See also *Gardner v. WCAB* (1992) 57 CCC 670 (an unpublished case) and *Otis Elevator Co. v. WCAB (Bodegraven)* (1984) 49 CCC 637 (writ denied). The dissent in *Flannery* noted that attempts to resurrect the psyche claim as a "compensable consequence" of the admitted orthopedic injury appeared to be an end run around the prior stipulated award, and would have disallowed the treatment. The defense may have done well here to raise LC 5815. Generally speaking, LC 5815 declares that any issue not decided by the board in an award " ... will be deemed to be decided adversely as to the party in whose interest such issue was raised." In *Hogan v. WCAB* (1984) 49 CCC 741 (writ denied) the WCJ failed to make a finding in the F&A on the issue of the need for future medical care. The board found it to be inferred under LC 5815 that no further medical care was necessary. Also, in *Keeley v. IAC (Henry)* (1961) 26 CCC 15, it was expounded that, if an original finding of the board is uncertain, if that finding may be made certain by reference to the record, the finding will be upheld. Likewise, upon claims of insufficiency of the board findings, it has been said that "the appellate court should read into the findings of the Board ... specific findings upon all factual issues that tend to support the award and which have substantial support in the evidence." *Liberty Mutual Insurance Co. v. IAC (Walden)* (1964) 29 CCC 287. But see *Santa Fe Energy Resources v. WCAB (Matney)* (1999) 64 CCC 1428 (writ denied), when an award issued for certain body parts (left forearm, lower back, right hip and right knee). Later, the applicant requested medical treatment for the left knee and left arm. The board rejected the defense argument that LC 5815 required that the applicant lose the issue and held that these body parts had never been considered by the WCJ, and that the case should be presented to the WCJ to decide if these body parts were injured.

[12] *Barnes v. WCAB* (2000) 65 CCC 780, 788.

[13] *Paris v. T.P.I.R./Mark Goodson Prod.*, 2010 Cal. Wrk. Comp. P.D. LEXIS 495.

[14] *See Anadite, Inc. v. WCAB (Aceves)* (2007) 72 CCC 648 (writ denied).

SECTIONS 6.32 THROUGH 6.35 ARE RESERVED FOR FUTURE USE

6.36 STATUTE OF LIMITATIONS AS AN AFFIRMATIVE DEFENSE AND WAIVER

The burden of proving that a claim is barred by the statute of limitations belongs to the employer. This includes the burden to show that estoppel does not apply.[1] Under LC 5405, the employer must prove that the statutory time has elapsed from any and all three of the points designated (that is, that the application for adjudication has not been filed within one year of the date of injury, the date of last indemnity benefits or last date of furnishing of medical benefits).[2] Under LC 5410 and LC 5803, the employer must demonstrate that the petition to reopen was not filed within five years of the date of injury. If the appeals board makes a general finding that the employer failed to sustain its burden of proof regarding the statute of limitations, it will be construed as a finding that no aspect of the claim will be barred by the statute of limitations. This means that if the appeals board finds that the employer failed to prove that an employee's claim is barred by the statute of limitations, it may not subsequently re-litigate the issue against lien claimants.[3]

The statute of limitations must be specifically raised by the employer and does not apply automatically when its conditions are met. The employer may waive its statute of limitations defense by not timely placing this matter in issue. The statute of limitations defense is a "use it or lose it" defense. When a statute of limitations bars a claim, it bars the employee's right to receive compensation. It does not bar the employee's right to file an application for adjudication of claim.

---

[1] *Sidders v. WCAB* (1988) 53 CCC 445.

[2] *Colonial Insurance Co. v. IAC (Nickles)* (1945) 27 Cal. 2d 437; *City and County of San Francisco v. WCAB (Quinn)* (1970) 35 CCC 390, 398.

[3] *Kaiser Foundation Hospitals v. WCAB (Kramer)* (1978) 43 CCC 661.

The employee has a right to file a claim for workers' compensation regardless of whether the claim is filed within the stated statutory period or beyond the stated time. What is the point of this? The employer may waive a statute of limitations defense by not presenting it before the submission of the cause for decision (LC 5409). When a statute of limitations defense is waived, an employee may be awarded benefits that otherwise would have been barred by the statute of limitations. But when the employer has prevailed on a statute of limitations defense, the WCAB does not have authority to award compensation after the statute of limitations has expired. A successful defense will defeat a claim, even in cases in which the employee would have otherwise prevailed on the merits.

So then, what constitutes waiver of the defense? First, per LC 5500, an answer is required after an application has been filed. The answer "shall be in writing" and shall delineate "all issues of disagreement." Per LC 5505, "evidence on matters not pleaded by answer shall be allowed only upon the terms and conditions imposed by the appeals board or referee holding the hearing." This statutory provision is restated in WCAB Rules of Practice and Procedure (`http://www.dir.ca.gov/wcab/WCABRulemaking.html`). Per CCR 10484, additional matters can be pleaded after the answer is filed, but "evidence on matters not pleaded by answer" will be allowed only at the discretion of the appeals board. If a statute of limitations defense is not raised in an answer or an answer is not filed, the employer risks waiving this defense. The employer has an additional opportunity in the process of litigation to raise the defense, but further success is dependent upon the judge's acquiescence at some later date. So the employer should raise the issue in its answer any time the defense appears appropriate.

Per LC 5409, the statute of limitations is an affirmative defense that operates to bar the remedy and not to extinguish the right of the employee. The defense may be waived if not presented before the submission of the case for decision.[4] CCR 10301 defines "submission" as "the closing of the record to the receipt of further evidence or argument." The appeals board has held that time for submission of a statute of limitations issue is at the time of the mandatory settlement conference

[4] *See Tarver (Page) v. WCAB* (1972) 37 CCC 483 (Court of Appeal opinion unpublished in official reports) (claim of new and further disability filed five years after the date of injury allowed when defendant did not raise statute of limitations under LC 5410 and LC 5803); *Pagones v. IAC (Hawkins)* (1937) 2 CCC 159 (waiver found when defense asserted that the statute of limitations was made orally at a hearing, but there was no proof of that); *City of Los Angeles v. WCAB (Johnson)* (2009) 74 CCC 1 (Court of Appeal opinion unpublished in official reports) (employer waived statute of limitations defense by not raising it in a timely fashion).

(MSC), and if the issue is not timely raised, it will be deemed waived.[5] As discussed further in Chapter 15, issues not raised at the time of the MSC are generally waived. Nevertheless, this remains in the WCJ's discretion; he or she has the power to raise the issue *sua sponte* (on the court's own motion) if it appears on its face that the claim is barred, even at the time of trial.[6] This is not a favored practice, however, and almost never occurs.

In an unpublished opinion, the Court of Appeal held that an employer did not waive the statute of limitations when it pleaded the defense in its answer, listed it as a disputed issue on the MSC statement, raised the issue orally at the MSC and again at trial, even though it was omitted on the settlement conference summary and trial issue sheet.[7] In another unpublished opinion, the Court of Appeal held that an employer did not waive the statute of limitations defense by raising it for the first time on reconsideration, when the WCJ unilaterally amended the applicant's cumulative trauma injury date after trial, and the defense was not viable before the WCJ issued his decision.[8] The appeals board has also held that a statute of limitations defense is not waived if the issue is raised on the first day of trial without an objection by the applicant.[9] But another unpublished opinion has held that the statute of limitations defense was waived when it was not mentioned at the MSC or trial, even though the defendant raised the issue in its answer and again in its DOR.[10]

In one case, it was held that letters extending the statute of limitations for a finite period of time did not constitute a waiver of the defense or estop the defendant from raising the statute.[11]

[5] *Memorial Hospital Association v. WCAB (Caldwell)* (1995) 60 CCC 779 (writ denied). See also *K-Mart/KM Administrators v. WCAB (Nelson)* (1995) 60 CCC 634 (writ denied) (waiver found when statute of limitations not raised until the day of trial).
[6] *Verwoerd v. WCAB* (1973) 38 CCC 411 (writ denied).
[7] *Sierra Pacific Services v. WCAB (Richardson)* (1994) 59 CCC 864 (Court of Appeal opinion unpublished in official reports).
[8] *Provigo Corp. v. WCAB (Heath)* (1995) 60 CCC 831 (Court of Appeal opinion unpublished in official reports).
[9] *Csapo v. WCAB* (1999) 65 CCC 71 (writ denied).
[10] *Guild v. WCAB* (1999) 64 CCC 175 (Court of Appeal opinion unpublished in official reports).
[11] *Adams v. WCAB* (2005) 70 CCC 881 (writ denied). See also *Padgett v. AON Corp.*, 2011 Cal. Wrk. Comp. P.D. LEXIS 237 (WCAB found no clear and convincing evidence that defendant intentionally relinquished its right to assert the statute of limitations defense).

6.37 TOLLING WHILE UNDER SUBMISSION TO INFORMATION AND ASSISTANCE OFFICER

LC 5454 provides for the tolling of all statutes of limitations when a matter is submitted to an I&A officer "for the period that the matter is under consideration by the information and assistance officer, and for 60 days following the issuance of his or her recommendation." This Labor Code statute is followed up by CCR 9928(d), which provides that in order to toll the statute of limitations pursuant to LC 5454, the officer must "notify in writing all parties to any misunderstanding, dispute or controversy of the fact that said Information and Assistance Officer has taken under consideration the misunderstanding, dispute or controversy submitted to him or her for a recommendation." In practice, tolling for this reason is rarely seen.

6.38 EXTENSION OF TIME FOR SPECIAL CASES

Certain classifications of people are special when it comes to the statute of limitations. Their special status confers the right to toll the statute of limitations for a period of time.

MINORS AND INCOMPETENTS

Per LC 5408, the statute of limitations does not run against anyone younger than 18 years of age or any incompetent unless and until a guardian or conservator of the estate or trustee is appointed. The California Supreme Court has stated, "Tolling provisions for minors 'effectuate a deep and long recognized principle of the common law and of this state: children are to be protected during their minority from the destruction of their rights by the running of the statute of limitations.' [citation.] 'Because a minor does not have the understanding or experience of an adult, and because a minor may not bring an action except through a guardian [citation], special safeguards [i.e., tolling provisions] are required to protect the minor's right of action.'" The court concluded that the purpose of LC 5408 is to protect minors and incompetent persons by putting them on equal footing with competent adult litigants, but it is not intended to give such applicants substantive rights that are not available to competent adults.[1]

[1] *Massey v. WCAB* (1993) 58 CCC 367, 372.

Appointment of Trustee or Guardian Ad Litem

The appeals board may appoint a trustee or guardian *ad litem* to appear for and represent any minor or incompetent and to receive and disburse compensation payments for the benefit of such minor or incompetent and his family (LC 5307.5 and LC 5408). If an applicant is a minor or incompetent, the application for adjudication filed with the appeals board must be accompanied by a petition for appointment of a guardian *ad litem* and trustee. When the minor has the right of nomination, the nomination shall be included in the petition (CCR 10402). If an employer has doubt as to whether the employee is competent, the employer may request a guardian to be appointed in order to protect a subsequent award from an attack that the proceedings were brought by or against an incompetent person who was not properly represented in court.[2]

Determining Incompetency

The term incompetent is not defined in LC 5408. The appeals board in one case identified incompetency as "not insanity, but rather inability to properly manage or take care of oneself or property without assistance."[3] This seems to indicate a very lazy standard that allows individual cases to fall well within the discretion of the individual WCJ. The term, however, refers to an applicant's mental capacity rather than physical capacity. So it has been held that the term does not define an applicant who is physically incapacitated but mentally competent.[4]

Medical evidence must be received to establish that an applicant is incompetent.[5] If an applicant is sufficiently psychologically impaired such that he or she is incapable or substantially compromised, the appeals board will toll the statute of limitations.[6] Per LC 5408, the appeals board has jurisdiction to determine the fact of the minority or incompetency of any injured employee.[7] If there is conflicting evidence as to whether an applicant is incompetent, the appeals board must resolve the conflict, and its findings will be upheld if supported by substantial evidence.[8]

---

[2] *Western Pipe and Steel Co. of California v. IAC (Fitzgerald)* (1926) 79 Cal. App. 215, 219; *Sun Indemnity Co. of New York v. IAC (McKinney)* (1948) 13 CCC 82, 85.

[3] *County of Santa Clara v. WCAB (McMonagle)* (1992) 57 CCC 377 (writ denied).

[4] *Francisco v. IAC* (1923) 192 Cal. 635; *Fox v. IAC* (1943) 8 CCC 194 (writ denied).

[5] *Sun Indemnity Co. of New York v. IAC (McKinney)* (1948) 13 CCC 82, 85; *Lamin v. City of Los Angeles, Police Department* (2004) 69 CCC 1002 (panel decision).

[6] *County of San Bernardino v. WCAB (Spencer)* (1996) 61 CCC 860 (writ denied); *Feeley v. Southern Pacific Transportation Co.* (1991) 234 Cal. 3d 949.

[7] This means that the state court may not interfere in the issue. *Callejo v. WCAB (Alcala)* (1977) 42 CCC 65 (writ denied).

[8] *Sun Indemnity Co. of New York v. IAC (McKinney)* (1948) 13 CCC 82, 85.

Application of the Statute of Limitations to Minors and Incompetents

The statute of limitations runs from the date of the appointment, or in the case of minors, the date the applicant turns 18.[9] For example, if a one-year statute of limitations would otherwise apply, the year begins the date a minor has his 18th birthday or a guardian *ad litem* is appointed, whichever comes first.[10] [11]

Sometimes an award issues after which an applicant is found during a hearing to have been a minor or to have been otherwise incompetent. In such cases, the award can be reopened for good cause. Also, the applicant may become incompetent after the award, within the five years from the date of injury, and thus be unable to file a timely petition to reopen. An applicant may, of course, file a petition to reopen any time within five years from the date of injury pursuant to LC 5804. But if the statutory period has expired, the applicant may file a petition to reopen; the statutes are tolled during the period of incompetence. So if an applicant receives an award, and becomes incompetent within the five years, the statute is tolled until he or she becomes competent or until a guardian is appointed. The cases on point allow for a reasonable period in which to file; this probably means that the time left over from the five-year period begins to run again.[12] Unfortunately, the courts have yet to clearly define a standard for this scenario.

Application of the Statute of Limitations for Death Benefits to Minors and Incompetents

In cases involving death benefits, LC 5406 provides that no proceedings to collect death benefits may be commenced more than 240 weeks from the date of injury. (Death benefits are covered in depth in Chapter 12.) The California Supreme Court has held that LC 5408 does not toll the 240-week period for minor claimants because it is a qualifying condition in the exercise of any right to death

---

[9] *Western Pipe and Steel Co. of California v. IAC (Fitzgerald)* (1926) 79 Cal. App. 215, 219; *Fogarty v. DIR* (1928) 206 Cal. 102; *Jordan v. IAC (Sears)* (1940) 5 CCC 194; *Royal Indemnity Co. v. IAC (Hitchcock)* (1948) 13 CCC 104.

[10] *Johnson v. Insurance Co. of North America* (1982) 10 CWCR 255 (panel decision). See also *Loveland v. WCAB* (1987) 52 CCC 401 (writ denied) (applicant who was injured when he was 17, but did not file an application for workers' compensation benefits until more than a year after he turned 18, was barred by the statute of limitations).

[11] In *Dulin v. IAC* (1944) 9 CCC 190, the court held that although a civil court may appoint a trustee or guardian *ad litem*, the statute of limitations does run until the appeals board makes an appointment. But as noted in *Massey v. WCAB* (1993) 58 CCC 367, LC 5408 has been amended, so *Dulin* is questionable on this point.

[12] *Gouanillou v. IAC* (1920) 184 Cal. 418; *Abbott v. IAC* (1936) 1 CCC 101.

benefits.[13] That is, the 240-week period between the injury and death simply determines whether any death benefit claim can be filed. If the employee dies more than 240 weeks from the date of injury, no claim for death benefits may be filed regardless of whether the applicant is a minor or incompetent. But if the employee dies within the 240-week period, the unexpired portion of the 240-week period begins to run against potential claimants and is subject to the tolling provisions of LC 5408.[14]

One employee sustained an injury May 5, 1999 and died May 15, 2003. A guardian was appointed for a minor applicant Aug. 25, 2003, but an application for death benefits was not filed until March 22, 2006. The appeals board held that the application for death benefits was untimely. The appeals board noted that the injured worker died approximately 200 weeks after her date of injury, so the minor applicant accrued a claim to the unexpired 40 weeks. LC 5408 tolled the statute of limitations until the date a guardian was appointed, Aug. 25, 2003, and the limitations period of LC 5406 began running again. So the application filed March 22, 2006 was untimely because it was filed more than 40 weeks after Aug. 25, 2003.[15]

TOLLING DURING MILITARY SERVICE

An employee who enters military service might be able to maintain that estoppel should apply during the period of service. The Soldiers and Sailors Civil Relief Act of 1940 (50 U.S.C. App. 525) allows for the suspension of any action, or the tolling of a statute of limitations, for a person serving in the United States armed forces.[16]

APPLICATION OF CIVIL PROCEDURE CODES

Generally, going to jail does not toll the statute of limitations; it is not legal incompetence.[17] Extensions provided in the California Code of Civil Procedure do not apply to workers' compensation proceedings, which has its own statutes

---

[13] *Massey v. WCAB* (1993) 58 CCC 367, 372.

[14] *Massey v. WCAB* (1993) 58 CCC 367, 372. *Massey* overrules the decisions of *Fisher v. WCAB* (1976) 41 CCC 677 and *Roblyer v. WCAB* (1976) 41 CCC 669, in addition to cases such as *Consolidated Freightways v. WCAB (Howell)* (1967) 32 CCC 320 (writ denied); *City of Oakland v. IAC (Barnett)* (1965) 30 CCC 398 (writ denied); *City of Los Angeles v. IAC (White)* (1964) 29 CCC 226 (writ denied).

[15] *Gonzales v. WCAB* (2008) 73 CCC 519 (writ denied). See also *Earley v. WCAB* (2003) 68 CCC 1707 (writ denied); *Gallegos v. WCAB* (1997) 62 CCC 1714 (writ denied).

[16] Of perhaps limited precedential value, due to the poor reporting, is the case of *Smethurst v. Schoonover* (1942) 8 CCC 38, in which an action was suspended, apparently because a key witness had joined the military.

[17] *Edwards v. IAC* (1942) 7 CCC 276 (writ denied); *California Contractors Network, Inc. v. WCAB (Hanss)* (2009) 74 CCC 780 (writ denied).

of limitations.[18] Unlike in civil cases, being absent from the state does not toll the statute of limitations in workers' compensation.[19]

[18] *Boyd v. WCAB* (1991) 56 CCC 219 (writ denied) refusing to apply CCP 352.
[19] Compare the federal case of *Abramson v. Brownstein* (9th Cir. 1990) 897 F. 2d 389 with *Pratali v. Gates* (1992) 4 Cal. App. 4th 632. In line with the *Boyd* case above, CCP 351 should not apply to California workers' compensation cases.

6.39 CLAIMS AGAINST MULTIPLE EMPLOYERS

In some cases, multiple employers may be responsible for an applicant's industrial injury. This situation generally occurs when an applicant files a cumulative trauma claim and two or more employers are liable within the statutory period defined in LC 5500.5. The courts have held that the filing of the application satisfies the statute of limitations only as to the employer who is named in the application. An applicant may not amend a claim to add additional employers beyond the time limitations in LC 5405 when the additional employers are not estopped from relying on the defense.[1] So the timely filing of an application against one employer will not bar another employer from asserting the statute of limitations.

The courts, however, have also held that the statute of limitations runs from the last payment of *any* compensation and not from the last payment by the party sought to be joined in the proceedings.[2] So an employer may be joined in a claim within one year of the last payment of disability or medical treatment made by another party. And in cases of cumulative trauma, the joinder rights of the named employer are not governed by LC 5405, but by LC 5500.5. That section allows a named employer to join other employers and pursue supplemental proceedings to apportion liability within one year following an award or

---

[1] See *Ingram v. DIR (Stoolfire)* (1930) 208 Cal. 633; *Bryant v. WCAB (Williams)* (1998) 63 CCC 286 (writ denied). But see *National Union Fire Insurance Co. v. WCAB (De La Rosa)* (2008) 73 CCC 1722 (writ denied).
[2] *SCIF v. IAC (Dean)* (1946) 11 CCC 30; *SCIF v. IAC (Rodgers)* (1945) 10 CCC 96.

settlement.[3] Joinder and contribution are discussed in depth in Section 5.8 Contribution Among Defendants.

[3] See *McCleary v. WCAB* (1994) 59 CCC 841 (Court of Appeal opinion unpublished in official reports) (employee barred from joining other defendants pursuant to LC 5405, but court noted that joinder rights of named employers were governed by LC 5500.5 rather than LC 5405).

6.40 DOCTRINE OF LACHES

Laches is a doctrine of law similar to the statute of limitations in that it bars a claim because of a delay in pursuing it. But unlike the statute of limitations, which bars a claim after a statutorily specified period of time, the doctrine of laches provides a defense to a claim in which a long delay in asserting the right or claim has prejudiced the adverse party.[1] So a claim not barred by the statute of limitations might be barred by the doctrine of laches.

Laches is an ancient legal doctrine. Historically and today it is a doctrine generally available only in cases involving equitable relief; that is, it pertains to remedies requiring parties to perform certain acts, rather than actions at law that seek monetary damages.[2] Several unpublished cases have questioned whether the defense is available in workers' compensation at all.[3] Nevertheless, the appeals board has held that laches is a valid defense in workers' compensation proceedings[4] and the defense has been discussed in several appeals board decisions. Furthermore, the California Supreme Court, in a footnote, has indicated that laches may be a viable defense in workers' compensation cases.[5] At present, it appears to be available to the defense.

---

[1] *Insurance Co. of the West v. WCAB (Morris)* (2002) 68 CCC 778 (writ denied).

[2] *Doerflinger v. WCAB* (1994) 59 CCC 834, 837 fn. 3 (Court of Appeal opinion unpublished in official reports).

[3] See *City and County of San Francisco v. WCAB (Powell)* (1967) 32 CCC 86 (Court of Appeal opinion unpublished in official reports); *Doerflinger v. WCAB* (1994) 59 CCC 834 (Court of Appeal opinion unpublished in official reports); *Mission Linen Supply v. WCAB* (1994) 59 CCC 849 (Court of Appeal opinion unpublished in official reports).

[4] See *Kaiser Foundation Hospitals/Permanente Medical Group v. WCAB (Valencia)* (1976) 41 CCC 730 (writ denied).

[5] *Kaiser Foundation Hospitals, Permanente Medical Group v. WCAB (Martin)* (1985) 50 CCC 411, fn. 11.

Laches is designed to stop parties from unreasonably delaying action in a case, and thereby hurting the chances of the opposing side to defend the case. In order to use the doctrine of laches to bar a claim, the party asserting the defense must demonstrate both an inexcusable delay and prejudice to the opposing party caused by the delay.[6] The doctrine of laches has been held inapplicable when there is only a few months delay.[7] But the appeals board has applied the doctrine when the delay was for six and seven years.[8]

Nevertheless, a delay alone does not constitute laches, as the key component to the laches defense is the prejudice resulting from the delay. Laches will bar a claim only if prejudice is demonstrated.[9] Prejudice is not presumed, it must be affirmatively demonstrated.[10] The defense is not viable when the party asserting the defense benefits from the other party's inactivity.[11]

Prejudice for the purposes of a laches defense has not been defined in any appeals board case. But in one case, the appeals board found the requisite prejudice and barred a claim for contribution by one insurer against another insurer using the doctrine of laches. In that case, an insurer admitted to a specific injury and cumulative injury, and the claim was resolved by F&A on Aug. 18, 1990. On Aug. 14, 1991, the insurer sought to join other insurance companies after concluding that it did not have coverage during the period of the cumulative injury. The WCJ denied relief on the grounds of laches. The WCJ noted that the insurer admitted coverage throughout the case, and then more than five years from the date of injury, claimed that it did not have coverage and attempted to shift coverage to other carriers. The WCJ found the situation prejudicial to the other carriers because they had absolutely no opportunity to participate in discovery, defend its interest at trial, call witnesses, obtain medical

[6] *Laing v. Occidental Life Insurance Co. of California* (1966) 31 CCC 498, 505. See *Morales v. Maintenance Match Inc.*, 2010 Cal. Wrk. Comp. P.D. LEXIS 489 (laches did not apply to bar CIGA's claim because solvent carrier failed to establish that CIGA's seven-year delay in seeking to join carrier was prejudicial).
[7] See *Aubry v. WCAB* (1993) 58 CCC 462 (writ denied).
[8] See *Kaiser Foundation Hospitals/Permanente Medical Group v. WCAB (Valencia)* (1976) 41 CCC 730 (writ denied); *Bell v. WCAB* (1987) 52 CCC 72 (writ denied).
[9] See *Travelers Indemnity Co. v. WCAB (Morales)* (2011) 76 CCC 601 (writ denied). See also *Brainard v. WCAB* (2003) 68 CCC 365 (Court of Appeal opinion unpublished in official reports); *New Century Chamber Orchestra v. WCAB (Simonds)* (2003) 69 CCC 421 (writ denied); *Jackson v. WCAB* (1981) 46 CCC 816 (writ denied); *Canas v. State of California*, 2009 Cal. Wrk. Comp. P.D. LEXIS 495; *Jaime v. Remedy Temp, Inc.*, 2011 Cal. Wrk. Comp. P.D. LEXIS 436.
[10] *Piscioneri v. City of Ontario* (2002) 95 Cal. App. 4th 1037, 1050. See *Godbolt v. Wherehouse Entertainment*, 2012 Cal. Wrk. Comp. P.D. LEXIS 69; *Kalous v. Shimmel, Hillshafer & Loewenthal*, 2012 Cal. Wrk. Comp. P.D. LEXIS 298.
[11] See *Ramsey v. WCAB* (1999) 64 CCC 1422 (writ denied).

reports or do anything at all until long after the outcome of the case had been decided.[12]

In addition, laches is only available when the party asserting the defense has "clean hands." For example, a lien claim filed more than five months after a compromise and release was not barred by the doctrine of laches because the defendant had knowledge of the potential lien claims, had failed to investigate them, failed to notify lien claimants of an applicant's workers' compensation claim, failed to disclose potential liens at the time of approval of a stipulated award or at the time of the C&R and had agreed to "pay all unpaid balances, for which there exists no bona fide dispute over defendant's liability."[13] In another case, the appeals board held that an employer could not rely on the laches defense when it failed to give the applicant notice of his right to workers' compensation benefits.[14]

The defense of laches must be raised at a mandatory settlement conference or it will be deemed to be waived.[15] The defense may not be raised in a trial brief if it was not raised at the MSC.[16]

---

[12] *Commercial Union Insurance Co. v. WCAB* (1995) 60 CCC 1026 (writ denied). But see *Wright v. WCAB* (2005) 70 CCC 95 (writ denied) (doctrine of laches barred applicant's applications for adjudication filed on 4/12/2004 related to industrial injuries on 10/28/62 and 5/12/65, because the applicant did nothing to prosecute claims for 34 years, defendants were severely prejudiced because insurer's file was closed in 1970, insurer's file was destroyed, and claims adjuster was deceased, and WCAB was prejudiced because it would be unable to determine which body parts applicant injured or the nature and extent of applicant's disability or need for medical treatment when medical records for the 1962 and 1965 injuries had been destroyed).

[13] *K-Mart v. WCAB (Acevedo)* (2003) 68 CCC 494 (writ denied). See also *Truck Insurance Exchange v. WCAB (Cyr-Remus)* (1997) 62 CCC 240 (writ denied) (laches not applicable when defendant did not serve lien claimant with C&R); *Town of Hillsborough v. WCAB (Sheehan)* (1996) 61 CCC 528 (writ denied) (laches did not bar lien claim when defendant must have known about the lien claim and did nothing); *Bethlehem Steel Corp. v. WCAB* (1985) 50 CCC 186 (writ denied) (lien claim not barred by laches when the employer failed to make any effort to pay for medical treatment despite its knowledge of such treatment); *Barrett Business Services, Inc. v. WCAB (Hathcock)*, 2012 Cal. Wrk. Comp. LEXIS 151 (writ denied) (laches did not apply when defendant did not have clean hands or show prejudice). But see *Blue Cross v. WCAB (Spratt)* (1997) 63 CCC 55 (writ denied).

[14] *New York Yankees v. WCAB (Montefusco)* (2001) 66 CCC 291 (writ denied).

[15] *Bowie v. WCAB* (1999) 65 CCC 59 (writ denied).

[16] *The Home Depot v. WCAB (O'Grady)* (2005) 70 CCC 1169 (writ denied).

6.41 RELAXED RESTRICTIONS FOR FILING DOCUMENTS SUBJECT TO THE STATUTE OF LIMITATIONS

Per CCR 10397, an application for adjudication of claim, a petition for reconsideration, a petition to reopen or any other petition or document subject to a statute of limitations or a jurisdictional time limitation will not be rejected for filing solely on the basis that:

1. The document is not filed in the proper office of the Workers' Compensation Appeals Board.[1]
2. The document has been submitted without the proper form, or it has been submitted with a form that is either incomplete or contains inaccurate information.
3. The document has not been submitted with the required document cover sheet and/or document separator sheet(s), or it has been submitted with a document cover sheet and/or document separator sheet(s) not containing all of the required information (CCR 10397(a)).

---

[1] Even before the adoption of CCR 10397 in 2008, the appeals board held that an application is timely filed for the purposes of the statute of limitations even if it is filed at the wrong office of the appeals board. See *Noble v. City of Oakland Police Department* (1982) 47 CCC 1 (appeals board *en banc*); *Main Tool & Die, Inc. v. WCAB (Allen)* (1999) 64 CCC 1488 (writ denied). Petitions for reconsideration were not rejected just because the documents were filed in the wrong place. See *County of Orange v. WCAB (Lean)* (2008) 73 CCC 1 (Court of Appeal opinion not published in official reports); *Scott Pontiac GMC v. WCAB (Olsen)* (2007) 72 CCC 346 (Court of Appeal opinion unpublished in official reports). In one unpublished case, the appellate court applied CCR 10397 to a petition to reopen filed before it was adopted, explaining that CCR 10397 was a procedural change that may be applied to a pending action. *Contreras v. WCAB* (2012) 77 CCC 1 (Court of Appeal opinion unpublished in official reports). In compliance with this decision, the appeals board returned the case to the trial level for further proceedings. *Contreras v. M&C Farm Labor,* 2012 Cal. Wrk. Comp. P.D. LEXIS 229.

But a document subject to a statute of limitations or a jurisdictional time limitation may be rejected for filing if it does not contain information sufficient to establish the case or cases to which the document relates or, if it is a case-opening document, sufficient information to open an adjudication file. If a document is rejected on the grounds that it does not contain sufficient information, the document is to be returned to the filing party with a notice of document discrepancy that it has not been accepted for filing. The notice must specify the nature of the discrepancy and the date of the attempted filing, and also state that the party has 15 days from the service of the notice to correct the discrepancy and resubmit the document for filing. If the document is corrected and resubmitted within 15 days, or at a later date upon a showing of good cause, it will be deemed filed as of the original date of submission (CCR 10397(b)).

Nothing in CCR 10397 precludes the discretionary or conditional acceptance of a filed document subject to a statute of limitations or a jurisdictional time limitation, even if it does not contain information sufficient to establish the case or cases to which the document relates or, if it is a case-opening document, sufficient information to open an adjudication file (CCR 10397(d)).

When a document subject to a statute of limitations or a jurisdictional time limitation has been accepted for filing in accordance with CCR 10397, but it cannot be processed by EAMS, a copy of the filed document may be served on the filing party or lien claimant, together with a notice of document discrepancy. The notice may specify the nature of the discrepancy and request that the party correct the discrepancy within 15 days after service of the notice. But a failure to timely correct the discrepancy will not nullify the acceptance of the document for filing (CCR 10397(e)).

Nothing in CCR 10397 will be deemed to excuse noncompliance with any other provisions of the rules of the appeals board. Any such noncompliance may still be a basis for the imposition of sanctions under LC 5813 and CCR 10561 (CCR 10397(f)).

According to the final statement of reasons for CCR 10397, the regulation was adopted in response to concerns regarding both the rejection of improperly filed or misfiled documents and the absence of notification to the filing party of the rejection so that corrective action could be taken. It was adopted to "minimize potential due process problems, not only relating to documents filed in the wrong place [citations], but also relating to filing defects that may not be the fault of the filer. [citation.]" CCR 10397, however, is limited only to documents that are subject to the statute of limitations or a jurisdictional time limitation. So these documents would not be affected by the rule:

1. noncase-opening settlements;
2. medical reports and medical-legal reports;
3. answers to applications and petitions;
4. amended lien claims; and
5. declarations of readiness and objections to them.[2]

[2] See http://www.dir.ca.gov/WCAB/WCABProposedRegulations/WCAB_RulesofPracticeandProcedure/WCAB_FSOR.doc, p. 14.

SECTIONS 6.42 THROUGH 6.44 ARE RESERVED FOR FUTURE USE

6.45 STATUTE OF LIMITATIONS FOR CLAIMS AGAINST THE SUBSEQUENT INJURIES BENEFITS TRUST FUND

There is no statute of limitations for filing a claim against the Subsequent Injuries Benefits Trust Fund (SIBTF). It's a state fund that was instituted to help workers with serious injuries caused by both industrial and nonindustrial factors who, as a result, are deprived of substantial permanent disability. This is discussed in Section 10.70 Subsequent Injuries Benefits Trust Fund.

Nevertheless, in *SIF v. WCAB (Talcott),*[1] the California Supreme Court held that an employee was not necessarily limited to five years from the date of injury as required by LC 5410. This was because if LC 5410 applied to claims against the fund, an employee may lose his or her cause of action even before the board is able to determine the facts on which the fund's liability is predicated. *Talcott* held that the statute of limitations for a claim against the fund is based solely on a reasonableness standard. That is, an employee has a reasonable time after he knows or should have known that there is a substantial likelihood that he will become entitled to benefits from the fund to file against it or join it in a proceeding.[2] If an employee knew or reasonably should have known before the expiration of the five-year period set forth in LC 5410 that there was a substantial

[1] (1970) 35 CCC 80, 84-87.
[2] *SIF v. WCAB (Talcott)* (1970) 35 CCC 80, 87; *SIF v. WCAB (Baca)* (1970) 35 CCC 94, 95. Before *Talcott,* the law was that the limitations applicable to proceedings against the fund were the same as those against the employer under LC 5410 and LC 5405. See *SIF v. IAC (Patterson)* (1952) 17 CCC 142; *SIF v. IAC (Ferguson)* (1960) 25 CCC 26; *SIF v. IAC (Clubb)* (1957) 22 CCC 240; *SIF v. IAC (Pranzitelli)* (1957) 22 CCC 132; *SIF v. IAC (Busch)* (1962) 27 CCC 14; *Lahti v. WCAB* (1966) 31 CCC 295 (writ denied); *SIF v. WCAB (Morgan)* (1966) 31 CCC 264 (writ denied).

likelihood that he would have a claim against the fund but did not file one, the claim will be barred.[3]

Whether an applicant should be reasonably deemed to have known that there was a substantial likelihood that he or she would be entitled to subsequent injuries benefits is a question of fact for the appeals board. The appeals board also must determine whether the applicant delayed an unreasonable time in filing subsequent injuries benefits after he or she was aware, from the appeals board's finding on the issue of permanent disability, that the fund probably would be liable.[4]

The courts have not fully outlined what constitutes a reasonable time but have held that claims against the fund filed five weeks[5] and two months[6] after receiving a permanent disability rating were reasonable. In one case, a claim filed seven months after the WCJ found the applicant's psychiatric condition was not a compensable consequence of her spinal injury was considered timely.[7] But in one case, an employee's claim was barred when it was filed more than one year after the last furnishing of compensation benefits; more than five years from the date of injury; and more than three years after the employee knew or should have known that he had a claim against the fund.[8]

[3] *SIF v. WCAB (Baca)* (1970) 35 CCC 94, 95; *SIF v. WCAB (Pullum)* (1970) 35 CCC 96, 97; *Shields v. WCAB* (1977) 42 CCC 77 (writ denied); *Jenkins v. WCAB* (1985) 50 CCC 593 (writ denied).

[4] *SIF v. WCAB (Woodburn)* (1970) 35 CCC 98, 99; *Formhals v. WCAB* (1972) 37 CCC 43 (Court of Appeal opinion unpublished in official reports).

[5] *SIF v. WCAB (Talcott)* (1970) 35 CCC 80.

[6] *SIF v. WCAB (Pullum)* (1970) 35 CCC 96, 97.

[7] *Duncan v. WCAB (May)* (2010) 75 CCC 1195 (writ denied).

[8] *Moore v. WCAB (Johnson)* (1977) 42 CCC 98 (writ denied).

6.46 STATUTE OF LIMITATIONS FOR CLAIMS UNDER LC 132a

LC 132a prohibits discrimination against workers who are injured in the course of employment. In workers' compensation practice, a petition for discrimination benefits under LC 132a is procedurally separate and distinct from an application for ordinary benefits.[1] Proceedings for increased compensation and/or for reinstatement and reimbursement for lost wages and work benefits under LC 132a are instituted by filing an appropriate petition with the appeals board (LC 132a(4)). LC 132a claims in general are handled in depth in Chapter 11 commencing with Section 11.7 Importance of LC 132a.

REQUIREMENTS FOR A PETITION UNDER LC 132a

CCR 10447 establishes the requirements for a petition under LC 132a. The petition must specify in detail the nature of each violation alleged and the facts supporting it. The petition must also state the relief sought. Each alleged violation must be pleaded separately so that the employer and the appeals board may be fully advised of the specific basis on which the charge is founded (CCR 10447). An alleged violation that was not raised in the petition may not be a basis for a finding of an LC 132a violation.[2]

A petition under LC 132a may be rejected by the appeals board if it does not put the parties and the appeals board on notice as to the specific bases on which the

[1] *Morehouse v. WCAB* (1984) 49 CCC 313, 318.
[2] *Duckson v. City of Long Beach* (1983) 48 CCC 511 (panel decision); *Duckson v. WCAB* (1984) 49 CCC 11 (writ denied).

LC 132a claim is founded.[3] But as long as the petition describes the alleged discrimination sufficiently, deviations in form will not cause it to be rejected. In one case, a petition was filed that mistakenly alleged termination at the hands of the third-party administrator rather than the employer itself. But the basis for the petition was spelled out, the employer was clearly on notice and the petition was allowed to stand.[4]

TIME LIMITS FOR FILING A PETITION UNDER LC 132a

A petition for penalties for discrimination under LC 132a "may not be commenced more than one year from the date of the discriminatory act or the date of termination of the employee" (LC 132a(4)). The date of termination for the purposes of LC 132a is the date of actual termination, not the date the employee received notice of termination.[5] The appeals board has held that the one-year period does not extend through the date the applicant exhausted the appeals process within the employer's organization — the date of the discriminatory act controls.[6] But the appeals board has held that when an employer engages in a discriminatory course of conduct, a claim filed within one year of the course of conduct is timely.[7]

A series of unpublished cases have elaborated on the one-year statute of limitations for filing an LC 132a claim, although none of them is controlling or even citable. In one case, the court held that a timely filed skeletal petition that was amended by a more specific pleading filed more than five years after the date of termination was not barred by the one-year period in LC 132a.[8] But in another opinion, the court held that an applicant could not amend a timely filed petition for penalties under LC 132a to include additional acts. The original petition had described one act of alleged discrimination, and the applicant wished to amend to add additional acts of discrimination. These additional acts took place more than a year before the proposed amendment. The court based its decision on CCR 10447, which requires applicant to specifically plead each violation in detail.[9]

---

[3] *Haynes v. WCAB* (1998) 63 CCC 1071 (writ denied).
[4] *San Diego Transit Corp. v. WCAB (Mayer)* (2007) 72 CCC 720 (writ denied).
[5] *St. Cyr v. WCAB* (1987) 52 CCC 528 (LC 132a claim timely when an employee was advised in a letter dated March 6, 1984 that she would be terminated effective March 15, 1984 and the claim was filed on March 15, 1985).
[6] *Jackson v. WCAB* (2004) 69 CCC 1035 (writ denied).
[7] *County of Los Angeles/Fire Department v. WCAB (Dulan)* (2000) 65 CCC 166 (writ denied); *Chevron Products Co. v. WCAB (Pernell)* (2004) 70 CCC 228 (writ denied).
[8] *Riddle v. WCAB* (1995) 60 CCC 170 (Court of Appeal opinion unpublished in official reports).
[9] *Alicea v. WCAB* (1999) 64 CCC 1213 (Court of Appeal opinion unpublished in official reports).

In one unpublished opinion, the court held that the statute of limitations for filing an LC 132a claim was tolled where the applicant had filed a civil action for wrongful discharge, and the LC 132a claim was timely when it was filed within two months after the demurrer to his civil action had been sustained.[10] Subsequently, the appeals board held that the statute of limitations for filing a claim under LC 132a was not tolled by timely filing a complaint in civil court alleging wrongful termination.[11]

In another unpublished opinion, an applicant timely filed an LC 132a claim but did not take any action on the claim until seven years later. The employer argued that the claim was barred by the doctrine of laches. But the court held that the claim was not barred because the employer provided no evidence that it was prejudiced by the delay in the applicant's prosecution of the LC 132a claim.[12] In any case, the statute of limitations was not violated.

Finally, in one unpublished opinion, the applicant sent a timely copy of an LC 132a petition to the employer, which filed an answer. At the hearing, the WCJ noticed that the file did not contain a copy of the LC 132a petition. An employee for the applicant's attorney stated that she could not swear under penalty of perjury that she mailed the petition to the WCAB, but it was her "firm belief" that she did because it was her "office procedure" to do so. The appeals board and ultimately the court found that the petition was timely because the fact that the original petition could not be found was "not unusual in view of the [WCAB's] clerical problems."[13]

As an affirmative defense, the statute of limitations may be waived if not timely raised.[14]

---

[10] *Snodgrass v. WCAB* (1985) 50 CCC 501 (Court of Appeal opinion unpublished in official reports).

[11] *Schaar v. WCAB* (1996) 61 CCC 135 (writ denied). This decision is questionable because it relied on *Portillo v. G.T. Price Products, Inc.* (1982) 131 Cal. App. 3d 285, which has been disapproved by the California Supreme Court in *City of Moorpark v. The Superior Court of Ventura County (Dillon)* (1998) 63 CCC 944.

[12] *Brainard v. WCAB* (2003) 68 CCC 365 (Court of Appeal opinion unpublished in official reports).

[13] *Torres v. WCAB* (1993) 58 CCC 417 (Court of Appeal opinion unpublished in official reports).

[14] See *May Co. v. WCAB (Banks)* (1992) 57 CCC 477 (Court of Appeal opinion unpublished in official reports).

6.47 STATUTE OF LIMITATIONS FOR CLAIMS OF SERIOUS AND WILLFUL MISCONDUCT

The Labor Code provides for penalties if an employee's injury occurs as a result of serious and willful misconduct. If an injury was caused by the employee's serious and willful misconduct, pursuant to LC 4551, the employee's compensation otherwise recoverable is reduced by one-half. If an injury was caused by the employer's serious and willful misconduct, LC 4553 provides that the amount of compensation is increased by one-half, together with costs and expenses not to exceed $250. Proceedings for increased or decreased compensation for serious and willful misconduct are instituted by filing an appropriate petition with the appeals board.

Serious and willful claims are discussed in depth in Section 13.40 Penalty for Serious and Willful Misconduct – Employer.

REQUIREMENTS FOR A PETITION FOR SERIOUS AND WILLFUL MISCONDUCT

An allegation that an injury was caused by either the serious and willful misconduct of the employee or of the employer must be separately pleaded (CCR 10440). That is, the filing of the application for adjudication to initiate a claim is not enough. Usually a separate petition alleging serious and willful misconduct is filed with the appeals board, although a separate application would seem to suffice.

The petition must set out in sufficient detail the basis on which the charge is founded so that the adverse party and the appeals board may be fully advised (CCR 10440).[1] If the charge of serious and willful misconduct is based on more than one theory, each must be stated separately (CCR 10445(a)). If the charge is predicated upon the violation of a safety order, the petition must include the correct citation or reference to the safety order, as well as all of the particulars required by LC 4553.1 (CCR 10445(b)).[2]

The reason a separate pleading is required for a serious and willful claim is that "the legal obligation to pay normal benefits is one obligation, while that to pay additional compensation by reason of serious and willful misconduct is an entirely distinct and further obligation."[3] "A claim for normal benefits and a claim for increased benefits by reason of serious and willful misconduct are not sought upon the same general set of facts, nor do they involve merely a difference or change in legal theory. The relief sought is not the same; the legal liability is not the same; and the 'proceedings' to recover the benefits as respectively provided are recognized as being different (LC 5407). Normal benefits automatically follow from an injury within a covered employment relationship, whereas the additional award based on serious and willful misconduct of the employer is an additional award."[4]

The employer may not reduce compensation pursuant to LC 4551 until the appeals board determines that the injury occurred as a result of the employee's serious and willful misconduct (LC 4552). Likewise, an employer is not obligated to pay increased compensation pursuant to LC 4553 until the appeals board decides the issue.

There are separate statutes for filing claims of serious and willful misconduct against an employer and an employee. The time limit for an employee's claim is covered by LC 5407, and the time limit for an employer's claim is covered by LC 5407.5.

---

[1] Before the adoption of CCR 10440, it was held that a claim for both ordinary benefits and a claim for increased benefits for serious and willful misconduct could be included in a single application if a definite step were taken to raise an issue of willful misconduct. An application setting up ordinary issues is not sufficient for the purposes of a serious and willful misconduct claim. *Peterson v. IAC (Barckley)* (1947) 12 CCC 180, 182.
[2] Before the adoption of CCR 10445(b), the appeals board held that the employee was not required to plead a particular safety order in order to receive an award under LC 4553.1. *K.C.A.C., Inc./Wilbur-Ellis Co. v. WCAB (Gallardo)* (2000) 65 CCC 1334 (writ denied); *La Deau Manufacturing Co. v. WCAB (De La Mora)* (1997) 62 CCC 522 (writ denied).
[3] *Lambreton v. IAC* (1956) 21 CCC 179, 183.
[4] *Lambreton v. IAC* (1956) 21 CCC 179, 182.

TIME LIMITS FOR EMPLOYEE'S CLAIM

LC 5407 provides that an employee must commence a claim for compensation on the grounds of serious and willful misconduct under LC 4553 within 12 months from the date of injury.

Strict Time Limit

As applied, this is a much stricter time limit than the one used for claims in general. This period of time is not extended by payment of compensation, agreement to terms of compensation or the filing of an application for compensation benefits under other provisions of the Labor Code. The five years to reopen an award on the grounds of new and further disability under LC 5410 do not extend the limitations provided in LC 5407 (LC 5410). Moreover, the time limit for filing is not extended by filing a civil action.[5] So even though an employee timely files an application for normal benefits, the employee may not amend the application more than a year after the injury to include a claim of serious and willful misconduct.[6]

The deadline is strict. In one case, an applicant argued that the one year should begin to run from the time he discovered the serious and willful violation, rather than from the date of injury. This standard was rejected.[7] There is an issue, however, of whether a serious and willful claim must be both timely filed with the appeals board, and served on the employer.[8]

Claims Amended After More than One Year

The courts are more liberal when the serious and willful claim is timely filed, but not pleaded with the specificity required, and amended later. This is so even if the amendment is made after the one-year period.[9] For example, one employee timely filed a claim alleging a violation of a safety order. More than a year after

---

[5] *Kallman v. WCAB* (1996) 61 CCC 1480 (writ denied).

[6] *Peterson v. IAC (Barckley)* (1947) 12 CCC 180; *Lambreton v. IAC* (1956) 21 CCC 179; *Boyd v. WCAB* (1984) 49 CCC 732 (writ denied).

[7] *Caro v. WCAB* (1977) 42 CCC 332 (writ denied). In *Caro* the applicant did not speak English and did not understand that the machine that injured him was improperly maintained until months after the injury. Note, however, that if the employer engages in deceitful practices to cause the delay in filing, and the employee reasonably relies on the misrepresentations, estoppel can apply and toll the statute. *McGee Street Productions/Hallmark Entertainment v. WCAB (Peterson)* (2003) 68 CCC 708.

[8] Compare *Fisher v. WCAB* (2001) 66 CCC 517 (writ denied) with *T and T Construction v. WCAB (Hillman)* (2012) 77 CCC 501 (Court of Appeal opinion unpublished in official reports).

[9] *Ray v. IAC (Wolgamott)* (1956) 21 CCC 327, 329-30.

the date of injury, the claim was amended to include other safety order violations. No statute of limitations violation was found.[10]

In another case, an application for adjudication filed for the underlying claim also recited that the employer's serious and willful misconduct was at issue. This was then amended more than year after the date of injury to specifically plead the facts and theories of the claim. It was held that the statute of limitations did not apply.[11] (Note, however, that this case was decided before the creation of CCR 10440, which specifically requires separate pleadings.) Also, an application alleging negligence may not be amended to include a serious and willful claim.[12]

Joinder of Parties After One Year

The appeals board may not generally allow joinder of a new party after the expiration of the one-year statute of limitations for the filing of a serious and willful misconduct claim. For example, in *McGee Street Productions/Hallmark Entertainment v. WCAB (Peterson),*[13] an employee suffered a fatal heart attack while working on a movie production on Feb. 17, 2000, and had both a general and special employer. The general employer, Entertainment Partners (Entertainment), handled payroll and regular workers' compensation benefits, and the special employer, McGee Street Productions (McGee Street), was the production company. (For a better understanding of these kinds of relationships, see Section 4.73 General and Special Employment).

The widow filed a workers' compensation claim against Entertainment. Also, within a year of the date of death, she filed a petition alleging serious and willful misconduct against Entertainment. More than a year after the death, the petition was amended to name both Entertainment and McGee Street. An order joining McGee Street was issued, and McGee Street objected. Later Entertainment was dismissed after settlement. The court then decided as a matter of law that the claim against McGee was barred, based on the unambiguous and plain language of LC 5407. It was found that the widow knew the identity of the employer who exercised the details of her husband's work. Therefore, because there was no evidence of true ignorance of the identity of the alleged employer, the serious and willful claim against McGee Street was barred by LC 5407.[14]

---

[10] *Bowers Manufacturing Co. v. IAC (Gonzalez)* (1966) 31 CCC 39 (writ denied).
[11] *Rubio v. WCAB* (1985) 50 CCC 160.
[12] *DeLeon v. WCAB* (1977) 42 CCC 272 (writ denied).
[13] (2003) 68 CCC 708.
[14] *McGee Street Productions/Hallmark Entertainment v. WCAB (Peterson)* (2003) 68 CCC 708, 713-14. See also *Denni v. WCAB* (2010) 75 CCC 1237 (writ denied).

Note that in *Peterson,* the court recognized that an employer is estopped from asserting the statute of limitations if it engaged in actions or misrepresentations that induced the employee to refrain from filing a claim until after the statute of limitations had run. But to prove estoppel, the employee must show reliance on some act, omission or statement of the employer. In *Peterson,* the court held that estoppel did not save the applicant because her grounds for estoppel were based on actions or statements made after the statute of limitations has expired.[15]

An example of estoppel that would toll the statute of limitations was provided in *Production Framing Systems v. WCAB (Dove).*[16] An applicant was employed by a general employer and sent to work for a special employer. He sustained an injury while working for the special employer. A supervisor for the special employer told the applicant that he was not employed by the special employer, and referred him to the general employer for treatment. The applicant filed an application for adjudication naming only the general employer as a defendant. The insurer for the general employer became insolvent and CIGA became involved. CIGA filed a petition to join the special employer as a party. The special employer argued that the claim was barred by the one-year statute of limitations in LC 5405.

The appeals board determined that the special employer was estopped from raising the statute of limitations as a defense. The board distinguished *Peterson,* noting that in this case, the special employer knew of the industrial injury before the general employer. The appeals board concluded that joinder of a special employer in an action after the statute of limitations has run is appropriate if the special employer was aware of the action from the outset. Also, the appeals board explained that the special employer was estopped to assert the statute of limitations as a defense because it told the applicant to submit the claim to the general employer, rather than to itself. The special employer was estopped to assert the statute of limitations because the applicant relied on the special employer's instructions to his detriment.[17]

Special Cases — Asbestos

In one case, the appeals board held a widow's claim for serious and willful misconduct was not barred by the statute of limitations when it was filed within a year of the employee's asbestos-related death. The employee died in June 1982

[15] *McGee Street Productions/Hallmark Entertainment v. WCAB (Peterson)* (2003) 68 CCC 708, 715.
[16] (2005) 70 CCC 735 (writ denied).
[17] *Production Framing Systems v. WCAB (Dove)* (2005) 70 CCC 735 (writ denied).

as a result of asbestos exposure from June 1954 to August 1973. In May 1983, the widow filed an application for increased benefits due to the employer's serious and willful misconduct. The widow admitted that both she and her husband knew that his mesothelioma was work related in January 1982, and that he was disabled at the time. Nevertheless, the appeals board in a split decision found that the claim was not barred. It held that the applicable statute of limitations was LC 5406.5, which covers asbestos-related deaths, and that the claim was timely filed because it was filed within a year of his death.[18]

TIME LIMITS FOR EMPLOYER'S CLAIM

Pursuant to LC 5407.5, the employer has 12 months from the date of injury to commence proceedings for the reduction of compensation on the grounds of serious and willful misconduct of the employee under LC 4551. This time limit, however, does not apply in any case in which the employee has commenced proceedings for the increase of compensation on the grounds of serious and willful misconduct of the employer under LC 4553. If an employee has filed such a claim under LC 4553, the employer may file a claim against the employee under LC 4551 more than one year from the date of injury.

[18] *County of Contra Costa v. WCAB (Vaughn)* (1986) 51 CCC 6 (writ denied).

6.48 STATUTE OF LIMITATIONS FOR DEATH BENEFITS

Following an employee's death from an industrial injury, his or her dependents have a right to death benefits as established in LC 4700 et. seq. The employer is required to give the dependents notice of benefits to which they may be entitled as a result of the employee's death (CCR 9812(h)). If the employer cannot determine if death benefits are payable, it may issue a delay letter (CCR 9812(h)(3)). Also, if the employer is denying death benefits, it must advise the dependents of the denial and the reasons for it (CCR 9812(h)(4)). Death benefits and the required notices are discussed in detail in Chapter 12.

DEPENDENT'S INDEPENDENT RIGHT

A dependent's right to statutory death benefits is not derived from the rights of the deceased employee. It is independent and severable from an employee's claim for *inter vivos* (while the employee is alive) workers' compensation benefits.[1] So a dependent must file an application for adjudication for a death claim, even if the deceased employee filed a workers' compensation claim while living. A dependent may not amend a timely filed application by a deceased employee to assert a claim for death benefits.[2] Moreover, a letter of intent to file a claim to defense counsel is not enough — an actual application for death benefits is required.[3] But if the application is timely filed with the appeals board,

[1] *Berkebile v. WCAB* (1983) 48 CCC 438, 441.
[2] *Clark v. WCAB* (1991) 56 CCC 331, 336.
[3] *Gonzales v. WCAB* (2008) 73 CCC 519 (writ denied).

proceedings will be timely commenced even if the application was not served on defendant until more than one year after the date of death.[4]

TIME LIMITS FOR FILING A CLAIM FOR DEATH BENEFITS

The statute of limitations for death benefits is established in LC 5406. It provides that except for LC 5406.5 and LC 5406.6 (which cover deaths from asbestos and HIV-related disease and are discussed in forthcoming sections), proceedings for the collection of death benefits may be commenced one year from:

1. the date of death when it occurs within one year from date of injury;
2. the date of last furnishing of any compensation benefits, when death occurs more than one year from the date of injury; or
3. the date of death, when death occurs more than one year after the date of injury and compensation benefits have been furnished.

But LC 5406 adds, "No such proceedings may be commenced more than one year after the date of death, nor more than 240 weeks from the date of injury."[5] In *Ruiz v. IAC,*[6] the California Supreme Court interpreted this language to mean that no proceedings for death benefits may be commenced more than one year after the date of death; *and* no such proceedings may be commenced more than 240 weeks from the date of injury.[7] In *Ruiz,* the employee contracted silicosis and the date of injury was fixed as July 24, 1949 in the workers' compensation claim. The applicant died 253 weeks after injury, and the widow filed for death benefits five weeks later. The court held that the claim was barred because it was "more than 240 weeks from the date of (her husband's) injury."[8]

So even if a claim for death benefits is filed within one year of the employee's death, it may still be barred if it is filed more than 240 weeks from the date of injury. Likewise, an application filed more than one year from the date of death,

---

[4] *Alhuniti v. Sears Holding Corp.*, 2010 Cal. Wrk. Comp. P.D. LEXIS 565.

[5] LC 5406 originally provided that a claim for death benefits could be commenced within "(a) One year from the date of death, and in any event within: (1) Two years from the date of injury, except as otherwise provided in this section. (2) 240 weeks from the date of injury, where the injury causing death also caused disability which continued to the date of death and for which a disability payment has been made, or agreed to be made, or [timely] proceedings for its collection had been instituted ... " This was interpreted as allowing an application for death benefits to be filed within one year after the date of death *or* within two years after the date of injury. See *Bianco v. IAC* (1944) 9 CCC 206. In apparent response to *Bianco,* the Legislature amended LC 5406 to add that "[n]o such proceedings may be commenced more than one year after the date of death, nor more than 240 weeks from the date of injury." See *Massey v. WCAB* (1993) 58 CCC 367, 369-371 for a discussion of this history.

[6] (1955) 20 CCC 265.

[7] *Ruiz v. IAC* (1955) 20 CCC 265, 266.

[8] *Ruiz v. IAC* (1955) 20 CCC 265, 267. See *Scott v. Fernando Canning Co.* (1956) 21 CCC 73 (panel decision).

although within 240 weeks from the date of injury, would be untimely.[9] If a claim for death benefits is barred by the statute of limitations, reimbursement for burial expenses would also be barred.[10]

Is this fair to applicants and their dependents? *Ruiz* recognized that because of the 240-week requirement, a death benefit claim may be barred before it ever arose. But the court added that the time limit in LC 5406 was not a normal statute of limitations, but was more in the nature of a qualifying condition to any right to death benefits.[11] The California Supreme Court has also stated the 240-week period "appears to reflect a legislative judgment that allowing a longer interval between injury and death would create unacceptable difficulties in proving industrial causation, as evidence grows stale and the possibilities of intervening causes increase."[12]

Date of Injury — Occupational Disease and Cumulative Trauma

Despite the seemingly clear language of LC 5406, there's considerable disagreement regarding the date of injury for the purposes of LC 5406. As discussed in depth in Section 6.14 One Year from Date of Injury, all occupational diseases and cumulative trauma injuries have a date of injury defined by LC 5412. That statute requires both compensable disability and knowledge of industrial causation.

The analysis of the proper date of injury for statute of limitations purposes under LC 5412 can be a complex and confusing enterprise. The reader should be advised that absent a study of the requirements of the statute, the concepts presented in this section will be very difficult to understand. Section 6.14 One Year from Date of Injury should be reviewed, as should Chapter 5, sections 5.5 - 5.9.

In *Arndt v. WCAB,*[13] the Court of Appeal held LC 5406 "is to be construed as requiring that a dependent's compensation claim, arising out of a worker's death from an industrially caused disease, must be commenced within one year from the 'date of death,' *or* the date that the applicant knew, or in the exercise of reasonable diligence should have known, that the death was of industrial causation" (emphasis added). But who is the "applicant"? Is it the deceased

[9] *Claverie v. WCAB* (1997) 62 CCC 1704 (writ denied).
[10] *Blum v. WCAB* (1972) 37 CCC 466 (writ denied).
[11] *Ruiz v. IAC* (1955) 20 CCC 265, 267-68.
[12] *Massey v. WCAB* (1993) 58 CCC 367, 370.
[13] (1976) 41 CCC 151, 159.

injured worker, or the dependent? The answer to that question can cause dramatic differences in the result.

In *Arndt,* the court found that a widow's application filed more than a year after her husband's death from asbestosis and more than five years after the injurious exposure was not barred by the LC 5406 statute of limitations. This was because the widow was considered to be the applicant for purposes of LC 5412. So it was her date of knowledge that was controlling. The widow neither knew nor could have known within one year of her husband's death, or within five years of his last injurious exposure, that his death was industrially related.[14]

Subsequently, in *Berkebile v. WCAB,*[15] the court confirmed that because a dependent's rights to workers' compensation death benefits are independent of and severable from the deceased employee's *inter vivos* rights, the decedent's knowledge of the industrial origin of the disability is not dispositive of the statute of limitations issue. Instead, the court held that it is the dependent's knowledge of the industrial nature of the decedent's condition that is pertinent to the date of injury for the purposes of a death claim. In *Berkebile,* the decedent worked for an employer from 1934 to 1942. He died in 1980, and a month later, his widow filed an application for workers' compensation death benefits based on his exposure to asbestos during the employment ending in 1942. Relying on *Arndt,* the court found that the statute of limitations did not bar the claim, because it was filed within one year of the date of death, and within 240 weeks of the widow's knowledge of the industrial nature of the decedent's fatal illness.[16] If the man had not died and had filed a claim, it would have been barred by the statute of limitations. But his widow's claim was not barred.

Issues Regarding Application of the Date of Injury

In *Massey v. WCAB,*[17] the California Supreme Court recognized that under LC 5406 and *Ruiz,* "a death benefit proceeding is untimely unless commenced within one year after the date of death and within 240 weeks from the date of injury." In a footnote, *Massey* acknowledged that under *Berkebile,* the date of injury may depend on the dependent's knowledge of the industrial nature of the injury causing death.[18] But the court also recognized that under *Ruiz,* the 240-week

---

[14] *Arndt v. WCAB* (1976) 41 CCC 151, 159. Note that since *Arndt,* LC 5406.5 was enacted (in 1980) to cover deaths from asbestos-related diseases. LC 5406.5 is discussed in Section 6.49 Statute of Limitations for Asbestos-Related Death.
[15] (1983) 48 CCC 438.
[16] *Berkebile v. WCAB* (1983) 48 CCC 438, 442.
[17] (1993) 58 CCC 367, 370.
[18] *Massey v. WCAB* (1993) 58 CCC 367, 368, fn. 1.

period in LC 5406 was a qualifying condition to the exercise of any right to death benefits, and that if the 240-week period has expired, no claim can arise.[19] In *Massey,* the employee suffered cumulative injuries resulting in a heart attack Oct. 19, 1979. The employee received workers' compensation benefits and died during heart surgery Oct. 28, 1987. *Massey* did not discuss when the dependents acquired knowledge of industrial causation, but held that the dependent minors' claims were barred because more than 240 weeks had passed between the injury and the death.[20]

So under *Ruiz* and *Massey,* the California Supreme Court has held that the 240-week period is a qualifying condition; a dependent may not bring a claim if an employee dies more than 240 weeks after an injury. Although the date of injury for the purposes of the 240-week period was not directly addressed in either case, both barred claims by dependents when the death occurred more than 240 weeks from the decedent's date of injury. But under *Arndt* and *Berkebile,* the Court of Appeal has held that dependents have an independent claim to death benefits and the date of injury is based on when the dependents knew or should have known that the decedent's death was industrial in nature. The appeals board has struggled in its application of these cases.

In some cases, the appeals board has relied on *Arndt* and *Berkebile* rationale and held that the date of injury under LC 5406 should based on the dependent's knowledge. For example, in *General Telephone v. WCAB (McCasland),*[21] the applicant claimed a cumulative trauma injury ending in May 1984, but his last day of work was March 31, 1984. He died June 29, 1988, and the widow filed an application for death benefits arising from the industrial injury May 3, 1989. Even though more than 240 weeks had passed between the last day of work and the decedent's death, the appeals board held that the claim was not barred by the statute of limitations noting "in a claim for death benefits arising out of occupational disease or cumulative injury, the date of injury is when the claimant, i.e., decedent's widow herein, knew or reasonably should have known that the decedent's injury or death was caused by the employment."[22]

---

[19] *Massey v. WCAB* (1993) 58 CCC 367, 372.

[20] Subsequent to *Massey,* the Court of Appeal in *State of California, Department of Highway Patrol v. WCAB (Sills)* (1995) 60 CCC 308 and the California Supreme Court in *Chevron U.S.A., Inc. v. WCAB (Steele)* (1999) 64 CCC 1 concluded that the date of injury in CT claims for the purposes of determining dependency status and the amount of the death benefit was the date the *deceased employee* first suffered disability from the injury, and either knew, or in exercise of reasonable diligence, should have known such disability was caused by employment.

[21] (1997) 62 CCC 513 (writ denied).

[22] *General Telephone v. WCAB (McCasland)* (1997) 62 CCC 513 (writ denied).

Similarly, in *State of California/Department of Corrections and Rehabilitation v. WCAB (Underwood),*[23] an employee retired June 1, 1990, and died of cardiac causes May 21, 1995. The widow claimed that she was unaware of the work-related nature of her husband's death until she met with a workers' compensation attorney in 2003. An application for adjudication was filed Dec. 10, 2004, 14 years after the decedent retired and nearly 10 years after his death. Nevertheless, the appeals board determined that the claim was not barred by LC 5406 because it was filed within 240 weeks of the date of injury — the widow first had knowledge that her husband's death was industrial was in 2003.[24]

In contrast, other cases have held that the date of injury in assessing whether the time limits for filing under LC 5406 are based on the decedent's injury. For example, in *Earley v. WCAB,*[25] the employee sustained a CT injury to his heart and cardiovascular system and a findings and award issued in 1984. In 2000, he died. Within one year of the death, a death claim was filed on behalf of his children. The applicants argued that the claim was timely under *Berkebile* because the children did not know of the industrial nature of their father's condition until his death. But the WCJ determined that the appeals board did not have jurisdiction over the claim under *Massey* because the death occurred more than 240 weeks from the date of injury. The WCJ found that under *Massey,* there was not a separate date of injury for the decedent's children when the decedent's date of injury was determined *inter vivos*. The appeals board dismissed the applicants' petition for reconsideration for lack of verification, but stated that it would have also denied it on the merits based on the WCJ's report.[26]

---

[23] (2006) 72 CCC 162 (writ denied).

[24] *State of California/Department of Corrections v. WCAB (Underwood)* (2006) 72 CCC 162 (writ denied). See also *City of Compton v. WCAB (Branscomb)* (2011) 76 CCC 991 (writ denied) (pursuant to LC 5406, date of injury to determine the statute of limitations is 240 weeks from the date of earliest concurrence of disability and knowledge of work-related nature of injury by the surviving spouse or other dependent); *Wiggins v. WCAB* (1991) 56 CCC 668 (Court of Appeal opinion unpublished in official reports) (widow's claim not barred by LC 5406 when there was no substantial evidence that the application was filed more than one year after she knew or should have known that her husband's death was industrial); *Maddon v. WCAB* (1984) 49 CCC 309 (Court of Appeal opinion unpublished in official reports) (despite the fact that the decedent's death occurred more than 12 years after he last worked for the employer, the widow's claim was timely because it was filed within one year of the date of death); *Duarte v. Stoesser Industries,* 2011 Cal. Wrk. Comp. P.D. LEXIS 157 (claim not barred because defendant failed to prove that dependent knew of the relationship between work and cancer sufficient to trigger the one-year statute of limitations). But see *Cohen v. WCAB* (1986) 51 CCC 211 (writ denied) (dependent's claim barred when her first knowledge of the industrial nature of her husband's condition as more than 240 weeks before date of death).

[25] (2003) 68 CCC 1707 (writ denied).

[26] *Earley v. WCAB* (2003) 68 CCC 1707 (writ denied). See also *Gallegos v. WCAB* (1997) 62 CCC 1714 (writ denied); *Cunningham v. WCAB* (1986) 51 CCC 495 (writ denied) (widow's claim filed more than 240 weeks after injury as determined in *inter vivos* claim barred).

In *Leverton v. WCAB*,[27] the decedent sustained a cumulative injury to his heart during the period ending in 2001. On Dec. 30, 2006, the injury ultimately caused his death. The widow filed a claim for death benefits in 2007. The parties disputed how to define the "date of injury" under LC 5406 for the purposes of the 240-week limitation. The employer argued that the date of injury was the employee's date of injury. The widow argued that the date of injury was based on a dependent's date of injury — the date the dependent knew or should have known of the employee's death and its industrial causation. The appeals board noted that it was not an easy decision but found that the death claim was barred because the date of injury in LC 5406 pertained to the employee's industrial injury. The appeals board added that "a whole line of cases define Labor Code Section 5406 as a bright line rule requiring death claims to be filed within 240 weeks of injury and that the injury referred to in the code is that of the applicant."[28]

So the appeals board has reached apparently conflicting decisions on how to apply the principles set forth in *Ruiz, Massey, Arndt* and *Berkebile.* Unless and until an appellate court resolves the issue, employers will continue to assert that the limitation period under LC 5406 is a qualifying condition based on the decedent's date of injury. And dependents will assert that the statute of limitations issue should be resolved based on their knowledge of industrial causation.

Date of Injury — Compensable Consequence Injuries

As discussed in Section 5.56 Compensable Consequence Injuries, an employee may sustain a subsequent injury that is found to be a compensable consequence of the original injury. If an employee dies as a result of a compensable consequence injury, is the time limit for filing a death claim governed by the date of the original injury or by the date of the subsequent consequential injury? The appeals board has addressed the issue in several cases, but, here again, it has

---

[27] (2009) 74 CCC 874 (writ denied).

[28] *Leverton v. WCAB* (2009) 74 CCC 874 (writ denied). See also *Palomares v. WCAB* (1974) 39 CCC 668 (writ denied) (widow's claim barred when it was filed eight years after her husband's death, even though it was filed within 30 days of the date she learned the death was industrial); *Morris v. State of California Department of Transportation,* 2011 Cal. Wrk. Comp. P.D. LEXIS 88 (240-week proviso refers to the time period from the date of the employee's injury to the date of death, not to the dependent's confirmed knowledge of the cause of her husband's death); *Brezensky v. WCAB* (2011) 76 CCC 1201 (writ denied) (date on which a dependent gains knowledge that the injured worker's death was industrially caused is irrelevant if the death occurs more than 240 weeks after the industrial injury; 240 week threshold must exist in order for any claim for dependent death benefits to accrue); *Lockett v. City of Los Angeles,* 2012 Cal. Wrk. Comp. P.D. LEXIS 193 (240 weeks ran from the end date of the employee's cumulative trauma date of injury; the qualifying condition for death benefits was not met because the employee did not die within 240 weeks of the date of injury).

reached seemingly inconsistent results. The majority of cases, however, hold that a compensable consequence injury is not given a new date of injury.

In *Wuagneux v. WCAB,*[29] an employee incurred an industrial injury to her back in 1978. In July 1988, she underwent surgery to her back, and died July 30, 1988. Her widower filed an application for death benefits alleging that the death was a result of heart and cardiovascular problems resulting from the back surgery. He argued that the 240-week limitation was not triggered by the original injury, but by the new injury from surgery. The appeals board found that the claim was barred because it was not commenced within 240 weeks from the date of injury. The appeals board commented that the death was not a "new injury," but was a consequence of the original injury.[30]

Similarly, in *Sedam v. WCAB,*[31] an employee sustained three industrial injuries in 1999, for which the employee received an award of 100 percent PD. On May 24, 2005, the employee was transported to consult on medication intoxication and dependence. The round-trip took eight hours and the employee developed deep vein thrombosis as a result. The employee died June 12, 2006 from cardiac arrest and pulmonary embolism, and the widow filed a claim for death benefits June 12, 2006. The appeals board concluded that the claim for death benefits was barred by the 204-week limitation of LC 5406. The appeals board explained that the May 24, 2005 incident was a medical consequence of the three industrial injuries, but not a new injury. The appeals board added that compensable consequence injuries relate back to the date of the original injuries; they were not given a new date of injury.

A contrary result was reached in *Long Beach Unified School District v. WCAB (McGhee).*[32] The employee sustained a cumulative trauma injury ending in 1990. He received an awarded for continuing treatment and temporary disability in 1998. On April 19, 1999, he died as a result of an accidental overdose of multiple medications. In October 1999, the widow filed an application for industrial death benefits. The appeals board held that the claim was not barred by the statute of limitations, finding that the death was a compensable consequence of the original injury, because the injury that resulted in death was the overdose of medication,

---

[29] (1991) 56 CCC 519 (writ denied).

[30] *Wuagneux v. WCAB* (1991) 56 CCC 519 (writ denied). A similar result was reached by the California Supreme Court in *Granell v. IAC* (1944) 9 CCC 301 in its decision denying death benefits to a woman who married the employee after the date of injury. He died as a result of surgery following an industrial injury, but the court fixed the date for the dependency determination on the date of the original injury and not the subsequent operation.

[31] (2011) 76 CCC 272 (writ denied).

[32] (2004) 69 CCC 1044 (writ denied).

not the psychiatric injury itself. So, pursuant to *Berkebile,* the appeals board held that the application was timely because it was filed within a year of the widow discovering that her husband's death was industrial.[33]

Note, however, that other cases have rejected *McGhee* and held that a death from a drug overdose alleged to be a compensable consequence of an industrial injury was to be barred if death occurs more than 240 weeks after the date of injury. In one case, the appeals board stated, "If the analysis in *McGhee* is accurate, and the date of injury in a death claim is the date of knowledge that the death was industrial, then no death benefits claim would ever be barred by the provision of Section 5406. Obviously, knowledge that the death was caused by the industrial injury could not exist prior to the death of the injured worker. If, for purposes of death benefits, the date of injury is the date the injured worker dies, the above-quoted portion of Section 5406 would be rendered meaningless. That result would be inconsistent with the Supreme Court's rulings in *Ruiz* and *Massey*."[34]

In another case, *K-Mart Corp. v. WCAB (Martinez),*[35] the appeals board did not decide the issue directly but relied on the fact that the parties stipulated to a date of injury for the subsequent injury. In that case, the employee sustained an admitted industrial injury to her right knee in 1997. In 2000, she fell at home and injured her right hip. The AME reported that the fall at home was a compensable consequence of her industrial injury. The claim was settled by way of stipulated award and the parties stipulated to injury in 1997 and in 2000. The applicant died in 2003 and her husband filed a claim for death benefits a month later, alleging that his wife's death was the result of the 2000 injury. In a split decision, the majority held that the claim was not barred by LC 5406. The appeals board relied on *County of Sacramento v. WCAB (Weatherall),*[36] which held that although a stipulation may be set aside based on inadvertence or mistake of fact, it may not be set aside simply because it produces a poor outcome for a party. The appeals board concluded that the stipulations in the case regarding the decedent's date of injury could not be set aside just because the evidence did not support the date of

[33] *Long Beach Unified School District v. WCAB (McGhee)* (2004) 69 CCC 1044 (writ denied)..
[34] *Clark v. Airborne Express/DHL,* 2011 Cal. Wrk. Comp. P.D. LEXIS 308. See also *Arias (Castro) v. Gardena Valley News,* 2011 Cal. Wrk. Comp. P.D. LEXIS 262 (accidental overdose did not trigger time period for filing a claim because a compensable consequence injury was not an injury under LC 5406). In *Nickles v. Coastal Products Co.,* 2010 Cal. Wrk. Comp. P.D. LEXIS 493, *McGhee* was cited by the applicant, but the appeals board concluded that a suicide, which was allegedly a compensable consequence of an industrial injury, was barred by LC 5406 because it occurred beyond the 240-week limitation period.
[35] (2006) 72 CCC 135 (writ denied).
[36] (2000) 65 CCC 1.

injury. It determined that the claim was not barred by LC 5406 because it was filed within 240 weeks of the 2000 injury.[37]

PROCEEDINGS FOR DEATH BENEFITS BY MINORS AND INCOMPETENTS

As discussed in Section 6.38 Extension of Time for Special Cases, pursuant to LC 5408, the statute of limitations does not run against any person younger than 18 or any incompetent unless and until a guardian or conservator of the estate or trustee is appointed. Nevertheless, the California Supreme Court held that LC 5408 does not toll the 240-week period for minor claimants because it is a qualifying condition in the exercise of any right to death benefits.[38] That is, the 240-week period between the injury and death simply determines whether any death benefit claim may arise. If the employee dies more than 240 weeks from the date of injury, no claim for death benefits may arise regardless of whether the applicant is a minor or incompetent. But if the employee dies *within* the 240-week period, the unexpired portion of the 240-week period begins to run against potential claimants and is subject to the tolling provisions of LC 5408.[39] The unexpired portion of the 240-week period is tolled until a guardian is appointed or a minor reaches the age of majority.

For example, an employee sustained an injury May 5, 1999 and died May 15, 2003. A guardian was appointed for a minor applicant on Aug. 25, 2003, but an application for death benefits was not filed until March 22, 2006. The appeals board held that the application for death benefits was untimely. The appeals board noted that the injured worker died approximately 200 weeks after her date of injury, and therefore the minor applicant accrued a claim to the unexpired 40 weeks. LC 5408 tolled the statute of limitations until the date a guardian was appointed, Aug. 25, 2003, and the limitations period of LC 5406 began running again. So the application filed on March 22, 2006 was untimely because it was filed more than 40 weeks after Aug. 25, 2003.[40]

---

[37] *K-Mart Corp. v. WCAB (Martinez)* (2006) 72 CCC 135 (writ denied). The dissent would have found the claim for death benefits was untimely because it was filed more than 240 weeks after the date of the 1997 injury. The dissent noted that there was no dispute that the 2000 injury at home was a compensable consequence of the earlier injury, rather than a separate industrial injury, and that *Weatherall* was not controlling.

[38] *Massey v. WCAB* (1993) 58 CCC 367, 372.

[39] *Massey v. WCAB* (1993) 58 CCC 367, 372. See also *Earley v. WCAB* (2003) 68 CCC 1707 (writ denied); *Gallegos v. WCAB* (1997) 62 CCC 1714 (writ denied). *Massey* overrules the decisions of *Fisher v. WCAB* (1976) 41 CCC 677 and *Roblyer v. WCAB* (1976) 41 CCC 669. Other cases previously holding that the 240-week period was tolled until the appointment of a guardian include *Consolidated Freightways v. WCAB (Howell)* (1967) 32 CCC 320 (writ denied); *City of Oakland v. IAC (Barnett)* (1965) 30 CCC 398 (writ denied); *City of Los Angeles v. IAC (White)* (1964) 29 CCC 226 (writ denied); *SCIF v. IAC (Flores)* (1960) 25 CCC 214 (writ denied).

[40] *Gonzales v. WCAB* (2008) 73 CCC 519 (writ denied).

Note that both the one-year and 240-week requirement of LC 5406 would be tolled for a minor or incompetent following an employee's death. A minor or incompetent might have as long as one year following the appointment of a guardian or the date the minor reaches the age of 18 to file a claim for death benefits. If an employee died with more than 52 weeks remaining in the 240-week period, the minor or incompetent would be entitled to a full year following the appointment of a guardian or the date the minor reaches 18 to file the claim. Typically, a claim for death benefits is filed contemporaneously with the appointment of a guardian. So if an employee dies within 240 weeks of an injury, the minor's claim for death benefits is usually timely.[41]

ESTOPPEL TO ASSERT THE STATUTE OF LIMITATIONS

As discussed in Section 6.17 Estoppel Based on Failure to Provide Notice, an employer may be estopped to assert the statute of limitations if it fails to give proper notice following an industrial injury. The same holds true under LC 5406. If an employer has appropriate notice of an injury, but fails to give the employee appropriate notice of workers' compensation rights, the employer may be estopped to assert the statute of limitations under LC 5406 if the employee dies without receiving the required notices.[42]

DEATH WITHOUT DEPENDENTS UNIT

If an employee sustains a fatal injury but has no dependents entitled to a death benefit, pursuant to LC 4706.5, the employer is required to pay benefits to the Department of Industrial Relations. The Death Without Dependents Unit (DWD) is charged with handling these claims. The employer is required to notify the administrative director of the death of every employee unless the employer has actual knowledge or notice that the deceased employee left a surviving dependent (LC 4706.5(f)). The form required for this purpose is DIA 510. It may be obtained from the DIR website: `http://www.dir.ca.gov/dwc/forms.html`. The appeals board has held that the DWD Unit is not barred by the statute of limitations for filing a claim for benefits resulting from an employee's death when the employer fails to notify the DWD Unit of an employee's death.[43]

---

[41] See *City and County of San Francisco v. WCAB (Shaughnessy, Maultsby)* (1969) 34 CCC 97 (claims not barred because they were commenced contemporaneously with appointment of guardians *ad litem* and the applicants were minors at the time of filing).

[42] See *Safeway Stores v. WCAB (Loader)* (1984) 49 CCC 574 (writ denied).

[43] *City of Los Angeles v. WCAB (Barrett)* (2006) 71 CCC 61 (writ denied).

AFFIRMATIVE DEFENSE AND WAIVER

As with other statutes of limitations, that under LC 5406 is an affirmative defense that may be waived if not timely raised.[44]

[44] *Aubry v. WCAB (Weathersbee)* (1997) 62 CCC 484 (writ denied).

6.49 STATUTE OF LIMITATIONS FOR ASBESTOS-RELATED DEATH

There is a special statute of limitations for asbestos-related death cases. Normally, under LC 5406, a death must occur within 240 weeks of the date of injury to be compensable; otherwise, it is barred by the statute of limitations. LC 5406.5 provides that in the case of the death of an asbestos worker or firefighter from asbestos, a dependent has one year from the date of death to file the application. This is regardless of the date of injury. Because "asbestos worker" is not defined, it probably means anyone injured by working with asbestos.

As discussed in depth in Section 6.14 One Year from Date of Injury, all occupational diseases have a date of injury defined by LC 5412 (requiring both disability and knowledge of injury). So the statute of limitation is tolled until the employee understands that he or she has an industrial injury; this can be years after the employment ends. In death cases, the dependent of the deceased injured worker has the date of injury defined by his or her own date of knowledge of industrial injury. Asbestos cases are no exception. The limitations period of LC 5406.5 is tolled until the dependent of the deceased asbestos worker knows, or in the exercise of reasonable diligence should know, that the worker's death was caused by the employment.[1] Whether a dependent knows or should have known in the exercise of reasonable diligence that the death was the result of his employment is a question of fact; the employer has the burden of proof on that issue.[2]

[1] *Clark v. WCAB* (1991) 56 CCC 331, 335-36; *Arndt v. WCAB* (1976) 41 CCC 151.
[2] See *Chambers v. WCAB* (1968) 33 CCC 722,724.

A dependent's right to death benefits are independent and severable from the rights of the deceased employee. So a new application must be filed by the applicant's survivors.[3] A decedent's failure to file a workers' compensation claim for injuries arising from asbestos exposure will not necessarily preclude a dependent from filing a claim for death benefits.[4] In fact, a dependent who timely files a claim for death benefits is also permitted to recover all unpaid and accrued benefits, including reimbursement for self-procured medical treatment, attendant care and temporary disability benefits.[5]

In one case, the court barred a widow's claim for death benefits pursuant to LC 5406.5 when it determined that she failed to file an application for death benefits within one year after she knew her husband's death was work related. The widow knew more than one year before she filed the application that her husband's death was industrially related because she signed his workers' compensation application several days before his death. Because he was too ill to sign it, she admitted that she read the application, she received the death certificate that listed emphysema as a cause of death and she testified that she believed his death was work related. [6] Death benefits are further discussed in Chapter 12.

[3] *Clark v. WCAB* (1991) 56 CCC 331, 335-36.

[4] *Plant Maintenance v. WCAB (Lecce)* (1995) 60 CCC 358 (writ denied); *Bethlehem Steel Corp. v. WCAB (Danley)* (2000) 65 CCC 710 (writ denied).

[5] *Manville Sales Corp. v. WCAB (Hobelheinrich)* (1994) 59 CCC 1093 (writ denied); *Plant Maintenance v. WCAB (Lecce)* (1995) 60 CCC 358 (writ denied); *Bethlehem Steel Corp. v. WCAB (Danley)* (2000) 65 CCC 710 (writ denied).

[6] *Clark v. WCAB* (1991) 56 CCC 331, 341.

6.50 STATUTE OF LIMITATIONS FOR HIV-RELATED DEATH

As with cases for death related to asbestos exposure, the Labor Code contains a specific provision covering death from an HIV-related disease. Normally, per LC 5406, the death must occur within 240 weeks of injury, or it is barred. But LC 5406.6 provides that the period within which to commence proceedings for death benefits for an HIV-related disease is one year from the date of death. That is so regardless of the date of injury, and can considerably extend the statute of limitations in these types of cases.

LC 5406.6 does not cover all employees. The statute of limitations only applies to the death of health-care workers, public safety officers and firefighters as defined in LC 3212,[1] and parole, probation, correctional officers and correctional counselors as described in Penal Code 830.5. LC 5406.6 applies only when these conditions are met:

1. A report of the injury or exposure was made to the employer or to a governmental agency authorized to administer industrial injury claims within one year of the date of the injury.
2. The worker has complied with the requisite notice provisions and the claim has not been finally determined to be noncompensable.
3. The employer provided, or was ordered to provide, workers' compensation benefits for the injury before the date of death.

[1] See Section 5.18 Presumption of Injury — Public Employees' Covered Conditions.

For the purposes of LC 5406.6, a "health-care worker" means an employee who has direct contact, in the course of his or her employment, with blood or other bodily fluids capable of transmitting HIV, who: (1) is employed by a provider of health care under Civil Code 56.05, including but not limited to registered nurses, licensed vocational nurses, certified nurses' aides, clinical laboratory technologists, dental hygienists, physicians, janitors or housekeeping workers; or (2) provides direct patient care.

6.51 STATUTE OF LIMITATIONS FOR FILING A LIEN

TIME LIMITS EFFECTIVE JAN. 1, 2003

LC 4903.5 became effective Jan. 1, 2003, and establishes the time limit for filing a lien claim for expenses under LC 4903(b), which relates to claims for medical treatment. It does not contain a time limit for any other type of lien.

LC 4903.5 was amended by SB 863, and currently provides that a lien for medical treatment must not be filed after three years from the date the services were provided.[1] If the services were provided on or after July 1, 2013, a lien must be filed no more than 18 months after the date they were provided. The statute of limitations established in LC 4903.5 covers all dates of injury, but the time limits are different depending on when the services were provided.[2]

If a lien is not timely filed, an employer would not be liable for any of the medical services provided. Furthermore, the injured worker is not liable for any underlying obligation if a lien claim has not been filed and served within the allowable period (LC 4903.5(c)).

---

[1] Former LC 4904.5 provided that a lien shall not be filed from the latest of: (1) six months from the date on which the appeals board or a workers' compensation administrative law judge issues a final decision, findings or order, including an order approving a compromise and release, or award, on the merits of the claim; (2) five years from the date of the injury for which the services were provided; or (3) one year from the date the services were provided.

[2] See *Medina v. Robinsons May*, 2012 Cal. Wrk. Comp. P.D. LEXIS 89; *Ravizza v. Albertson's*, 2010 Cal. Wrk. Comp. P.D. LEXIS 254; *Villatoro v. Kern Labor Contracting*, 2012 Cal. Wrk. Comp. P.D. LEXIS 321.

Date the Services Were Provided

Although after Jan. 1, 2013, LC 4903.5 specifies that the time limits start from "the date the services were provided," it is not entirely clear what this means. Does the time limit apply to each date of service? That is, if a lien is filed, are the services performed more than three years/18 months before the filing barred by LC 4903.5? Or is a lien timely filed as to all dates of service if it was filed within three years/18 months from the last date of service?

We have little guidance. The language of the statute before Jan. 1, 2013, refers to "the date of injury for which the services were provided." There are panel decisions interpreting this language, which is not exactly the same as its replacement. And, the panel decisions are in conflict.

In one case, the appeals board concluded that LC 4903.5 did not bar any reimbursement for home health-care services when they were provided continuously. The appeals board stated that time for filing was "unlimited at this time" because the services were ongoing.[3] But in another case, the appeals board reached an entirely different conclusion and upheld a WCJ's decision that a husband who filed a lien for home care services June 14, 2011, was allowed to recover for home health-care service only from June 14, 2010, forward. In that case, the appeals board rejected an argument that a lien can be filed any time and be considered timely when the services are ongoing.[4] These decisions cannot be reconciled plausibly, and the issue will need to be further clarified by the appeals board.[5]

Exception to the Limitations Period for Certain Providers

Notwithstanding these limits, certain medical providers may file a lien within 12 months after the entity knew or in the exercise of reasonable diligence should have known that an industrial injury was being claimed. Even in these cases, though, the lien may not be filed more than five years from the date the services were provided. These providers are:

1. a health-care service plan licensed per Health and Safety Code 1349;
2. a group disability insurer under a policy issued in California per IC 10270.5;

[3] *Allgreen Landscape v. WCAB (Mota)* (2012) 77 CCC 541, 542 (writ denied).
[4] *Medina v. Robinsons May*, 2012 Cal. Wrk. Comp. P.D. LEXIS 89.
[5] Note also that since these cases were decided, new and significant restrictions were made to home health-care liens. See Section 7.3 Scope of Care — Applied Cases.

3. a self-insured employee welfare benefit plan as defined by IC 10121 issued in California;
4. a Taft-Hartley health and welfare fund;
5. a publicly funded program providing medical benefits on a nonindustrial basis.

LC 4903.5 also does not apply to civil actions brought under the Cartwright Act, the Unfair Practices Act or the federal Racketeering Influenced and Corrupt Organization Act (LC 4903.5(d)).

Elimination of Zombie Liens

In many cases, an employer will issue partial payment on a medical provider's bill. Such payments commonly are made pursuant to the Official Medical Fee Schedule. So the employer is aware that its payments are short of those billed by the medical provider. Problems arise, however, when the medical provider initially writes off the difference without protest, then, years later, seeks payment for the difference of the balance. These were called "zombie liens" by some practitioners because they were dead and buried only to come back to life.[6]

In the past, the appeals board struggled with whether these zombie liens were viable. Some cases concluded the liens were viable by interpreting LC 4904(a)[7] and LC 4903.1(b)[8] as creating a loophole in the statute of limitations under LC 4903.5.[9] The cases held that the partial payments created a lien because the defendants had written notice of facts sufficient to constitute a lien, and that the statute of limitations in LC 4903.5 was tolled when the defendants failed to serve the lien claimants with the settlement documents.[10] Other cases, however, concluded that LC 4904(a) did not create an automatic notice of lien every time a

---

[6] WCAB's Final Statement of Reasons for CCR 10770, p. 4. A copy of this document may be found at http://www.dir.ca.gov/wcab/WCABProposedRegulations/WCAB_July2011/FinalStatementofReasons.pdf. As that document notes, for a general discussion of zombie liens see the Jan. 5, 2011 Liens Report of The California Commission on Health and Safety and Workers' Compensation, pps. 32-33 (http://www.dir.ca.gov/chswc/reports/2011/chswc_lienreport.pdf).

[7] LC 4904(a) states in pertinent part, "If notice is given in writing to the insurer, or to the employer if uninsured, setting forth the nature and extent of any claim that is allowable as a lien, the claim is a lien against any amount thereafter payable as compensation, subject to the determination of the amount and approval of the lien by the appeals board."

[8] LC 4903.1(b) states in pertinent part, "When a compromise of claim or an award is submitted to the appeals board ... the parties shall file ... any liens served on the parties."

[9] WCAB's Final Statement of Reasons for CCR 10770, p. 4.

[10] See *Tran v. Viet Nguyen Trucking Co.*, 2007 Cal. Wrk. Comp. P.D. LEXIS 42; *Campos v. St. Johns Regional Medical Center*, 2011 Cal. Wrk. Comp. P.D. LEXIS 416; *Reynoso v. Welcome Home*, 2011 Cal. Wrk. Comp. P.D. LEXIS 554; *Torres v. Marriott International (Vaughan)*, 2012 Cal. Wrk. Comp. P.D. LEXIS 392.

defendant pays less than the amount billed, and that defendants were under no obligation to serve settlements on such claimants.[11]

On May 21, 2012, the appeals board amended CCR 10770 to address the problem of zombie liens. CCR 10770(b)(3)[12] was adopted to interpret LC 4904(a) to mean that if a lien claim (or notice of any claim that would be allowable as a lien) is served on a defendant, this does not constitute the filing of a lien with the appeals board.[13] Furthermore, CCR 10770(b)(4) was adopted to interpret LC 4904(a) and LC 4903(1)(b) to mean that a defendant does not have "notice" that a lien is being asserted, and therefore has no duty to "file" a lien with the appeals board when an award is submitted if certain conditions are met.[14] CCR 10770(b)(4) provides that a defendant has no obligation to file a lien with the appeals board served under LC 4903.1(b) if:

A. the lien has been paid in full; or
B. a good-faith partial payment has been made; and
    i. the lien claimant concurrently was provided with a clear written explanation that both justifies the amount paid and specifies all additional information the lien claimant must submit as a prerequisite to additional or full payment, in conformity with the following, as applicable: (I) LC 4603.2(b)(1) and CCR 9792.5(c) for medical treatment liens; (II) LC 4622 and CCR 9794(b)(c) for medical-legal liens; and (III) CCR 9795.4(a) for interpreter liens; and
    ii. no additional written demand for payment is made by the lien claimant within 90 calendar days after the partial payment.

The provisions of CCR 10770(b)(3) and CCR 10770(b)(4) were adopted to give greater force to the statute of limitations provisions of LC 4903.5. They were intended to create more certainty and predictability in workers' compensation claims management and, ultimately, cause lien claimants to act promptly when

---

[11] See *Welch v. East Ventura Medical Group,* 2012 Cal. Wrk. Comp. P.D. LEXIS 108; *Cisneros v. Grimmway Enterprises,* 2011 Cal. Wrk. Comp. P.D. LEXIS 107; *Fields v. Raymond Interior Systems,* 2011 Cal. Wrk. Comp. P.D. LEXIS 530; *Segura v. Technicolor,* 2010 Cal. Wrk. Comp. P.D. LEXIS 448; *Ravizza v. Albertson's,* 2010 Cal. Wrk. Comp. P.D. LEXIS 254; *Villatoro v. Kern Labor Contracting,* 2012 Cal. Wrk. Comp. P.D. LEXIS 321; *Reznicsek v. The Kroger Co. dba Ralph's Grocery Store,* 2012 Cal. Wrk. Comp. P.D. LEXIS 432.

[12] CCR 10770(b)(3) states, "The service of a lien claim on a defendant, or the service of notice of any claim that would be allowable as a lien, shall not constitute the filing of a lien claim with the Workers' Compensation Appeals Board within the meaning of its rules of practice and procedure or within the meaning of Labor Code section 4903.1 et seq., including but not limited to section 4903.5."

[13] WCAB's Final Statement of Reasons for CCR 10770, p. 4.

[14] WCAB's Final Statement of Reasons for CCR 10770, p. 4.

there is a legitimate lien dispute.[15] So, in cases of partial payment, if a defendant has complied with the requirements of CCR 10770(b)(4), a lien claimant may not resurrect a zombie lien and avoid application of LC 4903.5 by relying on the provisions of LC 4904(a) and LC 4903(1)(b).

Note that the provisions of CCR 10770(b)(3) and CCR 10770(b)(4) do not apply to all lien claims. They do not apply to any notice of claim or lien claim of: (1) the Employment Development Department; (2) the California Victims of Crime Program; (3) any lien claimant listed as being excepted under CCR 10205.10(c)(5)(A)-(C);[16] and (4) any governmental entity pursuing a lien claim for child support or spousal support (CCR 10770(j)). Furthermore, CCR 10770(b)(3) and CCR 10770(b)(4) apply only in cases of partial payment.

Accordingly, as part of SB 863, the Legislature amended LC 4904(a) and LC 4903.1(b) to further compromise the viability of zombie liens. LC 4904(a) was amended to clarify that only notice of a claim allowable as a lien in favor of the Employment Development Department creates a lien against compensation.[17] And the language of former LC 4903.1(b) requiring parties to file any liens served on them at the time a C&R is submitted was eliminated altogether. Also, following receipt of a partial payment, LC 4603.2(e) requires medical providers to request a second review followed by an independent bill review (see Section 7.68 Second Review). So lien claimants may not rely on partial payments or failure to serve a C&R to relieve them of a failure to timely file a lien.

Waiver of Statute of Limitations

Because the statute of limitations is an affirmative defense, an employer may waive it under LC 4903.5 by not timely raising the issue.[18] Furthermore, an employer may be estopped from raising LC 4903.5 as a defense when its conduct or representations induces the claimant to refrain from filing the lien until after the statute of limitations has run.[19]

---

[15] WCAB's Final Statement of Reasons for CCR 10770, pps. 3-4.

[16] These are: (A) a lien claimant asserting a living expense lien under LC 4903(c); (B) a lien claimant asserting a burial expense lien under LC 4903(d); and (C) a nongovernmental lien claimant asserting a spousal or child support expenses lien under LC 4903(e).

[17] In some cases, the WCAB determined that LC 4904(a) does not apply only to EDD liens. See, e.g., *Hingtgen v. County of San Bernardino*, 2011 Cal. Wrk. Comp. P.D. LEXIS 536; *Zepeda v. Fremarc Designs*, 2008 Cal. Wrk. Comp. P.D. LEXIS 446.

[18] *Federal Express v. WCAB (Rozek)* (2004) 69 CCC 393 (writ denied).

[19] *Dicalite Minerals Corp. v. WCAB (Karr)* (2008) 73 CCC 686 (writ denied).

TIME TO FILE A LIEN

LC 4903.6 places restrictions on filing liens with the appeals board. It provides that, except as necessary to avoid violating the statute of limitations under LC 4903.5, the lien is not to be filed with the appeals board unless two conditions are met:[20] This is discussed in context in Section 15.89 Liens — Filing Procedure.

1. Sixty days have elapsed after the date of acceptance or rejection of liability for the claim, or expiration of the time for investigation of liability per LC 5402(b), whichever date is earlier.
2. Either:
    A. The time allowed for payment of medical treatment bills per LC 4603.2 has expired and, if the employer objected to the amount of the bill, the reasonable fee has been determined per LC 4603.6, and, if authorization for the medical treatment has been disputed per LC 4610, the necessity of the medical treatment has been determined per LC 4610.5 and LC 4610.6. Or
    B. The time allowed for payment of medical-legal expenses per LC 4622 has expired and, if the employer objected to the amount of the bill, the reasonable fee has been determined per LC 4603.6.

So a lien may not be filed or served until 60 days after the claim has been accepted or denied, or 60 days after the 90-day investigation period (see Section 5.16 Presumption of Injury — 90-Day Rule), whichever is earlier. Nor may a lien be filed and served until after the 45-day period defined in LC 4603.2 (see Section 7.67 Submission of Bills and Employer's Response) or the 60-day period for payment defined in LC 4622 has expired (see Section 14.65 Payment of or Objection to Medical-Legal Expenses).

If the employer disputes the amount of the bill, the lien may not be filed until the after the independent bill review process established in LC 4603.6 has been completed and it has been determined that the fee is reasonable (see sections commencing with Section 7.69 Independent Bill Review — Scope of Application). Also, if the employer disputes authorization in its entirety, the lien may not be filed until after the independent medical review process established in LC 4610.5 and LC 4610.6 has been completed and it has been determined that the treatment

[20] Former LC 4903.6 provided that a lien could not be filed until the expiration of: (1) 60 days after the date of acceptance or rejection of liability for the claim, or expiration of the time provided for investigation of liability per LC 5402(b), whichever date is earlier; or (2) expiration of the time provided for payment of medical treatment bills per LC 4603.2; or expiration of the time provided for payment of medical-legal expenses per LC 4622.

was medically necessary (see sections beginning with Section 7.37 Independent Medical Review — When to Use).

The prohibitions of LC 4309.6 do not apply to lien claims, applications for adjudication or declarations of readiness to proceed filed by or on behalf of the employee, or to the filings by or on behalf of the employer (LC 4903.6(d)).

TIME LIMITS BEFORE JAN. 1, 2003

Before the enactment of LC 4903.5, there was no statute of limitations for filing a lien.[21] But there is a rule that a lien claimant may not collect if the applicant would otherwise be barred by the statute of limitations — the lien claimant "stands in the shoes" of the injured worker.[22] Moreover, a lien could be barred by the doctrine of laches.[23] Laches is a very old legal doctrine that, in essence, holds that if a party delays a long time in pursuing its legal rights, and its opponent is materially prejudiced by the delays, then the right may be extinguished. For a complete discussion of this concept, see Section 6.40 Doctrine of Laches. Again, the appeals board has held that LC 4903.5 applies to injuries occurring prior to its enactment dates, and thus would not apply to injuries before Jan. 1, 2003.[24]

---

[21] *Town of Hillsborough v. WCAB (Sheehan)* (1996) 61 CCC 528 (writ denied); *State of California, Dept. of Corrections v. WCAB (Moncrief)* (1983) 48 CCC 830 (writ denied).

[22] *Kaiser Foundation Hospitals, Permanente Medical Group v. WCAB (Webb)* (1977) 42 CCC 302; *Permanente Medical Group/Kaiser Foundation Hospitals v. WCAB (Taylor)* (1989) 54 CCC 44 (writ denied); *Medina v. Santa Ana Plating,* 2010 Cal. Wrk. Comp. P.D. LEXIS 246. It works the other way, too. If the applicant's claim is not barred by the statute of limitations because of estoppel, then the lien claim is not barred either. *Kaiser Foundation Hospitals, Permanente Medical Group v. WCAB (Martin)* (1985) 50 CCC 411. It should be noted, however, that there is support for the idea that liens for medical-legal costs may survive an applicant being barred by the statute of limitations. *Anchor Glass Container v. WCAB (Franco)* (1995) 60 CCC 873 (writ denied); *Turudich v. IAC (Smale)* (1965) 30 CCC 316.

[23] *Kaiser Foundation Hospitals/Permanente Medical Group v. WCAB (Valencia)* (1976) 41 CCC 730 (writ denied) (lien denied for delay of six years); *Bell v. WCAB* (1987) 52 CCC 72 (writ denied) (lien denied for delay of seven years); *Midas Recovery Services, Inc. v. WCAB (Baker)* (1995) 60 CCC 783 (writ denied) (lien barred by laches when it was not filed before release and satisfaction of applicant's claim, nor within time to seek reconsideration of order approving a compromise and release).

[24] See *Medina v. Robinsons May,* 2012 Cal. Wrk. Comp. P.D. LEXIS 89; *Ravizza v. Albertson's,* 2010 Cal. Wrk. Comp. P.D. LEXIS 254; *Villatoro v. Kern Labor Contracting,* 2012 Cal. Wrk. Comp. P.D. LEXIS 321.

6.52 STATUTE OF LIMITATIONS FOR CONTRIBUTION FROM CO-DEFENDANTS

In cases involving occupational disease or cumulative trauma, more than one employer might be liable for an employee's injuries. The employee may elect to proceed against any one or more of the liable employers (LC 5500.5(c)). The employer who is elected against has a right to seek contribution from the other co-defendants following findings and award or settlement of the case. Per LC 5500.5(e), any employer held liable under the award may institute proceedings before the appeals board for the purpose of determining apportionment of liability or right of contribution. See Section 5.8 Contribution Among Defendants for a thorough discussion of these issues.

FILING A PETITION FOR CONTRIBUTION

An employer must file an appropriate petition to initiate proceedings for apportionment of liability or the right of contribution. Generally, an actual petition for contribution must be filed. Joinder of another employer or carrier subsequent to an award does not suffice as a petition for contribution under LC 5500.5(e).[1]

There seems to be a conflict about whether a petition for contribution is required if the settlement documents provide that the rights to contribution are reserved. Some cases have held that it is not enough to note in the settlement documents

[1] *General Accident Insurance Co. v. WCAB (Loterstein)* (1996) 61 CCC 648, 652.

that rights to contribution are reserved, and that a separate petition must be filed.[2] But in one case, the appeals board held that if a defendant has entered into a joint settlement agreement with an applicant and co-defendant that includes language reserving jurisdiction over contribution claims, that defendant is estopped from asserting the statute of limitation of LC 5500.5(e) by its stipulation.[3]

The appeals board also has concluded that a formal petition is not necessarily required, and that informal pleadings may serve as a petition. In one case, the appeals board explained that although the "normal" procedure was to file a petition for contribution and then a declaration of readiness to proceed for contribution proceedings, it also held that a DOR listing contribution as the issue sufficiently "instituted proceedings" before the appeals board.[4]

The appeals board, however, has held that a DOR filed by a defendant against whom contribution was being sought did not constitute initiation of proceedings for purposes of statute of limitations.[5] Also, the appeals board has held that a letter asking for the joinder of parties was not equivalent to a petition for contribution because it did not establish the specific relief sought.[6]

If the petition is filed, that is enough. If service is not performed on the parties, the statute of limitations is not violated, at least if the parties were aware of the impending effort to obtain contribution.[7]

PETITION FOR CONTRIBUTION — TIME TO FILE

The employer has one year following an award or order approving a settlement to file a petition for contribution. If the petition is not filed within the one-year

---

[2] *Dohm v. Old Town Deli & Golden Star Catering*, 2011 Cal. Wrk. Comp. P.D. LEXIS 527; *ARB, Inc. v. WCAB (Freeman)* (1999) 64 CCC 834 (Court of Appeal opinion unpublished in official reports); *Rudolf & Sletten, Inc. v. WCAB (Lyon)* (1998) 63 CCC 339 (writ denied). Also, in an unpublished opinion, the Court of Appeal held that an order of mandatory arbitration signed by a WCJ before approval of a compromise and release did not qualify as a petition for contribution. The court added that preliminary acts such as agreeing to assign the matter to a particular arbitrator or designating contribution as an issue to be decided in arbitration do not qualify as instituting proceedings to determine contribution. The court stated, "Once an employer is liable for an award, the formality of timely filing a petition — a document that puts the party against whom contribution is claimed — is required to trigger the right to have that claim adjudicated by the appeals board and thereby dispel any uncertainty about the status of the potential claim for contribution." *Council of Community Clinics v. WCAB (Cass)* (2005) 70 CCC 1225, 1229-30 (Court of Appeal opinion unpublished in official reports).

[3] *Scott v. Calemx/Armadillo Trading Co.*, 2012 Cal. Wrk. Comp. P.D. LEXIS 42.

[4] *Old Republic Insurance Co. v. WCAB (Bennett)* (2010) 75 CCC 168 (writ denied). See also *Chubb Services Corp. v. WCAB (Jannelle)* (2011) 76 CCC 363 (writ denied).

[5] *Dynacraft Industries v. WCAB (Poor)* (2012) 77 CCC 879 (writ denied).

[6] *Mission Insurance Co. v. WCAB* (1978) 43 CCC 1143 (writ denied).

[7] *Daugherty v. National Indem. Ins. Co.* (1982) 10 CWCR 137 (panel decision).

period, the opportunity to get contribution from the other co-defendants is forever lost.[8] LC 5500.5(e) even applies among multiple insurers for a single employer.[9] It also applies if the settlement is approved by an arbitrator per LC 3201.5 and LC 3201.7.[10] But it does not apply to elections made in successive injury cases because they are not subject to LC 5500.5.[11]

The one-year time limit for the filing of a petition for contribution is measured from the date of the WCJ's award, which is considered to be the WCAB's award — not from the date that reconsideration was denied. The filing of a petition for reconsideration does not toll or extend the one-year time limitation.[12] Even if the petition for reconsideration is granted, the time is not extended — if the award is affirmed.[13] But it seems that if an award is vacated and a new one issues, the one-year clock would start again,[14] as it would if the parties all agreed to reserve the issue and the appeals board issued an order to that effect.[15] Note that the one-year period begins as of the day of the award — not the day it was received. The "mailbox rule" — the rule that gives five extra days for mailing — does not apply to these types of petitions.[16]

Also, just because parties settle a case after an award issues, the time to file the petition for reconsideration is not extended. In one case, an award of benefits issued, and later, as the benefits were being paid out, the parties settled the case by compromise and release. It was held that the order approving the C&R by the WCJ did not extend the one-year statute of limitations.[17]

It is enough to timely file a petition for contribution. There is no requirement that the co-defendant be joined as a party within one year after an award issued.[18]

---

[8] See *Volk v. WCAB (Osborne)* (1975) 40 CCC 152 (writ denied). This is so even if there was no formal election. *Donaldson v. Zurich American Ins. Co.* (1992) 21 CWCR 16 (panel decision).
[9] *General Accident Insurance Co. v. WCAB (Loterstein)* (1996) 61 CCC 648, 652.
[10] *Perez v. Herrick Corp.*, 2012 Cal. Wrk. Comp. P.D. LEXIS 252.
[11] *Lucky Stores, Inc. v. WCAB (Ahern)* (1995) 60 CCC 1119 (writ denied); *Gordon v. Shaklee Corp.* (1989) 17 CWCR 132.
[12] *Republic Indemnity Co. of America v. WCAB (Johnson)* (1981) 46 CCC 88; *Rex Club v. WCAB (Oakley-Clyburn)* (1997) 62 CCC 441, 446; *Automatic Products, Inc. v. WCAB* (1982) 47 CCC 109 (writ denied). If the petition was filed after the vocational rehabilitation unit issued a determination, the one year would issue from that date. *M.B. Neves Trucking v. WCAB (Homan)* (1994) 59 CCC 770 (writ denied).
[13] *Employers Mutual Insurance Co. of Wisconsin v. WCAB (Schrimpf)* (1983) 48 CCC 636 (writ denied).
[14] *Miles v. Unicare Ins. Co.* (1984) 12 CWCR 237 (panel decision).
[15] *The Hartford v. WCAB (Renteria)* (1997) 62 CCC 1292 (writ denied).
[16] *SCIF v. WCAB (Militowski)* (1986) 51 CCC 59 (writ denied).
[17] *Industrial Indemnity Co. v. WCAB (Orvik)* (1997) 62 CCC 887.
[18] *Hite v. Tepco (Standard Abrasives, Inc.)*, 2012 Cal. Wrk. Comp. P.D. LEXIS 349.

Award Triggering Need to File a Petition for Contribution

The one-year statute of limitations provided by LC 5500.5(e) applies to any award of compensation benefits, not just the final award that disposes of all questions concerning the applicant's entitlement to benefits. But in *The Rex Club v. WCAB (Oakley-Clyburn),*[19] the Court of Appeal held that if a supplemental award is issued for new and distinct benefits, a petition for contribution filed within one year of the supplemental award is timely as to that award, even though more than one year has passed since the issuance of the original award.[20]

In *Rex Club,* the appeals board awarded temporary disability in November 1987 against one of several employers and determined that the award would continue indefinitely. The employee was awarded temporary disability indemnity until August 1989. In 1994, all issues were settled for $200,000 by way of compromise and release, and later that year the employer filed a petition for contribution. The Court of Appeal held that the November 1987 award of TD was an award of compensation benefits within the meaning of LC 5500.5(e). The court concluded that the employer could seek contribution from the $200,000 awarded only for new and distinct benefits, but could not seek reimbursement for any portion of the $200,000 attributable to the benefits awarded in the 1987 findings and award. Because the employer did not file a petition for contribution for the 1987 award of temporary disability, it could not receive contribution for those benefits, only for new and distinct benefits, such as permanent disability and vocational rehabilitation. The case was remanded to the appeals board to determine what portion of the compromise and release was attributable to new and distinct compensation benefits, and to permit the employer contribution only for those benefits.[21]

Accordingly, in a panel decision, a findings and award was issued in 2004. The employer did not file a petition for contribution within a year of the award. Later, the applicant filed a petition to reopen. This was settled for $25,000 by way of C&R in 2009, and the employer filed a petition for contribution within a year of the C&R. The appeals board concluded that the petition for contribution filed within one year of the supplemental award was timely as to that award even if it

---

[19] (1997) 62 CCC 441.

[20] *The Rex Club v. WCAB (Oakley-Clyburn)* (1997) 62 CCC 441; *Employers Insurance of Wausau v. WCAB (Duncan)* (1984) 49 CCC 333 (writ denied).

[21] *The Rex Club v. WCAB (Oakley-Clyburn)* (1997) 62 CCC 441, 447-48. See also *Industrial Indemnity Co. v. WCAB (Orvik)* (1997) 62 CCC 887 (Court of Appeal opinion unpublished in official reports) (due to late filing, contribution was allowed for only $500 worth of benefits; a past award was for $96,000). But see *Sierra Optical v. WCAB (Pimienta)* (2005) 71 CCC 92 (writ denied) (insurer's petition for contribution not timely when there was a stipulated award June 14, 2000, the case was resolved by way of C&R March 15, 2004, and the petition for contribution was filed Aug. 25, 2004).

was untimely as to the original award. It also found that the employer was entitled to a contribution against the C&R amount of $ 25,000.[22]

Furthermore, in one case, an applicant received a stipulated award of 49 percent PD in 2004. No petition for contribution was filed. In 2006, the applicant filed a petition for new and further disability, including a new claim of injury to the psyche as a compensable consequence. The parties then stipulated to increased permanent disability of 66 percent, and the defendant filed for contribution. The appeals board concluded that although the defendant could not receive contribution for benefits awarded in 2004, the new and further permanent disability arising from the original award and the new injury to the psyche were not an element of the initial award, and were new and distinct benefits subject to contribution.[23]

Effect of Prior Dismissal of a Party

It does not matter whether a party against whom the petition for contribution is filed had been dismissed from the case at the time of the filing. The liable employer is still permitted to file a petition for contribution against the previously dismissed party.

In one case, an applicant was employed by a temporary employer and later a permanent employer during the period of liability. The applicant elected to proceed against the permanent employer, and the WCJ dismissed the temporary employer due to this election. After the case was settled by way of compromise and release Dec. 7, 1998, the permanent employer filed a petition for contribution Feb. 10, 1999. After the case was referred to mandatory arbitration April 10, 2000, the temporary employer argued that the petition for contribution was barred by the statute of limitations, because it had not been rejoined as a defendant after dismissal by the WCJ. The temporary employer argued that although the petition was timely served, the fact that it was never formally rejoined meant that the petition was not served on a party defendant, and could never be timely served if it were now joined because the one-year statute of limitations had passed. The arbitrator found that the lack of rejoinder should not act to deny the permanent employer the right to proceed to contribution. The arbitrator concluded that a petition for contribution is timely filed even if it was not actually served on a party defendant within a year, if that party was aware of the claim for

---

[22] *Kent v. Control Components, Inc.*, 2009 Cal. Wrk. Comp. P.D. LEXIS 527.

[23] *Horton v. Crown Cork and Seal American Protection Insurance Co.*, 2012 Cal. Wrk. Comp. P.D. LEXIS 352.

contribution within one year. The appeals board adopted the arbitrator's report on reconsideration.[24]

Necessity of Petition for Contribution When Issue of Liability Is Decided

The appeals board will not always decide to use the mechanisms available in LC 5500.5. Sometimes the issues will simply be litigated at the appeals board with all parties present, and an award will issue that outlines the liabilities of each defendant. In such cases, there are no contribution proceedings, at least none that can be called such in light of LC 5500.5 or the arbitration requirements. Rather, the award simply issues, with parties allowed to appeal or ask the court to enforce the award, as they would in any case.[25] In these cases no petition for contribution need be filed, and if it is filed, it will be treated as a petition to enforce the award.

For example, in an unpublished opinion, an applicant sustained a cumulative trauma injury that fell under the coverage of two insurers, CCIC and Zenith. The WCJ issued a findings and award determining that CCIC was liable for 21 percent of the total liability and that Zenith was liable for 79 percent. The award also provided that CCIC would administer the benefits and seek contribution from Zenith. More than a year after the award, CCIC filed a petition for contribution. The court held that the petition was not barred by LC 5500.5, as such a determination was made in the F&A. The court concluded that the petition was for enforcement of the existing award, and the appeals board could enforce it through its continuing jurisdiction over awards and orders.[26]

Who Must File

In one case, the appeals board held that only the insurer that enters into a C&R is required to institute proceedings, pursuant to LC 5500.5(e), in order to preserve its right to contribution. An employee sustained a cumulative trauma injury while working for both Unilab/Quest Diagnostics (Unilab) and by Valley Health System (Valley). Unilab was self-insured for part of the period and its claims were administered by Sedgwick CMS (Sedgwick); it was insured part of the time

---

[24] *Manpower Temporary Services v. WCAB (Dunai)* (2000) 65 CCC 1177 (writ denied). The converse is also true — just because a party is already joined as a defendant does not mean that the one-year time limit for filing does not apply. *General Accident Insurance Co. v. WCAB (Loterstein)* (1996) 61 CCC 648.

[25] *California Compensation and Fire Co. v. WCAB (Custer)* (1992) 57 CCC 317 (Court of Appeal opinion unpublished in official reports).

[26] *California Compensation and Fire Co. v. WCAB (Custer)* (1992) 57 CCC 317 (Court of Appeal opinion unpublished in official reports).

by American Casualty Company (American Casualty), whose claims were administered by CNA Claimsplus (CNA). Valley was self-insured part of the time with its claims administered by Tristar Risk Management (Tristar), and was insured for part of the period by Zurich Insurance Co. (Zurich).

On Aug. 12, 2004, Sedgwick filed a lien claim seeking contribution for nearly $180,000. On April 25, 2005, the applicant settled her claim against all defendants by way of C&R; that document was signed for by the defendants only by CNA's attorney, with a proviso that the parties "reserve the right to contribution against each other." The C&R also required CNA to adjust lien claims, including Sedgwick's. On Aug. 10, 2005, Sedgwick filed a DOR that was served on Zurich and CNA for a conference on contribution. On Aug. 23, 2005, CNA filed a petition for contribution for $46,000 it spent on the applicant's benefits. Finally, on Nov. 13, 2006, Sedgwick filed a petition for contribution from CNA and Zurich. There was a dispute over whether Sedgwick's petition was timely. The arbitrator held that it was not. The appeals board held that Sedgwick could seek contribution.

The appeals board reasoned that Sedgwick was not held liable under the C&R, as it was not a signatory to it, and therefore was not required to file a petition for contribution to institute supplemental proceedings pursuant to LC 5500.5(e). Instead, the appeals board found that Sedgwick was entitled to file a lien pursuant to LC 4903(c), which it did in 2004. The appeals board added that even if Sedgwick was required to file a petition for contribution, CNA would be estopped from asserting the statute of limitations because the settlement reserved the right to contribution, and because it agreed to adjust all lien claims, including Sedgwick's.[27]

[27] *Zurich Insurance Co. v. WCAB (Goodrich)* (2010) 75 CCC 552 (writ denied).

6.53 STATUTE OF LIMITATIONS FOR PENALTIES UNDER LC 5814

With the changes brought about by the passage and implementation of SB 899, there's a statute of limitations to file a petition for penalties under LC 5814. Before SB 899, there was no defined statute other than the five-year statute of limitations in LC 5803 and LC 5804 to raise a penalty issue under LC 5814, unless it concerned penalty and enforcement of a previously issued award.[1]

LC 5814(g) establishes a two-year statute of limitations for the recovery of benefits under LC 5814. Specifically, LC 5814(g) states, "No action may be brought to be awarded to recover penalties under this section more than two years from the date the payment of compensation was due." The new LC 5814 was operative June 1, 2004, and LC 5814(h) provides that the penalty statute applies "to all injuries, without regard to whether the injury occurs before, on, or after the operative date."[2] So the statute of limitations defined in LC 5814(g) applies to all actions to recover penalties brought on or after June 1, 2004, regardless of the date of injury.[3] If the petition for penalty was filed before the June 1, 2004 operative date for delays occurring years earlier, then it would not be barred by the two-year statute of limitations, as it was timely when filed.[4] Penalties under LC 5814 are discussed in detail in Chapter 13 commencing with Section 13.11 Penalties Under LC 5814 — History and Purpose.

---

[1] *Santillan v. Kay Mart Co.* (1971) 36 CCC 12 (appeal board *en banc*).
[2] Although SB 899 was enacted April 19, 2004, the Legislature delayed implementation of the new LC 5814 and provided an additional period to avoid the two-year statute of limitations created by new LC 5814(g). *Green v. WCAB* (2005) 70 CCC 294, 305; *Abney v. Aera Energy* (2004) 69 CCC 1552 (appeals board *en banc*).
[3] *Abney v. Aera Energy* (2004) 69 CCC 1552, 1561 (appeals board *en banc*).
[4] *Pacific Steel & Engineering v. WCAB (Finley)* (2005) 70 CCC 1365 (writ denied).

6.80 STATUTE OF LIMITATIONS WORKSHEET — ORIGINAL JURISDICTION

NOTICE AND DISCLAIMER

Following is a checklist of sorts, designed to help the practitioner navigate the perilous waters of statutes of limitations in California. It is not, however, a substitute for legal counsel or for a diligent study of the law in light of the facts. This worksheet should be used to isolate the variables of a statute of limitations defense. The practitioner may then focus discovery, research and advocacy to achieve the best possible result.

This tool is to be used in conjunction with the "Sullivan on Comp" series of books, and in particular Chapter 6. That chapter is frequently referenced here by page.

INSTRUCTIONS

Eight elements must be analyzed to determine whether a statute of limitations defense applies. The first three are:

(1) the date of the filing of the application;
(2) the date of injury;
(3) the date of the last payment of benefits.

These elements determine if the application was timely filed with the appeals board. If so, there is no statute of limitations defense.

If the filing is not timely, the statute still may not apply under certain conditions. The next three elements concern tolling of the statute. They are:

(4) estoppel;
(5) the filing of the claim form;
(6) special cases.

These elements determine if the applicant has additional time to commence proceedings — what appears to be a late filing may still be timely.

The next element is:

(7) the possible application of the five-year statute of limitations.

In some circumstances, even when the statute of limitations applies, the applicant may pursue a claim for "new and further" disability. This consideration can effectively supplant the one-year statute of limitations defense.

The final element is:

(8) the concept of laches.

For cases in which the filing was timely and the statute does not apply, undue delay that prejudices the ability to defend the claim may result in a defense to the claim.

Begin with No. 1 and proceed through the entire worksheet in order unless specifically instructed to skip to another question or to end the analysis.

ELEMENTS 1 - 3: TIMELY FILING

Pursuant to LC 5405, the application must be filed within one year of the last payment of benefits or the date of injury, whichever is later (Chapter 6, pg. 33). Otherwise, it is barred by the statute of limitations.

Element 1 — Date of Filing

Filing the application commences proceedings (Chapter 6, pps. 29 - 31).

1. On what date was the application filed with the WCAB? ________________

Element 2 — Date of Injury

This is a tricky analysis and must be considered carefully. The courts may find that a specific injury date is part of a continuous, or cumulative, trauma for statute of limitations purposes (Chapter 6, pps. 51 -52).

2. Did the injury in question occur on a specific date or is it part of a continuous trauma (CT)? SPECIFIC / CT

   If specific, go to No. 3; if CT, go to No. 6.

Specific Injuries

3. On what date did the specific injury occur? ________________

   (Chapter 6, pps. 36 - 41)

4. Might this be a "latent effects" case? YES / NO

   Some authority allows for a delay of the date of injury for statute of limitations purposes if the employee does not know at first that the incident resulted in injury.

   (Chapter 6, pps. 36 - 41. A careful analysis is warranted on this point.)

   If yes, go to No. 5; if no, go to No. 10 and fill in the date of the incident from No. 3.

5. What was the date the applicant knew or should have known of the latent effect of the specific injury? ____________________

   This is the date of the injury, accounting for latent effects.

   Go to No. 10 and fill in this date, then continue with No. 11.

CT Injuries

6. Ensure that the injury in question is one CT, not more than one. This is a complex and subtle analysis. In cases of continuing exposure the courts may find more than one CT injury in order to avoid applying the statute of limitations defense to the applicant. This is discussed in depth in Chapter 6, pps. 48 - 51, and Section 5.6, subsection One Continuous Trauma or More.

   If there is more than one CT period, each must be analyzed separately.

7. What was the date of first disability? ____________________

   Usually this is the date the applicant first missed work, but can be whatever meets the definition of TD or PD. (For what constitutes compensable disability, see Chapter 6, pg. 42, and Section 5.5, subsection Compensable Disability.)

   Modified work or medical treatment is not in itself disability, but can be evidence of it.

8. What was the date the applicant knew or should have known of the industrial CT injury? ____________________

   Symptoms are not conclusive evidence (Chapter 6, pps. 42 - 47; Section 5.5, subsection Knowledge of Industrial Causation). Usually a physician's opinion is required. Applicant's actual knowledge, given experience and training, is enough.

9. What is the date of the CT injury? ____________________

LC 5412 defines the date of injury for purposes of statute of limitations as the date when both knowledge and disability first concur.

Fill in the later date from No. 7 and No. 8.

Date of Injury — Bottom Line

10. What is the date of injury? ____________________

For specific injuries, fill in the date from No. 3 or No. 5; for CT injuries, fill in the date from No. 9.

Element 3 — Date of Last Provision of Benefits

Indemnity Benefits

11. Were TD and/or PD benefits paid? YES / NO

(Chapter 6, pps. 55 - 56)

If yes, go to No. 12; if no, go to No. 13.

12. What was the date TD and/or PD benefits were last provided? ____________________

13. Were wages or disability benefits paid to the worker in lieu of indemnity benefits? YES / NO

(Chapter 6, pps. 56 - 57)

If yes, go to No. 14; if no, go to No. 15.

14. What was the last date that wages or disability benefits were paid in lieu of indemnity benefits? ____________________

15. Fill in the later date from No. 12 and No. 14; leave blank if both are blank. ____________________

This is the last date indemnity benefits were provided.

Medical Benefits

16. Were medical benefits provided directly through the workers' compensation system? YES / NO

    (For what constitutes provision of medical treatment, see Chapter 6, pps. 58 - 60.)

    If yes, go to No. 17; If no, go to question No. 18.

17. What was the last date medical benefits were provided through workers' compensation? ____________

18. Did the employer provide medical benefits through nonindustrial health insurance in lieu of providing it through the workers' compensation system? YES / NO

    (Chapter 6, pps. 60 - 62)

    If yes, go to No. 19; if no, go to No. 20.

19. What was the last date medical benefits were provided through the group carrier in lieu of workers' compensation? ____________

20. Fill in the later date from No. 17 and No. 19. ____________

    This is the date of last provision of medical care.

Provision of Benefits — Bottom Line

21. If you have not provided benefits so far, go to No. 25.

22. What was the date of the last provision of indemnity benefits? ____________

    Fill in the date from No. 15; leave blank if No. 15 is blank.

23. What was the date of the last provision of medical benefits? ____________

    Fill in the date from No. 20; leave blank if No. 20 is blank.

24. Fill in the later date from No. 22 and No. 23. This is the date of last provision of benefits. ________________

    If there is only one date, use it.

Timely Filed Application — Analysis

25. What is the date of injury (No. 10)? ________________

26. If benefits were provided, what was the date of the last provision of benefits (No. 24)? ________________

27. Fill in the later date from No. 25 and No. 26. ________________

28. What is the date of filing (No. 1)? ________________

29. Is the date from No. 28 more than a year later than the date from No. 27? YES / NO

    If yes, go to No. 31; if no, go to No. 30.

30. The application was filed – and the proceedings commenced – within the time limits specified in LC 5405. There is no statute of limitations defense.

    Laches, however, may still be considered as a defense.

    Go to No. 93.

31. The application was not filed within the one-year period, and it appears as though there is a statute of limitations defense.

    There may be other factors to consider; the analysis should continue.

ELEMENTS 4 - 6: TOLLING OF THE STATUTE

If the filing is not timely, there appears to be a statute of limitations violation. There are circumstances, however, in which the statute may be tolled. That is, the time the applicant has to file may be suspended for a certain period. This has the effect of extending the statute of limitations.

Element 4 — Tolling by Estoppel

Estoppel is an ancient legal doctrine that prevents parties from capitalizing on deceptive behavior on which others reasonably rely. The statute of limitations may be tolled if the employer engages in such behavior, either explicitly or by failure to provide required notices. Tolling ends when the misbehavior is corrected (Chapter 6, pps. 64 - 65).

Failure to Provide Notice

32. What was the date the employer first had knowledge of the injury? ________________

33. Did the employer, upon notice of injury, timely provide a claim form and notice of rights to the applicant as required by law? YES / NO

    (Chapter 6, pps. 66 - 68. For specifics about required notices, see Chapter 6, pps. 16 - 18. For what constitutes employer knowledge of injury, see Chapter 6, pps. 18 - 21.)

    If yes, go to No. 34; if no, go to No. 35.

34. Did the employer provide notices to the applicant that were incomplete or misleading? That is, did they suggest or imply that the applicant may be able to pursue his or her rights despite other notices provided? YES / NO

    (Chapter 6, pps. 68 - 69)

    If yes, go to No. 35; if no, go to No. 39.

35. Did the applicant have actual knowledge of his or her rights? YES / NO

Estoppel for lack of or improper notice does not apply if the applicant has knowledge of his or her rights (Chapter 6, pps. 72 - 76).

If yes, go to No. 39; if no, go to No. 36.

36. Was the lack of or inadequate notice cured? YES / NO

If yes, go to No. 37; if no, go to No. 45.

37. What was the date of the cure? ____________________

38. Fill in the span of time from the date of employer knowledge (No. 32) to the date of cure (No. 37); for example, 3/1/06 - 4/12/07. _________to_________

This is the period the statute will be tolled due to estoppel. There are other grounds for tolling, so the analysis must continue.

Misconduct or Misrepresentation

39. Did the employer mislead the employee or otherwise engage in misconduct? YES / NO

(Chapter 6, pps. 78 - 81)

If yes, go to No. 40; if no, go to No. 46.

40. What was the date of the misrepresentation or misconduct? ____________________

41. Did the employee rely on the misrepresentation of the employer? YES / NO

(Chapter 6, pg. 82)

If yes, go to No. 42; if no, go to No. 46.

42. Was the lack of notice or other misconduct cured? YES / NO

If yes, go to No. 43; if no, go to No. 45.

43. What was the date of the cure? ____________

44. Fill in the span of time from the date of the misrepresentation or misconduct (No. 40) to the date of cure (No. 43); for example, 3/20/06 - 4/12/07. ________to________

This is the period the statute will be tolled due to estoppel. There are other grounds for tolling, so the analysis must continue.

Go to No. 47.

45. Estoppel will apply until the lack of notice is cured by actual knowledge or notice, or until the misdeed or misrepresentation is corrected. The defense should make the correction(s) and be prepared to wait one year to start the entire analysis again.

The analysis ends here.

46. Estoppel does not apply to bar the statute of limitations.

Go to No. 47 to determine if there are other grounds for tolling.

Element 5 — Tolling by Filing the Claim Form

LC 5401(d) provides that the filing of a claim form tolls the statute of limitations until the claim is denied or is presumed compensable (90 days from the filing) (Chapter 6, pg. 26).

47. Was a claim form filed before the application? YES / NO

If yes, go to No. 48; if no, there is no tolling on this basis — go to No. 53 to continue the analysis.

48. What was the date the claim form was filed with the employer? ____________

49. Was the claim denied? YES / NO

(For what constitutes a denial, see Chapter 6, pps. 27 - 28.)

If yes, go to No. 50; if no, go to No. 52.

50. What was the date of denial? ____________________

This is the date the written denial is personally served, five days from the date the denial is placed in the mail or 20 days if the address is outside California.

(For criteria for the form and date of the denial, see Chapter 6, pps. 27 - 28.)

51. Fill in the span of time from the date the claim form was filed (No. 48) to the date of the denial (No. 50) to determine the period of tolling; for example, 3/1/05 - 5/24/05. _________to_________

Continue the analysis at No. 53.

52. Fill in the span of time from the date the claim form was filed (No. 48) to an end date 90 days later to determine the period of tolling; for example, 4/1/06 - 6/29/06. _________to_________

Element 6 — Tolling for Special Cases

Tolling may occur in special, rare cases. There are two kinds of special cases — minors or incompetents, and cases under review by an I&A officer.

Incompetents

53. Is the applicant an incompetent? YES / NO

(The definition is surprisingly slippery; see Chapter 6, pg. 161.)

If yes, go to No. 54; if no, this does not apply — go to No. 59.

54. Has a guardian *ad litem* been appointed by the appeals board? YES / NO

    (Chapter 6, pg. 161)

    If yes, go to No. 55; if no, go to No. 58.

55. What is the date the guardian *ad litem* was appointed? ____________

56. Fill in the date of injury (No. 10). ____________

57. Fill in the date of the injury (No. 10) through the date of the appointment of the guardian *ad litem* (No. 55); for example, 7/3/06 - 8/12/07 (Chapter 6, pg. 161). This is the period of tolling. ________to________

    Go to No. 59.

58. The statute of limitations remains tolled until the guardian *ad litem* is appointed. The parties must seek such an appointment to initiate the statute of limitations process. Once that is accomplished and a year has passed, the case may be reviewed again for a statute of limitations defense.

    The analysis ends here.

Minors

59. Was the applicant a minor (younger than 18) at the time of injury? YES / NO

    If yes, go to No. 60; if no, go to No. 67.

60. Is the applicant 18 or older now? YES / NO

    If yes, go to No. 61; if no, go to No. 63.

61. What is the date the applicant turned 18? ____________

62. Fill in the date of injury (No. 10) through the date the applicant turned 18 (No. 61); for example, 7/3/06 - 12/13/08. ________to________

This is the period of tolling.

Continue the analysis at No. 67.

63. Has a guardian *ad litem* been appointed by the appeals board? YES / NO

If yes, go to No. 64; if no, go to No. 66.

64. What is the date the guardian *ad litem* was appointed? ____________________

65. Fill in the date of injury (No. 10) through the date the guardian *ad litem* was appointed (No. 64); for example, 7/3/06 - 6/11/07 (Chapter 6, pg. 161). This is the period of tolling. ________to________

Continue the analysis at No. 67.

66. The statute of limitations remains tolled until either the applicant turns 18 or a guardian *ad litem* is appointed. Once either has occurred and a year has passed, the case may be reviewed again for a statute of limitations defense.

The analysis ends here.

Review by I&A Officer

67. Was the matter submitted to an I&A officer at the appeals board for review? YES / NO

(Chapter 6, pg. 159)

If yes, go to No. 68; if no, this does not apply, go to No. 72.

68. What date was the matter submitted to the I&A officer? ____________________

69. What date did the I&A officer submit recommendations on the disputed issue? ________________

70. Add 60 days to the date from No. 69. Fill in that date here. ________________

71. Fill in the date the matter was initially submitted to the I&A officer (No. 68) through the date the I&A officer submitted recommendations plus 60 days (No. 70). ________to________

This is the period of tolling.

Tolling the Statute — Bottom Line

72. The first step in determining the effect of tolling on the statute of limitations is to gather all periods in which tolling is appropriate for a given claim. Per the analysis above, fill in any dates of tolling from No. 38, No. 44, No. 51, No. 52, No. 57, No. 62, No. 65 and No. 71. (Most and possibly all of these lines will be blank.)

No. 38 ___________to___________

No. 44 ___________to___________

No. 51 ___________to___________

No. 52 ___________to___________

No. 57 ___________to___________

No. 62 ___________to___________

No. 65 ___________to___________

No .71 ___________to___________

73. Eliminate overlapping dates. For example, if there is tolling because notices were not provided 1/1/05 - 7/1/06, and because of submission to an I&A officer 1/1/06 - 9/1/06, there would be overlap. The tolling period would be 1/1/05 - 9/1/06.

Sometimes, per the example above, eliminating overlap results in one date of tolling. Sometimes, per the example below, there are multiple periods of overlap.

Suppose there are three dates of overlap:

from lack of notice (later cured):	1/1/05 - 7/1/06
from submission to the I&A officer:	1/1/06 - 9/1/06
from employer misrepresentation:	1/1/07 - 3/1/07

After eliminating overlap there are two periods: 1/1/05 - 9/1/06 and 1/1/07 - 3/1/07, for a total of two years of tolling.

After eliminating overlap, fill in the date(s) of tolling.

____________to____________

____________to____________

____________to____________

____________to____________

74. Eliminate dates that fall after the filing of the application — tolling may not occur for periods after proceedings have commenced. Suppose, per the example of No. 73, the application had been filed 2/1/07. The resulting dates of tolling would be 1/1/05 - 9/1/06 and 1/1/07 - 2/1/07. This would leave one year and 11 months of tolling.

Refer to No. 1 for the date the application was filed. Fill in the dates of tolling (that is, those before the filing).

____________to____________

____________to____________

____________to____________

____________to____________

75. Add up the number of days from all periods in No. 74. __________

76. Calculate the number of days from the date of injury (No. 10) through the date proceedings are commenced (No. 1). __________

77. Subtract No. 75 from No. 76. __________

    For example, if the application was filed two years after the date of injury (730 days) and there are fewer than six months of tolling (say, 180 days) the result would be 550 days. (If the result is a negative number, the terms of subtraction are probably reversed.)

78. Is the result more than 365 days (one year)? YES / NO

    If yes, there is no timely filing — go to No. 80; if no, there is timely filing — go to No. 79.

79. There is timely filing — tolling has given the applicant extra time to file the application. The statute of limitations does not apply to this case. The defense may consider the concept of laches.

    Go to No. 93.

80. There is no timely filing despite the tolling of the statute. The statute of limitations applies and the case may be defended. The applicant may try to use the five-year statute to obtain new and further disability and effectively circumvent the defense.

    Continue the analysis at No. 81.

ELEMENT 7 — THE FIVE-YEAR STATUTE

Generally, when benefits are provided, the applicant may seek "new and further disability" within five years from the date of injury under LC 5410 and LC 5803, even if the one-year statute of limitations applies (Chapter 6, pps. 86 - 88). This can have the effect of circumventing the one-year statute of limitations defense in whole or large part.

81. Were benefits provided? YES / NO

    If yes, go to No. 82; if no, go to No. 92.

82. What was the last date of benefits provided (No. 24)? ____________

83. What is the date of injury (No. 10)? ____________

84. Was there a denial? YES / NO

    If yes, go to No. 85; if no, go to No. 88.

85. What was the date of the denial (No. 50)? ____________

86. Was the date of the denial in No. 85 later than the last provision of benefits in No. 82? YES / NO

    If yes, go to No. 87; if no, go to No. 88.

87. If benefits were provided but the case was later denied, the applicant may not use the five-year statutes to seek new and further disability. The one-year statute remains effective.

    Go to No. 92.

88. Did the applicant seek new and further disability within five years of the date of injury (No. 83)? YES / NO

    (For the proper method of making this request, see Chapter 6, pps. 88 - 90.)

    If yes, go to No. 89; if no, go to No. 92.

89. Did the applicant truly sustain new and further disability? YES / NO

For a complete definition of new and further disability, see Chapter 6, pps. 99 - 102. WCAB cases have defined it as a "recurrence of temporary disability, a new need for medical treatment, or the change of a temporary disability into permanent disability."

If yes, go to No. 90; if no, go to No. 92.

90. Did the new and further disability occur within five years of the date of injury? YES / NO

(Chapter 6, pps. 103 – 106)

If yes, go to No. 91; if no, go to No. 92.

91. If the applicant who is otherwise barred by the one-year statute of limitations properly seeks within five years to obtain valid new and further disability, he or she is not barred from that disability or the accompanying medical care.

(For the extent of benefits allowable under this scenario, see Chapter 6, pps. 86 – 89.)

The analysis ends here.

92. The applicant may not seek benefits under the five-year statutes. The claim is wholly defensible because the statute of limitations has been violated.

The analysis ends here.

ELEMENT 8 — LACHES

Laches is an ancient equitable defense. If the party filing the application delays unreasonably, causing prejudice to the defense's case, the claim is barred, despite the fact that the statute of limitations is not violated. The concepts attendant to this defense are extremely fact-dependent and cannot be comprehensive in this format. Practitioners considering this defense must reference Chapter 6, pps. 167 - 169.

93. Did the applicant delay unduly in filing the application? YES / NO

    If yes, go to No. 94; if no, go to No. 96.

94. Did the delay cause the defense significant prejudice? YES / NO

    If yes, go to No. 95; if no, go to No. 96.

95. Did the defense have "clean hands"? YES / NO

    If yes, go to No. 97; if No, go to No. 96.

96. There is no laches defense. The defense must proceed on the merits.

    The analysis ends here.

97. A laches defense to the claim exists.

    The analysis ends here.

About Michael Sullivan & Associates

Michael Sullivan & Associates LLP is a dynamic, aggressive firm that provides high-quality litigation in defense of workers' compensation claims, employment issues and insurance litigation. It has offices throughout Southern California.

The firm is at the forefront of education in the California workers' compensation community. It regularly conducts seminars for its clients and other interested companies and organizations.

Michael Sullivan has written several widely distributed legal texts, including two books on the major reform legislation of Senate Bill 899, as well as analyses of prior reforms of Assembly Bills 227, 228, 486 and 749.

In 2012, the "Sullivan on Comp" team of authors wrote "Special Report: A First Look at SB 863," which has been widely read throughout the industry and is available for download at www.sullivanattorneys.com.

"Sullivan on Comp" is a comprehensive treatise on California workers' compensation law. The print edition is updated annually. Subscribers to "Sullivan on Comp" also have access to the content, continuously updated online, at WorkCompCentral.com.

Michael Sullivan & Associates LLP
Los Angeles | Orange | San Diego | Westlake Village
310.337.4480 | SullivanOnComp@sullivanattorneys.com
www.sullivanattorneys.com

CPSIA information can be obtained at www.ICGtesting.com
Printed in the USA
BVOW06s0939201115

427704BV00004B/26/P